AMC'S BEST DAY HIKES NEAR
WASHINGTON, D.C.

Four-Season Guide to 50 of the Best Trails in
Maryland, Virginia, and the Nation's Capital

SECOND EDITION

BETH HOMICZ & ANNIE EDDY

D0107721

Appalachian Mountain Club Books
Boston, Massachusetts

AMC is a nonprofit organization, and sales of AMC Books fund our mission of protecting the Northeast outdoors. If you appreciate our efforts and would like to become a member or make a donation to AMC, visit outdoors.org, call 800-372-1758, or contact us at Appalachian Mountain Club, 5 Joy Street, Boston, MA 02108.

outdoors.org/publications/books

Distributed by National Book Network.

Front cover photograph of Great Falls © Jeremy Bradford
Interior photographs © Beth Homicz and Annie Eddy, unless otherwise noted
Back cover photographs, from left, of Old Rag © Alex Ansley and of Bull Run © Kirybabe, all Creative Commons on Flickr
Maps by Ken Dumas © Appalachian Mountain Club
Book design by Abigail Coyle

Library of Congress Cataloging-in-Publication Data
Names: Homicz, Beth, author. | Eddy, Annie, author. Title: AMC's best day hikes near Washington, D.C. : four-season guide to 50 of the best trails in Maryland, Virginia, and the nation's capital / by Beth Homicz and Annie Eddy.
Description: Second Edition. | Boston, Massachusetts : Appalachian Mountain Club Books, [2017] | Includes index. | "Distributed by National Book Network"--T.p. verso. | The first edition lists Stephen Mauro as the first author on the title page.
Identifiers: LCCN 2016051245 (print) | LCCN 2016051721 (ebook) | ISBN 9781628420371 (paperback) | ISBN 9781628420388 (ePub) | ISBN 9781628420395 (Mobi) Subjects: LCSH: Hiking--Washington Metropolitan Area--Guidebooks. | Trails--Washington Metropolitan Area--Guidebooks. | Washington Metropolitan Area--Guidebooks.

The paper used in this publication meets the minimum requirements of the American National Standard for Information Sciences-Permanence of Paper for Printed Library Materials, ANSIZ39.48-1984. ∞

Outdoor recreation activities by their very nature are potentially hazardous. This book is not a substitute for good personal judgment and training in outdoor skills. Due to changes in conditions, use of the information in this book is at the sole risk of the user. The author and the Appalachian Mountain Club assume no liability for accidents happening to, or injuries sustained by, readers who engage in the activities described in this book.

Interior pages contain 30% post-consumer recycled fiber.
Cover contains 10% post-consumer recycled fiber.
Printed in the United States of America, using vegetable-based inks.

10 9 8 7 6 5 4 3 2 1   17 18 19 20 21

FSC
www.fsc.org
MIX
Paper from
responsible sources
FSC® C005010

DEDICATION

LOCATOR MAP

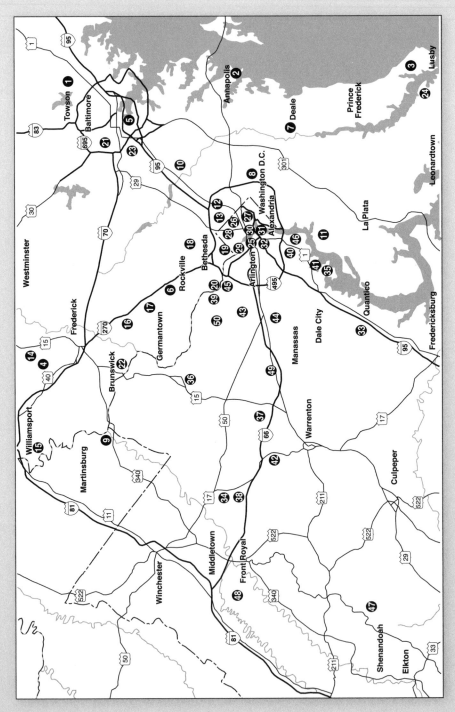

CONTENTS

APPENDIX

AT-A-GLANCE TRIP PLANNER

TRIP NUMBER	TRIP NAME	LOCATION	DIFFICULTY	DISTANCE	ELEVATION GAIN
MARYLAND					
1	Gunpowder Falls State Park: Wildlands Loop	Kingsville, MD	Moderate	5.3 mi	433 ft
2	Colonial Annapolis Historic District	Annapolis, MD	Easy	3.1 mi	87 ft
3	Calvert Cliffs State Park	Lusby, MD	Moderate	4.8 mi	330 ft
4	Annapolis Rock and Black Rock Cliff	Myersville, MD	Moderate	7.2 mi	840 ft
5	Baltimore Waterfront Promenade	Baltimore, MD	Easy-Moderate	3.75 mi	79 ft
6	Seneca Creek State Park: Clopper Lake	Gaithersburg, MD	Moderate	4.5 mi	400 to 500 ft
7	Jug Bay Wetlands Sanctuary	Lothian, MD	Easy-Moderate	5.3 mi	208 ft
8	Watkins Regional Park	Largo, MD	Easy	2.2 mi	45 ft
9	Harpers Ferry to Maryland Heights	Harpers Ferry, WV, via Maryland	Strenuous	7.6 mi	1,670 ft
10	Patuxent Research Refuge	Laurel, MD	Easy	2.1 mi	35 ft
11	Piscataway Park	Accokeek, MD	Easy	4 mi	Minimal
12	Greenbelt Park	Greenbelt, MD	Moderate	5.3 mi	350 ft
13	Lake Artemesia and Northeast Branch Trail	College Park and Berwyn Heights, MD	Easy	3.5 mi	20 ft
14	Catoctin Mountain Park and Cunningham Falls State Park	Thurmont, MD	Strenuous	10.4 mi	2,200 ft
15	Antietam National Battlefield	Sharpsburg, MD	Easy-Moderate	3.5 mi	400 ft
16	Sugarloaf Mountain	Dickerson, MD	Moderate-Strenuous	5.3 mi	1,375 ft
17	Black Hill Regional Park	Boyds, MD	Moderate	6.8 mi	320 ft
18	Matthew Henson Trail	Veirs Mill and Colesville, MD	Moderate	4.5 mi	235 ft
19	Capital Crescent Trail	Bethesda, MD, and Georgetown, Washington, DC	Moderate	8 mi	Downslope
20	Billy Goat Trail at Great Falls	Great Falls, MD	Strenuous	8.2 mi	650 ft

TIME	TRIP HIGHLIGHTS	FEE	GOOD FOR KIDS	DOG-FRIENDLY	PUBLIC TRANSPORT	WINTER SPORTS	WATER FEATURE
2.5 hrs	Secluded swimming hole		🚶	🐕		❄	≈
1.5 hrs	Quaint seventeenth-century streetscapes, city dock		🚶	🐕			≈
2 to 2.5 hrs	Miocene-era cliffs rich in shark teeth and other ancient fossils	$	🚶	🐕			≈
3.5 hrs	Two stunning overlooks		🚶	🐕			
2 to 2.5 hrs	Wharves, historic neighborhoods, industrial waterscape		🚶	🐕	🚌		≈
2.5 to 3 hrs	Mature hardwoods, excellent lakeshore views	$	🚶	🐕			≈
3 hrs	Wildlife, from snails and lizards to turtles and otters	$	🚶			❄	≈
2.5 to 3 hrs	Family fun: farm animals, wetland trail, carousel, nature center		🚶	🐕	🚌	❄	≈
4 to 4.5 hrs	Challenging, historic hike with gorgeous river confluence vistas			🐕			≈
4 hrs,	Hands-on nature center, wonderful array of flora and fauna, bald eagles		🚶	🐕			≈
1.5 to 2 hrs	Shoreline views, boats for rent, tobacco barns	$	🚶	🐕			≈
2 hrs	Excellent loop hike through secluded second-growth forest		🚶	🐕	🚌		
2 to 2.5 hrs	Birding trail, fishing piers, lake and river views; good for all ages		🚶	🐕	🚌	❄	≈
5.5 to 6 hrs	True mountain trails, pristine waterfall, rustic setting			🐕			≈
2 to 2.5 hrs	Quiet, beautiful rolling farm country; site of historic battle	$	🚶	🐕			≈
3 to 3.5 hrs	Challenging hike, wildflower-rich trails, farmland views			🐕			≈
3 hrs	Butterfly hotspot; ruined mill; lakeshore trail			🐕			≈
2.5 to 3 hrs	Peaceful trail with flora- and fauna-sighting opportunities		🚶	🐕		❄	≈
3 hrs	Views of C&O Canal, Potomac River, and old railway crossings		🚶	🐕	🚌	❄	≈
4 to 4.5 hrs	Spectacular hike to Mather Gorge overlooking Potomac River	$					≈

TRIP NUMBER	TRIP NAME	LOCATION	DIFFICULTY	DISTANCE	ELEVATION GAIN
21	Gwynns Falls and Leakin Park	Baltimore, MD	Easy	2.5 mi	217 ft
22	C&O Canal: Point of Rocks to Monocacy Aqueduct	Point of Rocks, MD	Moderate	12.2 mi	50 ft
23	Patapsco Valley State Park	Elkridge, MD	Strenuous	6.9 mi	1,300 ft
24	Greenwell State Park	Hollywood, MD	Moderate	4.5 mi	290 ft
WASHINGTON, D.C.					
25	Theodore Roosevelt Island and Potomac Heritage Trail	Arlington, VA, and Washington, D.C.	Easy	4.7 mi	160 ft
26	National Arboretum	Washington, D.C. (Northeast)	Easy–Moderate	8.2 mi	800 ft
27	Kenilworth Park & Aquatic Gardens	Washington, D.C. (Northeast)	Easy	2.5 mi	Minimal
28	Rock Creek Park	Washington, D.C. (Northwest)	Moderate	6 mi	840 ft
29	Around Georgetown	Washington, D.C. (Northwest)	Moderate	6.9 mi	800 ft
30	East Potomac Park and Hains Point	Washington, D.C. (Southwest)	Easy–Moderate	6.6 mi	30 ft
31	National Mall	Washington, D.C. (Southeast, Southwest)	Easy–Moderate	3.7 mi	Downslope
VIRGINIA					
32	Arlington National Cemetery and Marine Corps War (Iwo Jima) Memorial	Arlington, VA	Easy–Moderate	4 mi	600 ft
33	Prince William Forest Park	Triangle and Quantico, VA	Moderate–Strenuous	7.9 mi	600 ft
34	Sky Meadows State Park	Delaplane, VA	Moderate	5.8 mi	1,000 ft
35	Mason Neck State Park	Lorton, VA	Moderate	5.4 mi	250 ft
36	Banshee Reeks Nature Preserve	Leesburg, VA	Moderate	5.2 mi	215 ft
37	Bull Run Mountains Natural Area	Broad Run, VA	Moderate	3.5 mi	810 ft
38	G. Richard Thompson Wildlife Management Area	Delaplane, VA	Strenuous	8.8 mi	1,750 ft
39	Riverbend Park and Great Falls Park	Great Falls, VA	Moderate	6.8 mi	1,100 ft
40	Huntley Meadows Park	Alexandria (Hybla Valley), VA	Easy	1.5 mi	Minimal

TIME	TRIP HIGHLIGHTS	FEE	GOOD FOR KIDS	DOG-FRIENDLY	PUBLIC TRANSPORT	WINTER SPORTS	WATER FEATURE
1.5 hrs	Historic estate and outdoor art		🚶	🐕	🚌		≋
4 to 5 hrs	C&O Canal's largest aqueduct		🚶	🐕		❄	≋
3 hrs	Tranquil Cascade Falls	$		🐕			≋
2.5 to 3 hrs	Pine forests, farm fields, tidal creeks, sandy beaches	$	🚶	🐕			≋
2 to 2.5 hrs	Secluded, woodsy riverine island with cityscape vistas		🚶	🐕	🚌		≋
4.5 to 5 hrs	Bonsai, azaleas, 15 collections of flora from around the globe		🚶	🐕	🚌		≋
1.5 to 2 hrs	Human-made ponds teeming with waterlilies and lotuses		🚶	🐕	🚌		≋
2.5 to 3 hrs	Natural oasis of 1,700 wooded, hilly acres with challenging trails		🚶	🐕	🚌		≋
3.5 hrs	Secluded, shady hike through charming historic neighborhoods		🚶	🐕	🚌		≋
3.0 to 4 hrs	Memorials to great leaders, four bodies of water, cherry trees		🚶	🐕	🚌		≋
3 hrs	Art spaces, landscaped gardens, iconic memorials, Capitol Hill		🚶	🐕	🚌	❄	≋
3 to 4 hrs, including sightseeing	Tomb of the Unknowns, Kennedy graves, Custis-Lee mansion		🚶		🚌		
3 hrs	More than 15,000 protected acres, numerous trail options	$		🐕			≋
3 hrs	Stunning blend of wildflower meadows and woodlands	$		🐕			
2.5 to 3 hrs	Wide array of winged predators, including bald eagles	$		🐕			≋
2.5 hrs	Secluded, wild, little-known Virginia ramble		🚶	🐕		❄	≋
2 to 2.5 hrs	Closest mountain range to D.C., quartzite outcroppings, ruined mill		🚶				
4.5 to 5 hrs	2,300 feet above sea level, Virginia's best display of trilliums			🐕			≋
4 to 4.5 hrs	Dynamic views of the Potomac's Great Falls			🐕			≋
1 hr	Freshwater marsh supporting more than 200 species, prime birding		🚶	🐕			≋

TRIP NUMBER	TRIP NAME	LOCATION	DIFFICULTY	DISTANCE	ELEVATION GAIN
41	George Mason Plantation: River Trail	Lorton, VA	Easy	2.5 mi	86 ft
42	Wildcat Mountain Natural Area	Warrenton, VA	Moderate-Strenuous	3.4 mi	840 ft
43	Washington & Old Dominion Trail and Cross County Trail	Vienna, VA	Easy	12 mi	230 ft
44	Bull Run-Occoquan Trail	Manassas, VA	Moderate	7.8 mi	470 ft
45	Scott's Run Nature Preserve	McLean, VA	Strenuous	3.1 mi	710 ft
46	Mount Vernon Trail: Fort Hunt Park to Mount Vernon	Mount Vernon, VA	Moderate	8.2 mi	400 ft
47	Old Rag	Etlan, VA	Strenuous	8.8 mi	2,510 ft
48	Signal Knob	Fort Valley, VA	Strenuous	10.7 mi	2,680 ft
49	Manassas National Battlefield Park	Manassas, VA	Moderate	5.4 mi	900 ft
50	Meadowlark Botanical Gardens	Tysons Corner, VA	Easy	3.8 mi	360 ft

TIME	TRIP HIGHLIGHTS	FEE	GOOD FOR KIDS	DOG-FRIENDLY	PUBLIC TRANSPORT	WINTER SPORTS	WATER FEATURE
1.5 hrs	Wild birds of the Potomac wetlands	$	🧑‍🧒	🐕			≋
2 hrs	Scenic hiking in rustic Blue Ridge foothills						
4.5 to 5 hrs	Paved hike/bike path; historic Colvin Run Mill			🐕		❄	≋
4 hrs	Remote trail through rural lands	$		🐕			≋
2 to 2.5 hrs	Strenuous hike and scramble overlooking Potomac River			🐕			≋
3.5 to 4 hrs	Continual views of Potomac River			🐕			≋
6 to 7 hrs	One of the region's most popular hikes, rock scrambles	$					
7 to 7.5 hrs	Rugged loop with lovely views, greatest elevation gain			🐕			
3 to 3.5 hrs	Rolling hills, forested solitude, historic landmarks		🧑‍🧒	🐕		❄	≋
2 hrs	Easygoing trails, wildflowers, wetlands, Korean bell garden	$	🧑‍🧒				≋

ACKNOWLEDGMENTS

In my early tour-guiding days, master guides with ten or thirty years' experience coaxed my nascent enchantment with the federal city to blossom into full-fledged fascination. They taught me countless facts I hadn't known, then connected them via human-interest stories to concepts already understood. And they honestly embodied an oft-voiced creed that kept them young at any age: "There is always *so much more* to learn about Washington!" I still thank them with deep fondness, and I hope you too will feel the fascination—and the love—as you read, walk, and explore.

My warmest thanks go out to the true professionals at AMC Books—past, present, and future alike—who clearly love what they do, and who made this guidebook a gorgeous reality you now can hold in your hands, in print or digital form. Deserving of special gratitude is AMC's books project editor Shannon Smith, who has stepped up more times than I can count into greater responsibilities—and headaches!—while proving herself supremely capable and gracious at every turn. And co-author Annie Eddy has contributed a wonderfully fresh perspective and energy, and an appealing new embrace of the Baltimore and Annapolis areas, as well as several challenging new hikes in Maryland and Virginia. I'm grateful for a true team like this one.

Thanks are certainly due, and gladly offered, to the knowledgeable public servants who aided me greatly in my research and in orienting myself to their parks' offerings—too numerous to name here, but richly appreciated! A special recognition goes to the not-for-profit and volunteer associations whose members' bottomless contributions of love, knowledge, and hard work made them deeply felt along my hiking and research journeys, both literal and virtual.

Once again, I send a shout-out of gratitude to all the hikers, recreators, rangers, fisherfolk, maintenance workers, and volunteers I encountered along the trails—many of whom will always be anonymous, but whose good conversation, contagious enjoyment, and local wisdom were priceless.

My loving thanks go also to the dear friends, family members, and coworkers who've listened to my frustrations and lifted my spirits when the work on this book project weighed heavily upon me. Your goodwill and support have truly served to sustain me, and I couldn't have managed the effort but for you.

And lastly, to our readers and well-wishers: hearty thanks for buying the book and telling us both how you enjoyed it and how we could improve it. It's because of you that we've been able to keep the guidebook in print and, now, to offer this revised edition.

—Beth Homicz, April 2017

I am very grateful for my coauthor Beth's guidance and encouragement, and for her assurance that each hike would yield something magical of its own. Warm thanks go to Shannon, Jen, and the rest of the team for their support and enthusiasm.

As a transplant to Baltimore, I've fallen in love with this city and all the people here who are working to make the world a better place. Thanks to Heide Grundmann, Jo Orser, and all the Friends of Gwynns Falls and Leakin Park for their contagious enthusiasm—you guys could restore anyone's faith in the universe. At Waterfront Partnership, thanks to Amy Burke Friedman and Noelle Hewitt for their assistance. I owe eternal gratitude to Laurie Schwartz for her dedication to this city and for going out of her way to help me out.

Thanks also go to Robyn Stegman for trash wheel facts, to Ron Circe and Julie Paul for all the helpful information about Banshee Reeks Nature Preserve, to Viv Thompson for ideas, and to Steph Makowski for Annapolis parking tips and background information.

Special thanks go to Mac McComas and Becca Starr for their efforts in connecting me with reference materials and running tech support. Thanks also to the many wonderful people who joined me on these hikes, even when it was 97 degrees out: Mac, Becca, Liz, Bethany, Carolyn, Amber, Funmilayo, Guy, and my mom.

—Annie Eddy, April 2017

PREFACE

If we do say so ourselves, this revised second edition of *AMC's Best Day Hikes near Washington, D.C.,* presents a truly delectable sampling of the abundant menu to be savored by day-hikers in our area.

For this second edition, we've moved in a couple of new directions, literally, by reaching east and north toward Maryland's largest city, Baltimore, and the state's charming capital, Annapolis. We've set a fresh, energetic course by adding both more urban walks—such as Baltimore's Gwynns Falls and Leakin Park (Trip 21) and a walking tour of Annapolis' quaint streets and waterfront (Trip 2)—and more challenging mountainous options, such as Virginia's Signal Knob (Trip 48). We've also added a new hike along the C&O Canal towpath in rural Maryland, from Point of Rocks to Monocacy Aqueduct (Trip 22), and a tourist favorite: a guided walk through the historic hills of Arlington National Cemetery and up to the Marine Corps War Memorial, also known as the Iwo Jima statue (Trip 32). Two new essays, on the industry of Baltimore and the lost home of the Lee family, add a dash of spice and sugar.

At the same time, we've kept the best of our hikes from the original edition, with an eye toward showcasing the area's most distinctive and memorable offerings for lovers of the outdoors—experiences you simply won't find elsewhere. Options such as southern Maryland's Calvert Cliffs State Park (Trip 3), Shenandoah National Park's Old Rag (Trip 47), and northeast D.C.'s National Arboretum (Trip 26) are a few of the stick-to-your-ribs staples we couldn't imagine leaving out of the blend due to the incomparable enjoyment they provide.

"Water, water everywhere!" is a phrase particularly appropriate to the Washington, D.C., area. From experience, we know how a water element, whether a singing stream or an old-school swimming hole, can enhance a hike and the relaxation one hopes to find in it. So we've added an icon in our trip descriptions and At-a-Glance reference chart that calls out the hikes offering a year-round water feature, quenching that thirst for inner peace.

We sincerely hope you will delight in the trail mix we've cooked up this time around. Go ahead: Take a big bite and take a hike—or better yet, take all 50.

—Beth Homicz & Annie Eddy, April 2017

INTRODUCTION

WELCOME TO WASHINGTON, D.C.

The nation's capital region affords a rich, pleasing, and challenging variety of terrain and ecology, with abounding wildlife, extraordinary vistas, and sites that speak to our historical roots. Parks of all sorts—arboretums, meadows, forests, mountains, aquatic gardens, wildlife management areas, canals, Colonial-era streetscapes, funky urban art spaces, waterfront wharves, and Civil War battlefields—are all within an enjoyable 90-minute drive; many of them are just a short Metrorail ride from downtown. Forty-two of the 50 hikes included here offer a year-round water feature, be it a creek, a waterfall, a bay, or a river. Moreover, many of these havens welcome hikers at no charge. Even the most overworked and underpaid political operative, legislative staffer, or White House intern can manage to squeeze in an occasional getaway to green spaces and quiet places. The nearness of such oases is one of the region's saving graces, as commuter traffic becomes tougher and tougher to outsmart.

Washington, D.C., is cradled in a bowl at the falls point of the Potomac River, upstream from which large watercraft cannot pass. These waters are brackish, a mix of salt and fresh water. In Colonial days, many settlements were established at river falls points: Fredericksburg and Richmond in Virginia, for instance, situated at the falls of the Rappahannock and James rivers, respectively, where the Piedmont plateaus wend their way down to the tidal waters. All waterways in the region flow into the Chesapeake Bay and, eventually, to the Atlantic Ocean.

Because of this blend of geographic and hydrologic features, you find a wonderful spectrum of level strolls within the boundaries of the nation's capital, such as along the National Mall and through East Potomac Park, and interesting, shady inclines, such as those in Rock Creek Park and Georgetown. But as you venture afield from D.C. into the Piedmont (foothills) of Virginia, Maryland, and West Virginia, the terrain and geology—and the whitewater rapids—are stunning and varied from the falls upstream. Riverbend Park, Billy Goat Trail at Great Falls, and the confluence of the Shenandoah and Potomac rivers at Harpers Ferry, for instance, all provide a window into primeval times and the power of water rushing through chasms in ancient rock.

Rolling from the tidewater up to the base of the Appalachian Mountains—represented by Virginia's Blue Ridge and Maryland's Catoctin mountains—the Piedmont offers rich clay soils, verdant hills, excellent horse pasture, and wildflowers galore. The well-worn Appalachians beckon hikers ever upward with the mountains' serene, rustic, down-home beauty; their rich offerings of fauna and fall colors; and their marvelous vistas. These gifts await you at Maryland's Catoctin Mountain Park and Cunningham Falls State Park, Virginia's Sky Meadows State Park and G. Richard Thompson Wildlife Management Area, and other sites featured in this book. Three hikes included here—Annapolis Rock and Black Rock Cliff, Harpers Ferry to Maryland Heights, and Sky Meadows State Park—traverse short segments of the revered, rugged Appalachian Trail, which stretches 2,190 miles from Georgia to Maine.

The Washington, D.C., region also bears the memories—some would say the ghosts—of the shared human history familiar to most of us, if sometimes vaguely recalled from our school days. From Harpers Ferry in what is now West Virginia to Arlington National Cemetery and Mount Vernon, from Manassas to Antietam, the D.C. area provides hikers with countless opportunities to take a walk through sites humming with the vibrations of iconic American experiences.

When it comes to family-friendly local parks, gardens, and trails—well, we doubt any other metropolitan area can beat this one for appeal. Be sure to check out standbys (and standouts!) like Meadowlark Botanical Gardens, Watkins Regional Park, and Huntley Meadows Park. Don't miss our new offerings, such as Jug Bay Wetlands Sanctuary and Banshee Reeks Nature Preserve, for sheer enjoyment and learning—for young and old alike.

Again, welcome to the Washington, D.C., region. We think you'll enjoy the day-hiking choices available here. No wonder millions of people from all over the world come here to visit, to live, to work—and to recreate. We're glad you are among them.

HOW TO USE THIS BOOK

With 50 hikes to choose from, you may wonder how to decide where to go. The locator map at the front of this book will help you narrow down the trips by location, and the At-a-Glance Trip Planner that follows the table of contents will provide more information to guide you toward a decision.

Once you settle on a destination and turn to a trip in this guide, you will find a series of icons that indicate whether the hike is a good place for kids, whether dogs are permitted, whether the location is good for winter sports, whether the location is accessible via public transportation, if it has a water feature, and whether fees are charged.

Information on the basics follows: location, rating, distance, elevation gain, estimated time, and maps. The ratings are based on the authors' perception and are estimates of what the average hiker will experience. You may find them to be easier or more difficult than stated. The estimated time is also based on the authors' perception. Consider your own pace when planning a trip.

The elevation gain is calculated from measurements and information from USGS topographic maps, landowner maps, and Google Earth. Information is included about the relevant USGS maps as well as where you can find trail maps. The boldfaced summary provides a basic overview of what you will see on your hike.

The Directions explain how to reach the trailhead by car and, for some trips, by public transportation. GPS coordinates for parking lots are also included. When you enter the coordinates into your device, it will provide driving directions. Whether or not you own a GPS device, it is wise to consult an atlas before leaving your home.

In the Trail Description, you will find instructions on where to hike, the trails on which to hike, and where to turn. You will also learn about the natural and human history along your hike as well as information about flora, fauna, and any landmarks and objects you will encounter.

The trail maps that accompany each trip will help guide you along your hike, but it would be wise to also take an official trail map with you. They are often— but not always—available online, at the trailhead, or at the visitor center.

Each trip ends with a More Information section that provides details about the locations of bathrooms, access times and fees, the property's rules and regulations, and contact information for the place where you will be hiking. A Nearby section includes information about where restaurants or shops can be found near the trailheads.

TRIP PLANNING AND SAFETY

While elevations in and around Washington, D.C., are relatively low compared with other regions of the East Coast and the hikes detailed in this guide aren't particularly dangerous, you'll still want to be prepared. Some of the walks traverse moderately rugged terrain along rocky hills, while others lead to sandy beaches, ponds, and fields where you'll have extended periods of sun exposure and to areas where walking is slow in soft sand.

You will be more likely to have an enjoyable, safe hike if you plan ahead and take proper precautions. Before heading out for your hike, consider the following:

Select a hike that everyone in your group is comfortable taking. Match the hike to the abilities of the least capable person in the group. If anyone is uncomfortable with the weather or is tired, turn around and complete the hike another day.

Plan to be back at the trailhead before dark. Before beginning your hike, determine a turnaround time. Don't diverge from it, even if you have not reached your intended destination.

Check the weather. If you are planning a ridge or summit hike, start early so that you will be off the exposed area before the afternoon hours, when thunderstorms most often strike, especially in summer. Hikers at coastal locations should be prepared for wind year-round, especially during winter, when windchill is a concern. Compared with inland locations, the climate is generally cooler along the immediate coast during warm months and milder in winter. Significant storms—including heavy winter snowfalls, spring rainstorms, and tropical storms in late summer and fall—may cause flooding, potentially dangerous ocean tides, and other hazards. When exploring beaches or other areas along the coast, be sure to check tide tables in advance and keep an eye on the water at all times.

Bring a pack with the following items:

- ✓ Water: Two quarts per person is usually adequate, depending on the weather and the length of the trip.
- ✓ Food: Even if you are planning just a one-hour hike, bring some high-energy snacks such as nuts, dried fruit, or snack bars. Pack a lunch for longer trips.
- ✓ Map and compass: Be sure you know how to use them. A handheld GPS device may also be helpful, but it is not always reliable.
- ✓ Headlamp or flashlight, with spare batteries

- ✓ Extra clothing: rain gear, wool sweater or fleece, hat, and mittens
- ✓ Sunscreen
- ✓ First-aid kit, including adhesive bandages, gauze, nonprescription pain-killers, and moleskin
- ✓ Pocketknife or multitool
- ✓ Waterproof matches and a lighter
- ✓ Trash bag
- ✓ Toilet paper
- ✓ Whistle
- ✓ Insect repellent
- ✓ Sunglasses
- ✓ Cell phone: Be aware that cell phone service is unreliable in rural areas. If you are receiving a signal, use the phone only for emergencies to avoid disturbing the backcountry experience for other hikers.
- ✓ Binoculars (optional)
- ✓ Camera (optional)

Wear appropriate footwear and clothing. Wool or synthetic hiking socks will keep your feet dry and help prevent blisters. Comfortable, waterproof hiking boots will provide ankle support and good traction. Avoid wearing cotton clothing, which absorbs sweat and rain and contributes to an unpleasant hiking experience. Polypropylene, fleece, silk, and wool all wick moisture away from your body and keep you warm in wet or cold conditions. To help avoid bug bites, you may want to wear pants and a long-sleeve shirt.

When you are ahead of the rest of your hiking group, wait at all trail junctions until the others catch up. This avoids confusion and keeps people from getting separated or lost.

If you see downed wood that appears to be purposely covering a trail, it probably means the trail is closed due to overuse or hazardous conditions.

If a trail is muddy, walk through the mud or on rocks, never on tree roots or plants. Waterproof boots will keep your feet comfortable. Staying in the center of the trail will keep it from eroding into a wide hiking highway.

Leave your itinerary and the time you expect to return with someone you trust. If you see a logbook at a trailhead, be sure to sign in when you arrive and sign out when you finish your hike.

After you complete your hike, check for deer ticks, which carry the dangerous Lyme disease.

Poison ivy is always a threat when hiking. To identify the plant, look for clusters of three leaves that shine in the sun but are dull in the shade. If you do come into contact with poison ivy, wash the affected area with soap as soon as possible.

Wear blaze-orange items in hunting season. For Virginia hunting season see: dgif.virginia.gov/hunting/regulations/, and for Maryland hunting season see: dnr.maryland.gov/huntersguide/Pages/default.aspx.

Biting insects are present during warm months, particularly in the vicinity of wetlands. They can be a minor or significant nuisance, depending on seasonal and daily conditions. One serious concern is the eastern equine encephalitis virus (commonly referred to as EEE), a rare but potentially fatal disease that can be transmitted to humans by infected mosquitoes. The Mid-Atlantic's many swamps provide ideal mosquito habitats; the threat is generally greatest in the evening hours, when they are most active.

A variety of options are available for dealing with bugs, ranging from sprays that include the active ingredient N,N-diethyl-meta-toluamide (commonly known as DEET), which can potentially cause skin or eye irritation, to more skin-friendly products. Head nets, which often can be purchased more cheaply than a can of repellent, are useful during especially buggy conditions.

LEAVE NO TRACE

The Appalachian Mountain Club is a national educational partner of Leave No Trace, a nonprofit organization dedicated to promoting and inspiring responsible outdoor recreation through education, research, and partnerships.  The Leave No Trace program seeks to develop wildland ethics—ways in which people think and act in the outdoors to minimize their impact on the areas they visit and to protect our natural resources for future enjoyment. Leave No Trace unites four federal land management agencies— the U.S. Forest Service, the National Park Service, the Bureau of Land Management, and the U.S. Fish and Wildlife Service—with manufacturers, outdoor retailers, user groups, educators, organizations such as AMC, and individuals.

The Leave No Trace ethic is guided by these seven principles:

1. *Plan Ahead and Prepare.* Know the terrain and any regulations applicable to the area you're planning to visit, and be prepared for extreme weather or other emergencies. This will enhance your enjoyment and ensure that you've chosen an appropriate destination. Small groups have less impact on resources and the experiences of other backcountry visitors.

2. *Travel and Camp on Durable Surfaces.* Travel and camp on established trails and campsites, rock, gravel, dry grasses, or snow. Good campsites are found, not made. Camp at least 200 feet from lakes and streams, and focus activities on areas where vegetation is absent. In pristine areas, disperse use to prevent the creation of campsites and trails.

3. *Dispose of Waste Properly.* Pack it in, pack it out. Inspect your camp for trash or food scraps. Deposit solid human waste in cat holes dug 6 to 8 inches deep, at least 200 feet from water, camps, and trails. Pack out toilet paper and hygiene products. To wash yourself or your dishes, carry water 200 feet from streams or lakes and use small amounts of biodegradable soap. Scatter strained dishwater.

4. *Leave What You Find.* Cultural or historic artifacts, as well as natural objects such as plants and rocks, should be left as found.

5. *Minimize Campfire Impacts.* Cook on a stove. Use established fire rings, fire pans, or mound fires. If you build a campfire, keep it small and use dead sticks found on the ground.

6. *Respect Wildlife.* Observe wildlife from a distance. Feeding animals alters their natural behavior. Protect wildlife from your food by storing rations and trash securely.

7. *Be Considerate of Other Visitors.* Be courteous, respect the quality of other visitors' backcountry experiences, and let nature's sounds prevail.

AMC is a national provider of the Leave No Trace Master Educator course. AMC offers this five-day course, designed especially for outdoor professionals and land managers, as well as the shorter two-day Leave No Trace Trainer course, at locations throughout the Northeast.

For Leave No Trace information and materials, contact the Leave No Trace Center for Outdoor Ethics, P.O. Box 997, Boulder, CO 80306. Phone: 800-332-4100 or 303-442-8222; fax: 303-442-8217; web: lnt.org. For information on the AMC Leave No Trace Master Educator training course schedule, see outdoors.org/education/lnt.

MARYLAND

From the serene yet rustic Catoctin Mountain to the shining
Chesapeake Bay, the topography
of Maryland offers rich variety
and memorable appeal. Its urban centers also beckon—from
the industrial, bohemian edge
in Baltimore to the quaintly narrow seventeenth-century streets

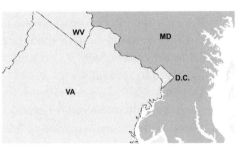

of the state capital, Annapolis. Maryland is one of the smaller states in the
nation, in terms of landmass, yet it's nearly as wide east to west as its big northern neighbor, Pennsylvania. The hikes described in this section cover a goodly
share of that geographical range.

Establish your hiking home base along the winding western shore of the Chesapeake, as the colonists did, a few dozen miles east and south of Washington,
D.C. There, Calvert Cliffs State Park rewards intrepid hikers with miles of sandy
cliffs safeguarding Miocene-epoch fossils and sharks' teeth. Greenwell State Park
along the Patuxent River showcases a fascinating spectrum of habitats, from
pine woods to sandy beaches and tidal creeks. Piscataway Park offers Mount
Vernon views and a Colonial-era working farm. Jug Bay Wetlands Sanctuary,
new to this edition, appeals to all ages with its wide variety of wildlife.

Peaceful retreats ring the bustling Washington, D.C., metro area. These
havens include Watkins Regional Park, a family-friendly destination with
a nature center, a farmstead housing peacocks and other critters, and even
a carousel. Lake Artemesia and Northeast Branch Trail in College Park is a
wonderful hike for bird-watching a short walk away from the Metro. Matthew
Henson Trail is a suburban-to-rural, hard-surface trail with chances to surprise deer and other shy fauna.

Greenbelt Park provides surprising seclusion and good hiking for a nature
spot just outside the Beltway, the interstate highway ring around Washington,
D.C. A bit farther afield to the northeast is Patuxent Research Refuge, which
offers an easy lakeshore hike, a wildlife center, and peaceful fishing. Capital

Crescent Trail from Bethesda into Georgetown is an appealing rail-trail mix of urban hustle and steampunk style, with plenty of shady stretches and river views tossed in.

North and west of the nation's capital, stretching upward into higher elevations, you can savor the rugged, rocky beauty of Catoctin Mountain National Park and its neighbor, Cunningham Falls State Park. Sugarloaf Mountain, a privately owned monadnock, or standalone mountain, that Franklin D. Roosevelt once coveted for a presidential retreat, showcases outcroppings of ancient quartzite. Don't miss Patapsco Valley State Park, one of the more demanding Maryland trips in this guide, which rewards hikers with the lovely Cascade Falls. New to this edition is the Annapolis Rock and Black Rock Cliff hike, which isn't anywhere near the city of Annapolis—in fact, it's one of the Appalachian Trail-linked trips—but its gorgeous overlooks make it well worth the drive.

Closer to the capital, Seneca Creek State Park and Black Hill Regional Park offer more-moderate trails within wide stretches of unspoiled lands. Billy Goat Trail at Great Falls is a challenge for most any hiker looking for a good climb, and it's only a few miles beyond the Beltway. Gunpowder Falls State Park offers old-fashioned swimming holes popular with Washington, D.C., and Baltimore folks alike.

If you're interested in historic sites, make tracks for Antietam National Battlefield's quiet, solemn meadows and antique stone bridge. The nearby Harpers Ferry hike, which starts and ends just inside the West Virginia panhandle (and briefly joins the AT), provides stunning views of the point where the Shenandoah River and the Potomac River join. Devotees of transportation history will particularly enjoy a hike along the historic Chesapeake & Ohio (C&O) Canal from Point of Rocks to Monocacy Aqueduct.

For those of a more citified bent, we've enhanced this edition with three new urban-centered Maryland trips. Stroll along Baltimore's bayside waterfront, through historic neighborhoods and commercial landmarks. Also in Baltimore is Gwynns Falls and Leakin Park, popular with fans of *The Blair Witch Project* and *The Wire*, offering historic ruins and "nature art" composed of organic and found materials. Circling back to Chesapeake Bay, and backward into history, take in a walking tour of Colonial Annapolis and discover her hidden charm.

A special note: Maryland's Department of Natural Resources maintains the system of state parks, forests, and wildlife sanctuaries, which is among the best in the nation. All of the state parks listed in this section have well-maintained trails, and most have historical sites and excellent visitor centers. Detailed, waterproof topographic maps of Maryland's state parks are available for purchase online at shopdnr.com/alltrailguides.aspx.

GUNPOWDER FALLS STATE PARK: WILDLANDS LOOP

The streams and rivers of Maryland's Gunpowder Falls State Park offer opportunities for wading or swimming—refreshing relief from D.C.'s sticky summers.

DIRECTIONS

From I-495 (Capital Beltway), take Exit 27 for I-95 north toward Baltimore. Take Exit 67 and turn left onto White Marsh Boulevard. Drive 0.5 mile and turn right onto Honeygo Boulevard. In 3.3 miles, turn right onto US-1/Bel Air Road. After 0.9 mile, the parking area will be on the right. *Global Positioning System (GPS) coordinates*: 39° 25.671' N, 76° 26.603' W.

TRAIL DESCRIPTION

Spanning 18,000 noncontiguous acres in Maryland's Baltimore and Harford counties, Gunpowder Falls State Park boasts 120 miles of trails along the Gunpowder River and in the Big and Little Gunpowder valleys. Hammerman Area is a popular day-use park with a lifeguard-staffed swimming beach. For a more tranquil experience, head to the park's Central Area. Here, Wildlands Loop in the Sweathouse Branch/Wildlands Area carries you through forests of Virginia pine, oak, hickory, and beech trees with modest elevation change. Cross several tributaries on the way to a pristine swimming hole on the Sweathouse Branch and finish with the last mile hugging the banks of Gunpowder River. Following heavy rains, the trail may be muddy in some areas, but it is not especially rugged. In spring, look for marsh marigolds, periwinkle, and Virginia bluebells.

From the parking area, pass a large sign bearing a map of the park and head down the stairs; turn right onto the gravel path, passing through the tunnel beneath Bel Air

LOCATION
Kingsville, MD

RATING
Moderate

DISTANCE
5.3 miles

ELEVATION GAIN
433 feet

ESTIMATED TIME
2.5 hours

MAPS
USGS Gunpowder Neck; Maryland Department of Natural Resources does not currently sell a formal map of Gunpowder Falls State Park's Central Area, but black-and-white maps are free at park headquarters; online: dnr2.maryland.gov/publiclands /Documents/Central_Sweathouse.pdf

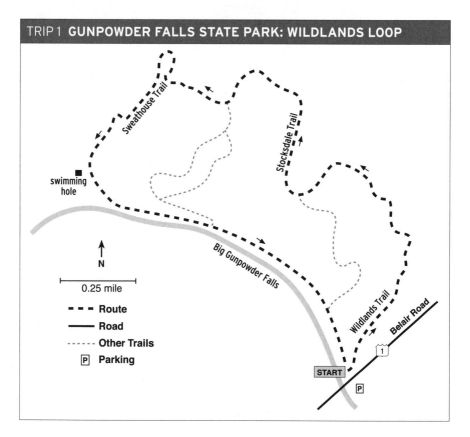

swimming
hole

N

0.25 mile

- - - **Route**
—— **Road**
----- **Other Trails**
P **Parking**

Sweathouse Trail

Stocksdale Trail

Big Gunpowder Falls

Wildlands Trail

Belair Road

1

START

P

Road. The pink-blazed Wildlands Trail splits off almost immediately at a post marker; turn right to begin your loop on Wildlands Trail. Tall trees fringe the dirt trail. Climb steeply at first then circle to the left beside the road. Continue to climb moderately as you wind through the forest, gaining elevation. The slope falls away to the right, with Bel Air Road still in view. After the trail levels out, you descend gently before rising again. In summer, ferns abound in this forested area. Pink blazes are infrequent, but the trail is wide and distinct. Pass through a level area then climb gently as a residence comes into view between the trees. Follow Wildlands Trail left then circle uphill to the right, crossing over a dip in the land before curving right again and descending through a sparsely forested area.

Soon after, the trail crosses the first creek. The water here is generally shallow and rocks provide stepping-stones, but use caution in spring or following heavy rains, when the water may be higher. The trail rises away from the streambed, briefly with some steepness. One mile into your hike, you reach the second creek crossing; in summer, this crossing is barely more than a mud puddle. Look left for a grotto of ferns nestled beneath the trees. With Bel Air Road now distant, this forested section of the trail is peaceful, if a little unvaried. As the trail turns a corner to the left, you may catch the scent of pine from the tall specimens that line the trail, forming the appearance of a corridor.

Wildlands Trail ends at a "T" intersection with the blue-blazed Stocksdale Trail. Turn right to continue on the second leg of the loop. Stocksdale Trail becomes slightly rockier, but this section is gently paced. Enter a more densely vegetated area as the trail turns left. Cross the third, often dry, streambed in a rocky section of the trail. At the 2-mile mark, a pair of wooden posts point all hikers to the left to bypass a residence.

Climb gently to an intersection and turn right onto the yellow-blazed Sweathouse Trail. Descend a slope into an arrestingly beautiful area where ferns grow densely beneath vine-laden beech and Virginia pine trees. Native wildflowers include Virginia bluebell, mullein, hepatica, and anemone. The trail cuts through lush undergrowth with red clay underfoot, narrowing even more before dropping and winding along the edge of a steep slope that descends to your left, where you can see and hear the running water of the Sweathouse Branch. Descend and approach the branch, reaching it at about 2.5 miles. From this point, the trail parallels the water along the short cliff that overlooks it. Cross a small, shallow tributary; the trail is narrow here as it continues to follow the Sweathouse Branch to the right. At 3 miles, turn right toward a tiny, stony beach at a shallow area of the branch—a good place to pause if you would like to get your feet wet, but a better swimming area is still to come. Cross on the rocks; this is a slightly more challenging crossing than the ones that preceded it, but it is safe most of the year. Continue along the opposite side of the branch.

Shortly after a still section of water, the trail turns right, climbing away from the water, parallel to a tributary choked with fallen trees. Take a sharp left turn, crossing this tributary, and then climb steeply but briefly, weaving to the right around the ridge before descending. The creek remains in view in the distance, far down the slope.

At a "Y" intersection with a double yellow blaze, Sweathouse Trail continues to the left; take a right onto the unblazed splinter trail to descend steeply to a pristine, turquoise swimming hole at the base of the Sweathouse Branch's mini-rapids. If you wish to swim, use caution; due to the possible presence of sharp rocks or broken glass, it is best to wear water shoes. Closely supervise children, swim and wade at your own risk, and never swim alone.

To rejoin Sweathouse Trail, climb back up to the "Y" intersection and continue on the yellow-blazed trail to the left of the double-blazed tree. At an unmarked intersection, turn left, following yellow blazes, and cross the Sweathouse Branch over a shallow, rocky area. Hang right to continue on Sweathouse Trail. Soon after, look to the right through vine-laden trees to see where the Sweathouse Branch joins with the slow, calm waters of Gunpowder River. The flat dirt trail remains level but becomes rockier as you continue to walk parallel to the river. Many small turnoffs to the right offer stunning views of Gunpowder River. Look for herons stalking fish in the clear waters; the river is home to small-mouthed bass, catfish, eel, carp, and brown trout.

When you reach the sign for Bel Air Road, you are now 0.8 mile from the parking lot. Stocksdale Trail departs sharply to the left; continue straight on the unblazed segment of Stocksdale Trail that returns to the Bel Air Road parking area. This well-traveled section is flat, with the river constantly in view on your right and large boulders on the left. Aquatic plants grow in profusion in the slow-moving water. Cross a tributary on an elevated trail section as cars begin to come into earshot. When the blue-blazed trail splits off to the left, continue straight. The trail turns to gravel, passes through a fenced section, and arrives back at the intersection with the pink-blazed Wildlands Trail. Head back through the tunnel under the road and climb the stairs to your left to the parking lot.

MORE INFORMATION

The parking area often fills up on weekends. Overflow parking is available across Bel Air Road near the Gunpowder Lodge. The Central Area of the park is open between sunrise and sunset. Dogs are welcome but must remain leashed. The restored gristmill in historic Jerusalem Mill Village serves as headquarters for Gunpowder Falls State Park. For more information, call the office at 410-592-2897 from 8 A.M. to 4 P.M. Monday through Friday, except on state holidays.

The calm Gunpowder River landscape is a draw for hikers.

NEARBY

Gunpowder Falls State Park's Central Area encompasses the historic Jerusalem Mill. In the eighteenth and nineteenth centuries, the operations of the gristmill supported a bustling Quaker settlement. The historic village hosts a variety of events throughout the year, including a large Civil War encampment for reenactors in early summer. Contact the park office for this year's event dates. The Visitor Center and Museum are open on Saturdays and Sundays from 1 P.M. to 4 P.M., and the Blacksmith Shop offers demonstrations of iron-working techniques during the same hours.

2

COLONIAL ANNAPOLIS HISTORIC DISTRICT

Explore the rich heritage of Maryland's capital city, Annapolis, on this tour of its quaint historic downtown neighborhood.

DIRECTIONS

From I-495 (Capital Beltway), take US 50 east to Exit 24 and merge onto I-70 south. After 1.2 miles, turn slightly right then slightly left onto Northwest Street. After 0.2 mile, turn left onto Church Circle. Take a right onto Duke of Gloucester Street; after 0.2 mile, turn left onto Green Street, followed by a left onto Main Street and a left onto Gorman Street. The parking garage (Noah Hillman Garage) is at 150 Gorman Street. *GPS coordinates*: 38° 58.638′ N, 76° 29.361′ W.

TRAIL DESCRIPTION

Annapolis is rich with history; many of its structures date from the eighteenth century. Although it is a bustling capital city, it has the feel of an old-fashioned small town. The Colonial Annapolis Historic District, located in the city's downtown, is designated as a National Historic Landmark. The streets that surround the joined circles containing the State House and St. Anne's Church are full of significant structures with tales to tell.

Parking at the Noah Hillman Garage costs $5 for 1 to 2 hours, $8 for up to 3 hours, and $11 for up to 4 hours. If this garage is full when you arrive, the Gotts Court Garage on 25 Northwest Street is also conveniently located.

Exit the Noah Hillman Parking Garage onto Gorman Street; turn left and take another left on Conduit Street. Immediately on your right at the corner is the John Callahan House (164 Conduit Street), which dates from the eighteenth century. Its builder, John Callahan, served as the register for land records for the western shore of

LOCATION
Annapolis, MD

RATING
Easy

DISTANCE
3.1 miles

ELEVATION GAIN
87 feet

ESTIMATED TIME
1.5 hours

MAPS
USGS Annapolis; online: visitannapolis.org/map

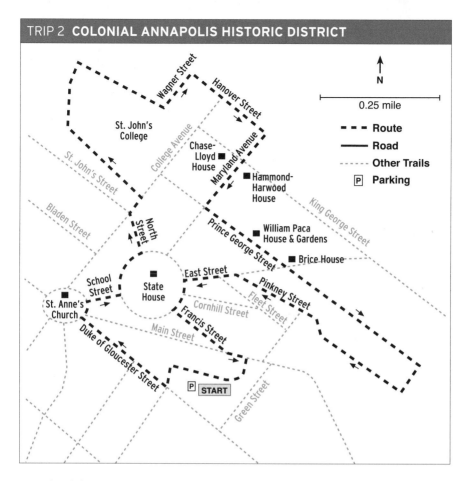

Maryland during the Revolutionary War. Mann's Tavern on the opposite corner (162 Conduit Street) was the site of the 1786 Annapolis Convention, in which delegates from 12 states called for a constitutional convention.

At the top of the short hill, cross Conduit Street and turn right onto Duke of Gloucester Street. When you arrive at Church Circle, cross Main Street and turn left on the inner sidewalk that circles historic St. Anne's Church. The original church building dated from 1704, but the current church, which replaced an enlarged building that had burned to the ground, dates from 1859. Built in the Romanesque Revival style, the current building is an active Episcopal parish serving residents of Annapolis and surrounding areas.

Crossing Main Street again, exit the circle on School Street, following signs for State Circle. As you pass the Maryland Government House on the left, pause to appreciate its lovely, well-curated gardens. Bear left onto State Circle, passing the State House on the right. Maryland's State House is the oldest state capitol building still in use in the United States. The Continental Congress met here from 1783 to 1784; it is the only state house to ever serve as the U.S. Capitol.

Magnolia blossoms frame the historic St. Anne's Church. The building, which dates from 1859, still houses an active Episcopal parish. Photo by MarylandReporter, Creative Commons on Flickr.

Take a left onto North Street, passing several shingled homes. Cross College Avenue to arrive at St. John's College, which got its start in 1696 as King William's School, a grammar and prep school. In 1784, Maryland chartered St John's College as its first institution of higher education; four signers of the Declaration of Independence number among its founders. Head diagonally into the campus on a brick path. Pass the Greenfield Library/State of Maryland Records Hall on the left. Turn slightly left toward Campbell Hall before you reach McDowell Hall; pass Campbell, head down the stairs, and continue straight on a brick path with the quad to your right and Mitchell Gallery on your left. The path passes under a low concrete arch at the entrance to Mellon Hall with the diminutive McKeldin Planetarium on the right. Pass the rainwater garden and Spector Hall on the left. As you reach Gilliam Hall, you will emerge in view of College Creek.

Turn right and walk along the lip of the slope. Trace the edge of the field, heading left to view the memorial to Sons of the Revolution: unknown French soldiers and sailors who died in the Revolutionary War. Behind the memorial is the path down to Hodson Boathouse. Turn right and walk along the sidewalk parallel to King George Street (MD 450). Pass the college's private tennis courts on the right. When you reach the parking area for Iglehart Hall, turn left to exit to King George Street and then turn right. Cross to take a left on Wagner, a quiet street with brick sidewalks that slope steeply downhill. Turn right onto Hanover at the bottom of the hill and climb back up the slope in view of the iconic green dome of the Naval Academy Chapel. The wall of the Naval Academy complex borders Hanover Street on your left. As you approach the entrance to the academy, turn right onto Maryland Avenue.

Historical houses cluster on either side of this brick-paved, tree-lined avenue. On your left is the Hammond-Harwood House, now a museum. Renowned architect William Buckland, who also designed Gunston Hall on the George Mason Plantation, built this structure for a 25-year-old tobacco planter, Matthias Hammond. Although Hammond never lived there, choosing instead to live on his plantation in Gambrills, Maryland, the Hammond-Harwood house is nonetheless an architectural treasure, featuring some of the finest plasterwork and wood carving of its era. The house served as the center for the St. John's College decorative arts program in the 1920s, and the Hammond-Harwood House Association purchased it in 1940 for the purpose of preserving the site.

On your right is the Chase-Lloyd House, which is open for tours from 2 P.M. to 4 P.M. Monday through Saturday, except in January and February. This residence was built in the Georgian style in 1774, also by Buckland. The land the house sits on had previously been owned by Samuel Chase, who would go on to sign the Declaration of Independence.

With the State House in sight ahead, turn left onto Prince George Street, which is lined with beautiful historic row homes. The William Paca House and Gardens, on the left at 186 Prince George Street, is a five-part Georgian mansion dating from the 1760s. William Paca was another signer of the Declaration of Independence, and he went on to become the third governor of Maryland. In 1901, the tennis champion William Larned purchased the house and converted it into a hotel. Historic Annapolis, a preservation organization, and the State of Maryland later bought and restored the property and its gardens. Self-guided garden tours are available for a $5 entrance fee.

Cross East Street and notice the James Brice House (42 East Street) on the corner. James Brice was a lawyer, a planter, and a governor of Maryland. His historic home, built in 1767, is among Annapolis's largest Georgian mansions. Continue straight past a dead end sign to where Prince George Street terminates at Spa Creek. Turn right on the boardwalk and cross over to Annapolis's City Dock. Circle the edge of the water then cross Randall Street onto Market Space, which shortly becomes Pinkney Street. Immediately on your right is the Waterfront Warehouse, a replica of an eighteenth-century dockside warehouse that is now a museum. The Artisan's House, located on your left at 43 Pinkney Street, likely dates to the early 1700s and may have housed troops during the Revolutionary War. Land records show the house served as state barracks for Maryland in 1777.

Emerge on East Street and take a left toward Spire Street. Return to State Circle, heading to the left; take another left onto Francis Street down a brick slope.

Bear left to continue onto Main Street, and immediately cross to Hyde Street. The parking garage is ahead on Gorman Street.

MORE INFORMATION

Learn more about Annapolis' many historic structures from Historic Annapolis (annapolis.org). Tips and information on arts, culture, and events can be found at downtownannapolis.org.

NEARBY

On a hot day, make sure to pause at City Dock to enjoy some ice cream or coffee and look out over the waterfront, known to locals as "Ego Alley" because of the many expensive boats that pass through or anchor there.

Annapolis also has a rich military history. You may wish to take a few extra hours for a tour of the United States Naval Academy to see the campus grounds and U.S. Navy historical artifacts. Personal identification is required to enter the Naval Academy.

3

CALVERT CLIFFS STATE PARK

Calvert Cliffs State Park offers a perfect circuit hike, with a halfway point at a stretch of Miocene-epoch cliffs rich in sharks' teeth and other ancient fossils.

DIRECTIONS

Calvert Cliffs State Park is located on the western shore of Chesapeake Bay, near the mouth of the Patuxent River. From I-95/I-495 (Capital Beltway), take Exit 11 onto MD 4 east (Pennsylvania Avenue) in the direction of Upper Marlboro. Travel approximately 36 miles, during which MD 4 becomes MD 4/MD 2. Turn left onto MD 765, approximately 14 miles south of the town of Prince Frederick. Follow MD 765 a short distance to the park. Parking is located around the central picnic area (25 spaces) or at a side lot (40 spaces). *GPS coordinates*: 38° 24.576′ N, 76° 27.099′ W.

TRAIL DESCRIPTION

Calvert Cliffs State Park is a uniquely Chesapeake Bay treasure, containing 100-foot-high cliffs formed 10 to 20 million years ago during the Miocene epoch, when a warm, shallow sea covered southern Maryland. As the sea receded, the exposed cliffs began to erode. More than 600 species of fossils have been identified from the sands of Calvert Cliffs, including whale ear bones and skulls; crocodile snouts; the dental plate of a ray; and shark teeth from mako, snaggletooth, requiem, sand, tiger, and cow varieties, as well as the extinct megalodon. Remnants of these prehistoric creatures still frequently turn up today and collecting fossils from the beach is allowed. More recently, but still more than 400 years ago, Captain John Smith noted these cliffs on a map dated 1612, naming

LOCATION
Lusby, MD

RATING
Moderate

DISTANCE
4.8 miles

ELEVATION GAIN
330 feet

ESTIMATED TIME
2 to 2.5 hours

MAPS
USGS Cove Point; Maryland Trail Guide available for purchase online at shopdnr.com/calvertcliffsstatepark.aspx

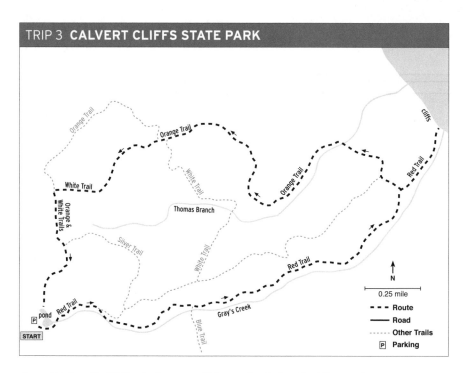

Orange Trail

Orange Trail

White Trail

White Trail

Orange Trail

cliffs

Red Trail

Orange & White Trails

Thomas Branch

White Trail

Silver Trail

Red Trail

N

0.25 mile

- - - Route

—— Road

······ Other Trails

P Parking

pond

P

Red Trail

Gray's Creek

Blue Trail

START

them Rickard's Cliffes in honor of his mother's family. The park contains 1,079 acres and has 13 miles of hiking trails.

Begin this hike on Red Trail (also called Cliff Trail), to the right of a pond adjacent to the picnic area. This trail runs 1.8 miles to the cliffs on the Chesapeake Bay. (Access to the cliff tops is closed due to landslides.) Cross a bridge over the edge of the pond near the picnic area and follow the trail left to cross Gray's Creek. White oaks and chestnut oaks rise overhead. Holly bushes and mountain laurel spread out at eye level, and beach sand dusts the trail underfoot. Turn right onto a gravel service road and walk 50 yards to a right turn to continue on Red Trail. Follow the small rapids of Gray's Creek as it carves its way between ridges. Pass intersections with Yellow Trail, at 0.2 mile, and Blue Trail, at 0.6 mile.

At 1.1 miles, the creek reaches an open tidal marsh replete with sunflowers, broadleaf arrowheads (a variety of edible tuber), cold-hardy swamp mallow, invasive arrow arum, spatterdock, and white water lilies. At 1.3 miles, a platform leads out over the marsh to a panoramic and aromatic viewpoint and, farther along, fecund pools of more broadleaf arrowhead and water lilies. At 1.6 miles, the trail reconnects with the service road then passes a network of beaver dams—the structures responsible for converting gentle Gray's Creek into a sprawling marsh. At 1.8 miles, you'll come to Chesapeake Bay and the stunning Calvert Cliffs.

The cliffs are the park's most rewarding sight and most powerful attraction. Over 100 feet high, Calvert Cliffs contain the highest concentration of Miocene

Warm-season visitors enjoy the sandy Chesapeake Bay beach at Calvert Cliffs State Park, where ancient fossils and shark teeth have been found. Photo by Alliecat1881, Creative Commons on Flickr.

fossils on the East Coast. Scientists, rock hounds, and children are equally drawn to the cliffs in search of these ancient traces of life dating from millions of years ago. Don't be surprised to find people searching with the serious-minded fervor of prospectors!

Please keep in mind that the cliffs are fragile, eroding at a rate of 3 feet per year. The area directly beneath the cliffs is closed due to the potential for injury from landslides, and it is illegal to climb or hike onto the cliffs, or to collect fossils beneath them. Swimming and collecting, however, are allowed at the beach.

Return via Red Trail and turn right onto the service road, climbing 90 feet before a right turn onto Orange Trail, marked by a wooden pole and GPS coordinates. Plunge down the other side of the hill to a 150-foot-long bridge over Thomas Creek Bog, constructed in 1999 as part of an Eagle Scout project. The bridge affords access to the heart of the freshwater marsh, where sweetgum maples overhead filter prismatic sun rays onto a surface dappled with water lilies, arrowheads, and swarms of swift-moving dragonflies in summer.

After crossing the bridge, turn 90 degrees to the left and pass through a pine grove, following the edge of the bog as it narrows to a creek bed. Pass a connector trail that comes in from the left (leading to White Trail) and, just after it, begin a steep, 80-foot scramble to the top of a ridge. Turn left along the top of the ridge and pass sweetgums and top-heavy pawpaw trees before linking up with White

Trail at 3.6 miles. Proceed straight ahead on White Trail and after a short distance, begin a roller-coaster ride of a hike over folded terrain.

Climb the side of a ridge, tracing the hill's contours, and soon enter a grove of monumental yellow poplars and more leafy pawpaw trees. At 4.3 miles into the hike, reach a clearing with cornfields and turn left, passing the intersection of White Trail and Orange Trail near a meadow filled with purple milkwort and Queen Anne's lace—the best place in the park to see swallowtail butterflies feasting on nectar. From here, White and Orange trails run together for the rest of your hike. At 4.6 miles, pass an intersection with Silver Trail and a large fire-warning siren, then pass some large-leafed paulownia and black locust trees on the left—species not found anywhere else in the park. Finally, turn right past a gate onto the service road and follow it the final 0.1 mile back to the parking lot.

MORE INFORMATION

The park entrance is located at 10540 H. G. Trueman Road, Lusby, MD 20657. Entry to the park is $5 per car. Weather-resistant trail maps are available for sale at the gate. Dogs are allowed in the park, on leash. There is also a recycled-tire playground, probably the ultimate stop for children visiting the park. Portions of Calvert Cliffs State Park are open to hunting, including areas crossed by Orange Trail, so be alert and wear bright colors during fall deer season and spring turkey season.

One of Maryland's most popular parks, Calvert Cliffs receives large numbers of visitors during summer weekends and holidays. The park closes when it reaches capacity, and traffic is turned away from the park entrance. If you are traveling with a crowd during summer, plan to carpool together or at least arrive at the same time. For more information, visit dnr.maryland.gov/publiclands/Pages/southern/calvertcliffs.aspx or call 301-743-7613.

NEARBY

Middleham Chapel, an Episcopal church constructed in 1748, is situated just north of the park entrance on MD 765. Also nearby are Flag Ponds Park (farther north on MD 2) and the Battle Creek Cypress Swamp Sanctuary, a 100-acre site that is one of the northernmost habitats of the bald cypress tree. A few miles north on MD 2 in Solomons, the Calvert Marine Museum is a popular family-friendly attraction offering a woodcarving shop (admission fee applies). Other options include tours of the Drum Point Lighthouse and charming exhibits centering on maritime history, paleontology, and estuarine biology of the Chesapeake Bay region. A marsh walk leads to a river otter habitat.

4

ANNAPOLIS ROCK AND BLACK ROCK CLIFF

One of Maryland's most popular day hikes, this out-and-back on the Appalachian Trail offers stunning views from two lookouts.

DIRECTIONS

From I-495 (Capital Beltway), take I-270 north for 29.1 miles. Take Exit 32 to merge onto I-70 west. After 11.5 miles, take Exit 42 onto MD 17 north. After 0.7 mile, turn right to continue on MD 17 north. After 0.4 mile, turn left onto US 40 west. Drive 3 miles; the parking area is on the left. *GPS Coordinates: 39° 32.133' N, 77° 36.245' W*

TRAIL DESCRIPTION

As the Appalachian Trail (AT) passes through Myersville, Maryland, its fortuitous proximity to the road allows day-hikers to take advantage of two impressive viewpoints on the South Mountain Ridge—Annapolis Rock and Black Rock Cliff—with less than 1,000 feet of climbing. Falling within the region designated as South Mountain State Park, this hike attracts a mix of long-distance hikers, day-trippers, and families with young children. The South Mountain Ridge is located along a migration route for eagles, hawks, and owls; keep an eye out for these winged travelers.

The parking area by the side of US 40 is fairly expansive but fills up on weekends as day-trippers flock to this popular trailhead so plan on arriving early. Begin on the paved section of the connector trail, past the Appalachian Trail sign. When the old section of road terminates at a highway barrier, turn left at the blue-blazed post. Follow the rocky path as it curves around to the narrow, covered pedestrian bridge over I-70. Do not cross the bridge; turn right immediately before it, following the sign that indicates a distance of 2.2 miles to Annapolis Rock.

LOCATION
Myersville, MD

RATING
Moderate

DISTANCE
7.2 miles

ELEVATION GAIN
840 feet

ESTIMATED TIME
3.5 hours

MAPS
USGS Myersville; Appalachian Trail Guide, from Potomac Appalachian Trail Club, Map 6 or MD DNR: Appalachian Trail from Maryland Department of Natural Resources; also available at Appalachian Trail Conservancy, 799 Washington Street, Harpers Ferry, WV, 25425; online: dhweb.com/cvb/smra14/ (pages 10–11)

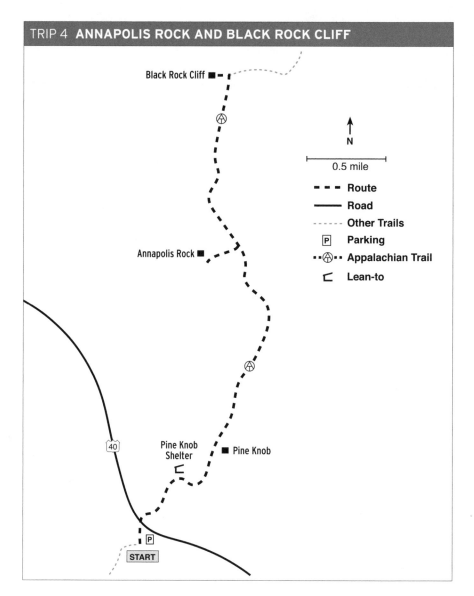

Black Rock Cliff ■ ▪

N

0.5 mile

▪ ▪ ▪ Route
━━━ Road
▬▬▬ Other Trails
P Parking
▪▪Ⓐ▪▪ Appalachian Trail
⊏ Lean-to

Annapolis Rock ■

40

Pine Knob
Shelter

■ Pine Knob

P

START

The level path follows noisy I-70, separated from the busy traffic by some elevation and a chain-link fence. Walk under the US 40 bridge then curve to the right, away from the traffic, as the trail rises steeply into the forest. Pass a placard welcoming you to the Appalachian Trail as the path curves left. Soon after, an unmarked splinter trail departs to the right; stay straight, following the AT's white blazes.

The trail crosses a utility cut under power lines before returning to the cover of trees. At 0.5 mile, the first connector trail for the Pine Knob shelter branches off to the left, followed shortly by the second connector trail to the same shelter. Pass both of these side trails, continuing to follow the AT. The elevation gain is

A hiker observes the view from Black Rock Cliff. This vista, just off the Appalachian Trail, offers one of the most scenic overlooks in South Mountain State Park. Photo by Annie Eddy.

steep for the next half-mile as the trail becomes rockier. Ascend over logs crossing the trail before turning right and left on switchbacks. Pass an unmarked trail that departs to the right, staying on the AT as it curves to the left.

At 1.1 miles, the trail levels out as you crest South Mountain Ridge. Ferns blanket the forest floor and fringe the trail, and the ground rises on either side of the path, giving the ferns the appearance of height. The trail descends briefly before leveling out into a sandy track bordered by rocks. Begin to climb again, more gently now. A large rock outcrop on the right, 100 yards from the trail, offers an obstructed view down into the forest below the ridge. Pass through another grove of ferns as the view begins to gradually open up on the right before the trail curves back into the woods.

At 2.3 miles, arrive at the intersection with Annapolis Rock connector trail. Turn left, following blue blazes, to descend 0.25 mile to the viewpoint. Pass the caretaker's campsite on the right. Soon after, a sign welcomes you to Annapolis Rock Backpacking Campground, with paths leading to campsites on either side and to a privy on the right. As you approach the cliff, a fence separates the trail from a reforestation area. Arrive at the lookout, which offers a sweeping view to the west. Greenbriar Lake, the site of a popular day-use beach within Greenbriar State Park, is visible to the southwest.

Return to the intersection with the AT and turn left to continue 1 mile north to Black Rock Cliff. The trail remains level for some time. To the left, sky is visible through the trees where the ground slopes away. An unmarked turnoff to the left leads 100 yards off the trail to a smaller but still impressive vista. Continue toward Black Rock Cliff, passing a reforestation area posted with a "No Camping" sign. Soon after, at 3.6 miles, a sign marks the turnoff for the connector trail to Black Rock Cliff. Take a left on the connector and proceed 75 yards to the overlook. This viewpoint offers a panoramic view to the west, looking over scree and dead trees to the distant farms, fields, and bustling highway.

To return, take a right (south) from the Black Rock Cliff connector trail, retracing your steps back to the US 40 parking area.

MORE INFORMATION

Hunting is allowed in South Mountain State Park, although not within 150 yards of the Appalachian Trail. Pets are allowed. For more information, visit dnr.maryland.gov/publiclands/Pages/western/southmountain.aspx or call 301-791-4767.

NEARBY

History buffs should make a stop at nearby South Mountain State Battlefield, the site of Maryland's first major Civil War battle. The aftermath of the Battle of South Mountain precipitated the Battle of Antietam, the bloodiest day in our nation's history (see Trip 15: Antietam National Battlefield). Washington Monument State Park on South Mountain boasts hiking trails, mostly part of the Appalachian Trail, around the nineteenth-century monument.

5

BALTIMORE WATERFRONT PROMENADE

Take a tour of Baltimore's historic waterfront, passing boats, luxury homes, and the iconic Domino Sugars sign, then make your return trip by water taxi to see the shorefront from another angle.

DIRECTIONS

From I-495 (Capital Beltway), take the Baltimore-Washington Parkway to MD 295 north. Continue on MD 295 north for 11.5 miles. Take the I-95 north exit then take Exit 56 and merge onto Keith Avenue. After 0.5 mile, Keith Avenue becomes South Clinton Street; continue for 1 mile more. Turn left onto Boston Street. The parking lot for Canton Waterfront Park will be on your left. *GPS coordinates:* 39° 16.628′ N, 76° 34.318′ W.

TRAIL DESCRIPTION

Baltimore's Waterfront Promenade, maintained by the Waterfront Partnership, covers 7 miles along Baltimore Harbor through the Canton, Fells Point, and Harbor East neighborhoods. The Promenade terminates at historic Fort McHenry, where Francis Scott Key wrote the lyrics to the U.S. national anthem while under siege by British troops. For the best views of the sparkling waters of Baltimore Harbor and its boats and luxury condominiums, start at Canton Waterfront Park, travel through Canton and Fells Point toward Harbor East, then catch the Water Taxi back to your car.

Parking is free at Canton Waterfront Park. The lot is relatively large, and how busy it is depends on events taking place in the park. After walking west in the park, you may wish to pause to pay respects at the Korean War Memorial. Once you're ready, begin on the Promenade by heading west along the brick walkway that hugs the waterfront.

LOCATION
Baltimore, MD

RATING
Easy to moderate

DISTANCE
3.75 miles

ELEVATION GAIN
79 feet

ESTIMATED TIME
2 to 2.5 hours

MAPS
USGS Baltimore East; online: Waterfront Partnership of Baltimore, baltimorewaterfront .com/getting-around/visitor (located under "Walk")

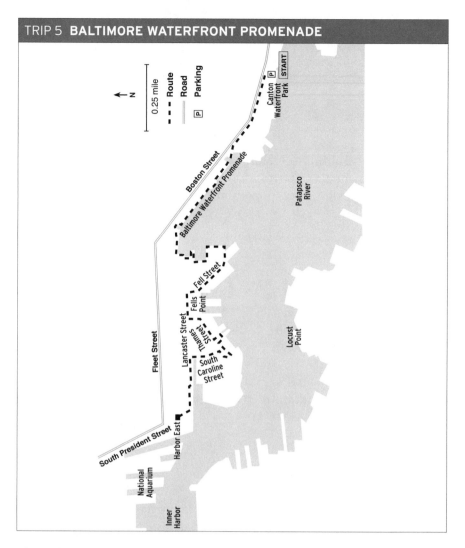

Throughout the hike, follow the green Waterfront Partnership signs that feature a map of your route. Maps are also available online; when in doubt, follow the edge of the water.

The walkway turns left at 0.4 mile; follow the brick walkway and signs onto Tindeco Wharf with its many boat moorings. Continue along the wharf; when you see the Safeway grocery store on the right across the road, the brick walkway turns left. Soon after, the backside of the iconic, neon Domino Sugars sign comes into view across the water. Domino has been refining sugar in Baltimore's Inner Harbor for 95 years; today, 6.6 million pounds of sugar per day is refined there. The Promenade turns right at the Captain James Crab House. Emerge at the intersection of Boston Street and Aliceanna Street; turn left onto the sidewalk then left again opposite Chester Street, toward Chester Cove. Bearing right through the Cove, pick up the brick walkway and continue onto the boardwalk at the Chester Cove sign. Weave along the dock at Union Wharf, keeping an eye out for warped boards.

Continue onto the boardwalk by the Inn at Henderson's Wharf. Soon after, emerge onto the Broadway Pier, passing the Urban Pirates shopfront; depending on the time of day, you may see *Fearless*, Baltimore Harbor's pirate-themed tour boat, docked or passing by. If you smell bread baking, that's because the famed H&S Bakery, which has been operating in Baltimore since 1943, is nearby. The cobbled streets indicate you are entering Fells Point, Baltimore's historic waterfront neighborhood. Cross Thames Street at the intersection of South Ann Street to avoid construction on the waterfront and continue along Thames Street on the brick sidewalk, heading west. You are likely to encounter crowds here at the Broadway Square plaza, where you may wish to pause for a cold lemonade.

Turn left, crossing back over Thames Street toward the water taxi stop, to continue along the water around Bond Street Wharf. When you pass Water Taxi Stop No. 8, you have gone almost 3 miles. Circle around to the right, following the brick walkway. Soon, 0.1 mile later, the promenade reaches Thames Street Wharf and passes a bust of Frederick Douglass, who escaped slavery in

On the Baltimore Waterfront Promenade, the beloved trash wheel, affectionately nicknamed Mr. Trash Wheel, is the first invention of its kind to prevent trash from local riverways from entering the harbor. A 2016 campaign by residents resulted in the addition of an oversized pair of googly eyes.

Baltimore and later returned to construct the Douglass Place row homes in Fells Point, which offered rental housing to black people at the time. Also visible are the remains of the nineteenth-century marine railway, where shipbuilding materials were transported and boats launched. This is one of three spots on the Promenade where fishing is allowed, and you may see residents availing themselves of this opportunity.

Continue along the Promenade. At the end of Thames Street Wharf, the Domino Sugars sign is now visible from the front. Look for detour signs, if necessary, to avoid ongoing construction in this area. Parts of the Promenade in Fells Point and Harbor East remain under development, and the route is subject to minor changes, which will be marked. Developers who build along the waterfront must maintain the Promenade route, but during active construction, the route may need to leave the water's edge briefly. If you encounter construction, follow detour signs to head several blocks north into the city, and then rejoin the Promenade.

As you enter the Harbor East neighborhood, luxury high-rise apartments line the waterfront, and the Four Seasons hotel rises up on the right. At 0.1 mile later, take a moment to view and learn about Baltimore Harbor's beloved trash wheel, which uses a combination of water and solar power to filter trash out of the harbor. A 2016 campaign by residents resulted in the addition of a pair of oversized googly eyes to the personified "Mr. Trash Wheel," and a campaign to build a second wheel in Canton, this one known as "Professor Trash Wheel," is in the works. You are now at Water Taxi Stop No. 7, where you can catch the boat back to Canton Waterfront Park and your car. The Water Taxi costs $8 for a one-way pass; check hours, which vary seasonally, at baltimorewatertaxi.com. For a land-based route back to your car, catch the number 31 city bus, which runs every 20 minutes, at the corner of President Street and Eastern Avenue for a fare of $1.60. Get off at the intersection of Boston Street and Ellwood Avenue to return to your car.

MORE INFORMATION

The Waterfront Promenade is almost completely exposed to sun, which makes this a walk better suited for cooler weather. Although the wind off the harbor is often refreshing, Baltimore's summer heat and humidity can be grueling. Make sure you have access to ample hydration if you choose to visit in July or August.

NEARBY

For a more ambitious trip, follow the Promenade's full 7 miles to Fort McHenry. The Promenade departs from the water in several areas, but your patience will be rewarded with a stunning vista overlooking the harbor at the fort, where you can take a tour and learn about Francis Scott Key's writing of the U.S. national anthem.

SUGAR, SPICE, EVERYTHING NICE: INDUSTRY IN BALTIMORE TOWN

Strolling along Baltimore's streets and wharves, you're exploring a maritime city dating back more than 300 years, to the 1706 establishment of a port intended to service the tobacco trade between Great Britain and its colonies. Named in 1729 for Maryland's first proprietary royal governor, Cecil Calvert, Lord Baltimore, the city grew rapidly with the success of its port. Mills built behind the wharves soon made Baltimore a top processing center for sugar crops imported from the Caribbean.

Fells Point, the natural harbor's deepest point, grew into the colony's main shipbuilding center and later emerged as a national leader in the construction of clipper ships. The gold rush to California brought many orders for fast ocean-going vessels, and after the Civil War, a special ship was designed here to accommodate coffee trade with Brazil. Meanwhile, overland pioneers provisioned themselves with canned goods produced in Baltimore. Waterfront areas in the neighborhoods of Fells Point, Canton, Federal Hill, and Locust Point housed canneries that packed food for domestic markets and global export—a new industry in which Baltimore led the world by the 1870s.

Baltimore boasted the nation's first railroad, the Baltimore & Ohio (B&O), chartered in 1827. In 1830, Peter Cooper's "Tom Thumb" engine made the journey over the railroad's first 13 miles of track in one hour. The line reached the Ohio River in 1852, comprising 380 double-tracked miles and opening up unprecedented trading opportunities between the Atlantic seaboard and the Midwest.

Culturally and commercially, Baltimore has always been something of an edgy juxtaposition: a southern town that seems northern in its eagerness for industry and innovation. Baltimore lies closer to the Mason-Dixon Line than other major southern cities such as Richmond and Atlanta. Plentiful working-class jobs drew nearly two million mostly European immigrants in the late nineteenth and early twentieth centuries. For decades, Baltimore was an immigrant intake point second in volume only to Ellis Island. Jobs plus proximity to the North also made the city a haven for escaped slaves and free blacks seeking their own American dream. Competition for laborers' jobs among black people and those European immigrants occasionally led to unrest.

Baltimore inaugurated the first post office system in the Colonies in 1774, as well as the new nation's first chartered municipal water company in 1792. Further enhancing the convenience of urban life and the city's up-and-coming reputation, Baltimore introduced lighting fueled by hydrogen coal gas, which was piped through wooden mains in 1816. The first such "rings beset with gems of light," as a contemporary advertisement phrased it, were showcased at Rembrandt Peale's museum of art and curiosities. The museum exists today as the Municipal Museum (still known to locals as Peale's Museum) on

Holliday Street. Gas streetlights soon followed at Market and Lemmon streets (now Baltimore and Holliday).

Another shining example of Baltimorean industry was the various incarnations of Kirk-Stieff-Schofield Silver, once the oldest continually operating silversmith in the United States. In 1828 the firm revived an old technique known as *repoussé* (French for "pushed again"), a process of tracing and chasing patterns on sheet silver using so-called snarling irons and small hammers, eventually raising lovely, detailed designs that became known to Victorian-era Americans as Baltimore silver.

Other nice things crafted in Baltimore included soldiers' and sailors' uniforms, which laid the groundwork for a full-fledged men's clothing industry—another innovation, as most clothing of the day was home-sewn or tailor-made rather than ready-to-wear. Many early immigrants were skilled in needlecrafts and quickly could begin to earn a good living, even working as cottage-industry contractors. Oehm's Acme Hall began manufacturing clothing for men and women in 1850, employing 500 people. Rosenfeld's New York Clothing House, also established in 1850, got its start making police and firefighter uniforms. By 1860, the manufacture of men's clothing became Baltimore's leading industry, in terms of both dollars earned and individuals employed. Of course, the well-dressed man or woman wanted to be well accessorized, so Franz Bechler opened a local umbrella factory in 1828. His products sported carved wooden shafts and spokelike whalebone ribs. The firm also produced walking canes and whips for driving horse-drawn buggies.

Past visitors to Baltimore often noticed savory aromas in the air—a pleasant form of pollution produced by the spice-processing plant of McCormick and Company, founded in 1889 in downtown Baltimore and located there for its first 100 years before moving to the suburbs. The Fortune 1000 company today owns the iconic Old Bay Seasoning brand, among other household names. And the sugar trade lives on downtown, in the building bearing the beloved Domino Sugars sign.

But Baltimore's industrial past has given way to a service economy, and many factory jobs with solid wages are long gone. There's hope, though: In September 2016, city officials approved a $660 million bond deal for a massive waterfront redevelopment project, championed by the Under Armour clothing company founder, Kevin Plank. The project, comprising new company headquarters, shops, housing, offices, and manufacturing spaces, is projected to create 26,500 permanent jobs.

6

SENECA CREEK STATE PARK: CLOPPER LAKE

This hike travels underneath towering mature hardwoods—first following Great Seneca Creek to Clopper Lake then circling the lake—and offers excellent shoreline views across open water.

DIRECTIONS

From the I-495 (Capital Beltway) inner loop, take Exit 38 (from the outer loop, take Exit 35) onto I-270 north toward Frederick. Take Exit 10 and stay in the right lane to turn right onto MD 117 (becomes Clopper Road). Travel west approximately 2 miles and turn left into the park, followed by an immediate right into the visitor center parking lot. *GPS coordinates*: 39° 9.054′ N, 77° 14.858′ W.

TRAIL DESCRIPTION

Seneca Creek State Park is a 16.5-mile-long stretch of preserved land running along both sides of Great Seneca Creek. Comprising 6,500 acres, the park starts just outside of Gaithersburg's town limits and continues south to Riley's Lock, the creek's confluence with the Potomac River, near the McKee-Beshers Wildlife Management Area. The Clopper Lake area is in the northern section of the park. The park's trail system is extensive: The 25-mile Greenway Trail follows Great Seneca Creek for its entire distance, and the Schaeffer Farm area has 10 miles of loops popular with mountain bikers and equestrians. Traveling under the tall ceilings of old-growth deciduous trees and viewing several crumbling nineteenth-century mills provides a pleasantly humbling experience.

Start your hike at the visitor center off Clopper Road. The circa-1855 Grusendorf Log House stands nearby on land that was the former estate of Francis C. Clopper, who, along with his descendants, built several mills on Great Seneca Creek. One of these mills, just to the north near

LOCATION
Gaithersburg, MD

RATING
Moderate

DISTANCE
4.5 miles

ELEVATION GAIN
400 to 500 feet

ESTIMATED TIME
2.5 to 3 hours

MAPS
USGS Seneca; Maryland Trail Guide (shopdnr.com/ SenecaCreekStatePark.aspx); online: dnr2.maryland.gov/ publiclands/Pages/central/ seneca.aspx

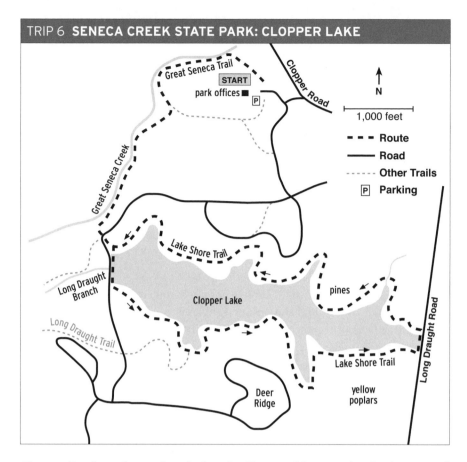

Clopper Road, made woolen clothes for Union soldiers in the Civil War, and another near the creek's confluence with the Potomac River cut the red sandstone used to construct the Smithsonian Castle in Washington, D.C.

At the intersection of the entrance road and the parking lot, start on the 1.2-mile, orange-blazed Great Seneca Trail. The trail immediately descends 100 feet, running parallel to MD 117 through a draw (a small valley running across a ridge or streambed) with power lines, a tunnel of dense shrubbery, and a series of knolls supporting great sycamores and oaks. Throughout this hike, try to distinguish sycamores (mottled bark with cream-colored underbark) from maples (hard, close-grained bark).

Upon reaching the intersection with Great Seneca Creek, turn left. The 0.6-mile stretch along the creek passes through a lush deciduous forest and is frequently muddy from floods. The branches of massive oaks, sycamores, maples, and beeches form a lofty, leafy ceiling 40 feet overhead. At a point where a beaver-dammed island splits the water into two channels, the trail bends left under a few large maples and passes through an aromatic pine grove. Enter an open draw, cross a wooden bridge over seasonal runoff, and return to deep-green pines.

The trail emerges into a second draw, recrossing the power lines encountered earlier. Downy woodpeckers enjoy the poles, and spring and summer wildflowers, with their distinctive woody smell, attract spicebush and tiger swallowtail butterflies. Go past the intersection with Old Pond Trail and over a bridge that spans a trickling tributary. A wide lane runs along the power lines for several hundred yards, parallel to the edge of the forest, then plunges back into the woods. The moss-covered path winds left and right on a high ridge over Seneca Creek before veering sharply left for an 80-foot ascent to a park road. The road marks the endpoint of Great Seneca Trail.

Cross the road in the direction of Clopper Lake (southeast). Turn right onto the blue-blazed Lake Shore Trail, which encircles the 90-acre lake. Stream-fed fingers, which you'll cross via wooden walkways, reach out from Clopper's north and south sides. This hike offers excellent opportunities to see red-shouldered hawks, ospreys, and barred owls fishing for dinner, as well as great blue herons roosting in the treetops. The tree diversity—maples, oaks, sycamores, pines, cedars, hickories, beeches, and yellow poplars—makes for a great variety of reds, oranges, and yellows rimming the lake in autumn against a backdrop of

Autumn sunshine casts reflections through the hardwoods lining the shores of Clopper Lake, in Seneca Creek State Park. Photo by Mr. TinDC, Creative Commons on Flickr.

evergreens. Note that park officials have rerouted the trail away from the immediate shore to higher ground in some areas to restore the natural lakeside environment. Head for higher ground whenever the trail forks; the first tree on the correct route is always clearly marked with a blue blaze.

As you loop around the third spur on the lake's north side (after 2.7 miles), continue past the boating center. Stay on Lake Shore Trail until you complete the loop around Clopper Lake. At the intersection with Great Seneca Trail, take a right and retrace your steps along Great Seneca Creek, back to the visitor center and parking area.

MORE INFORMATION

The park entrance is located at 11950 Clopper Road, Gaithersburg, MD 20878. The entrance fee is $3 per person ($5 out-of-state; no fee November–March). The Clopper Lake Boat Center has canoes, kayaks, and paddleboats available for rent and offers nature tours via its Heron Pontoon Boat in the summer. The center also rents fishing poles, sells bait, and offers classes in fishing. Check the U.S. Geological Survey (USGS) gauging station on MD 28 for water levels, which should be at 2.1 feet or higher. A 32-acre Frisbee golf course is available. Find scorecards and golf discs in the visitor center. For more information, visit dnr2.maryland.gov/publiclands/Pages/central/seneca.aspx or call 301-924-2127.

NEARBY

Magruder Trail, Black Hill Regional Park (see Trip 17), and Little Bennett Regional Park all offer great hiking trails nearby. For an excellent topographical map of Seneca Creek State Park, visit shopdnr.com/SenecaCreekStatePark.aspx.

7

JUG BAY WETLANDS SANCTUARY

A hidden treasure along the tidal Patuxent River in southern Maryland, this pristine wildlife sanctuary offers a peaceful ramble with stunning views of the wetlands from its boardwalks and many opportunities for glimpsing birds and other wildlife.

DIRECTIONS

From I-495 (Capital Beltway), take Exit 11A for MD 4 South/Pennsylvania Avenue toward Upper Marlboro. Continue along MD 4 south for 10.5 miles. Turn right onto Plummer Lane and continue 0.5 mile, then turn right onto Wrighton Road. After 0.6 mile, turn left onto the Jug Bay Entrance Road. Continue onto Blue Shirt Road 0.5 mile to the parking lot by the McCann Wetlands Study Center. *GPS Coordinates*: 38° 47.082′ N, 76° 42.100′ W.

TRAIL DESCRIPTION

Jug Bay Wetlands Sanctuary is made up of 1,700 acres of tidal freshwater marshes, forested wetlands, upland forests, riparian (riverbank) forests, fields, and open water. Please note that the sanctuary is not open every day; visitors are welcome from 9 A.M. to 5 P.M. on Wednesday, Friday, Saturday, and Sunday from March through November. From December through February, the sanctuary is also closed on Sundays.

Check in and pay to park at the McCann Wetlands Study Center. Parking is $6 per car by cash or check only. The small museum area is worth a pause to flip through the informative binders, previewing some of the sanctuary's plants and wildlife. Make sure to pick up a copy of the detailed map. Your route will take you on the map's brown loop, followed by a modified version of the red loop, returning to the Wetlands Center on Utility Road.

LOCATION
Lothian, MD

RATING
Easy to moderate

DISTANCE
5.3 miles

ELEVATION GAIN
208 feet

ESTIMATED TIME
3 hours

MAPS
USGS Bristol; Map available at the McCann Wetlands Study Center; online: jugbay.org/files/uploads/Trailmap-Sanctuary.pdf

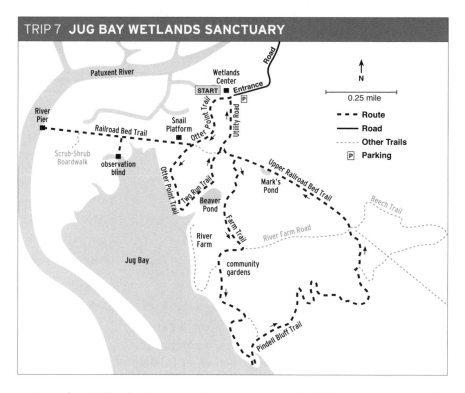

From the Wetlands Center, walk through a small field toward the sign for Otter Point Trail. The broad observation deck on the right offers a sweeping view of the wetlands and gives you the opportunity to spot ospreys and eagles. In summer, look below to see the water crowded with spatterdock, also known as cow lilies, with their heart-shaped leaves. In autumn, ducks often congregate in this area. This view is even more beautiful in winter, when visibility is least obstructed.

Returning to Otter Point Trail, proceed along the wide, flat, sandy path through shady woods. Turn right at the sign for Railroad Bed Trail. This out-and-back diversion from the loop takes you past two of the sanctuary's most impressive observation areas. As you walk along this gravelly, elevated spur, look to either side to see water nearby, almost level with the trail at high tide. The Snail Platform, a wooden dock with a bench overlooking a peaceful marshy area, is on the right; watch for Oxyloma snails clinging to the cattails and arrow arum stalks. You also may see ospreys flying overhead and swallowtail butter-flies passing through.

Continue on Railroad Bed Trail as it becomes grassier and mossier. On quiet days, watch for the flick of a white-tailed deer on the path. Turn left onto a boardwalk that carries you 250 feet into the wetlands to the observation blind, an enclosed viewing area with windows surrounded by open porches. Wildlife is less likely to be startled by your presence when viewed from a blind. Peer among the vegetation for muskrats, otters, and turtles, and listen for the clicking *kid-dik* call of the rail and the *ho-ho-ho* of the least bittern.

Retrace your steps on the boardwalk, then turn left where the boardwalk joins the path to continue on your way on Railroad Bed Trail. Soon you pass the marked turnoff to the Scrub Shrub boardwalk, which brings you to a bench in the midst of shrub wetlands. In summer, an overgrowth of wild rice often renders this boardwalk impassable, but in winter it is a pleasant, peaceful spot for observation.

Continue on Railroad Bed Trail; soon, you pass the Bill Steiner Canoe Shelter on your left. Immediately after, Railroad Bed Trail turns to boardwalk and terminates at the River Pier Boat Launch with a wide view of the water and the Mount Calvert Historical and Archaeological Park across the Patuxent River.

Turn back to retrace your steps to the intersection with Otter Point Trail; turn right to continue along the red loop. Dappled sun falls between tall trees and shorter holly plants on this flat section of trail. A sign and a bench mark the turnoff to the right to the swamp blind (another, smaller blind). Walk along this narrow, curving connector boardwalk through the freshwater tidal swamp—populated with ash trees—to the viewing shed. Watch out for wasps, which sometimes nest within the structure. Return to Otter Point Trail. Shortly after, the trail will terminate at Otter Point, an area with a picnic table and a view of Jug Bay, perfect for a snack or a lunch break.

Go left from Otter Point to pick up the white-blazed Two Run Trail, which traces the bluff above Two Run Branch. Look to the right to see the peaceful, algae-covered Beaver Pond with its viewing platform; you may spot a heron. Two Run Trail climbs gently up a root-covered slope through the forest and curves around the hilltop to the left, offering another view of the north end of Beaver Pond. At the intersection of Railroad Bed Trail and Two Run Trail, turn right to continue down a set of wooden stairs on Two Run Trail. Arrive at the intersection of Two Run Trail and River Farm Road. Go right on the boardwalk, crossing a shallow stream. Tiny lizards, such as race runners and skinks, tend to congregate in this area. You may see them running ahead of you and snaking up trees. At the boardwalk's end, climb a staircase with rope railings.

Here you see the sign for Upper Railroad Bed Trail (but do not follow it). Go right on Farm Trail, which carries you up another set of stairs. Climb gently, following white blazes. Farm Trail widens into a sunny clearing. On the right is a view down to the stream, and you can see the red farm building in the distance between the trees. The trail then widens and forms a "T" intersection with a sandy road. Head right on Pindell Bluff Trail toward the farm and picnic area. This section of road is shared with vehicles but quickly opens onto the farm property. Pass to the left, between the South County Community Garden and the River Farm building, and continue through the grassy lawn, keeping to the left of the Pindell Bluff Trail sign, with the community garden on your near left.

Located at the end of a 75-foot boardwalk off Railroad Bed Trail, Jug Bay's observation blind offers views of waterfowl and turtles among the cattails.

At the edge of the mowed field, another sign marks where Pindell Bluff Trail reenters the trees as a shady forest path. This well-blazed section of trail winds through the trees, fringed on either side with beds of young pines. Listen for the sounds of mourning doves and woodpeckers. At the next intersection, continue to the right on Pindell Bluff Trail and soon emerge to view Jug Bay. Its muddy waters may appear almost white in sunlight. Hang left to hug the water, elevated on a slight rise. Here the forest is less dense; look for a fern grove through the trees on the left. Circle right, around the edge of the ridge, and descend to overgrown Pindell Point.

Here the trail hairpins. Take the lower trail to the left, doubling back below the same ridge you just descended. At the next intersection, turn right to continue on Pindell Bluff Trail via a narrow bog bridge, which may be slippery. Proceed up a brief but very steep incline to crest the ridge. The trail flits back and forth, with views of the Pindell Branch of the Patuxent River on the right through the trees. The route is not always distinct but remains well blazed. Watch for eastern box turtles, which often pass through these woods. The trail rejoins the river briefly then climbs gently into a grassy section of forest. Beds of young pines give way to dense fern groves.

At a signed intersection with Beech Trail, turn left to stay on Pindell Bluff Trail. Emerge on Farm Road; cross the road, and follow the sign to Upper Railroad Bed Trail. This grassy, mossy trail is flanked by tall trees. It remains very flat and straight as you continue, while the forest rises and a lush bed of ferns encroaches onto the path.

At the next intersection, stay left on Upper Railroad Bed Trail. The trail, knotted with roots, narrows as it sinks between two small swells, then rises again before passing the intersection of a staff-only trail on the right. Soon you see water on two sides: the Two Run Branch on the right, a little way down a slope, and the small, murky Mark's Pond on the left.

At the intersection with Farm Trail, stay straight. Retrace your steps down the stairs and along the boardwalk over the creek; at the intersection with Two Run Trail, turn right onto the north section, which climbs up steep wooden stairs before turning into a wide dirt pathway, winding past the fences that mark the edges of deer enclosures.

Climb gently to the intersection of Middle Trail, Two Run Trail, and Utility Road. Turn left to take Utility Road uphill to the Wetlands Center through a section of mockernut hickory trees. Look for lovely, thin-leafed willow oaks and black walnuts as you walk the short distance back to the Wetlands Center and parking area.

MORE INFORMATION

Dogs, horses, fishing, and biking are not permitted at Jug Bay Wetlands Sanctuary, but picnicking is allowed. The minimal elevation change and the many opportunities to spot wildlife, in combination with the thoughtfully curated museum at the McCann Wetlands Center, makes this an ideal hike for children and families. The Jug Bay Wetlands Sanctuary can be reached at 401-741-9330; more information is available at jugbay.org.

NEARBY

If you haven't had your fill, Glendening Nature Preserve, the northern part of Jug Bay Wetlands Sanctuary, offers more miles of hiking trails. Beaver Rock Trail and Red Oak Trail in this area offer opportunities for butterfly sightings, as the winged insects pass through forests and a cultivated cactus garden. Parking is free in the Glendening Nature Preserve.

8

WATKINS REGIONAL PARK

Peacocks and pollywogs, owls and llamas, a *Wizard of Oz*-themed playground, gentle hiking, and family fun await you in this pleasant park. In summer, an antique carousel, miniature golf, and a small-scale train ride add festivity to your visit.

DIRECTIONS

From I-95/I-495 (Capital Beltway), take Exit 15A for MD 214 (Central Avenue) eastbound. Drive approximately 3 miles (past Six Flags theme park) and turn right onto MD 193 (Watkins Park Drive). The park entrance is about 1 mile ahead on the right. Follow the park road toward the nature center, past the playground and farm parking, and turn left at a "T" intersection to arrive at the nature center parking lot on your left. *GPS coordinates*: 38° 53.292′ N, 76° 47.035′ W.

By public transportation, take Metrorail's Blue line to the Largo Town Center station. Catch the C26 bus, which brings you within 0.25 mile of the park entrance. Exit at the intersection of Watkins Park Drive and Keverton Drive. From there, you can take Loop Trail or Spicebush Trail to the nature center.

TRAIL DESCRIPTION

Watkins Regional Park has lots going on: history, live animals (wild and domesticated, from bullfrogs to peacocks), camping, picnic shelters, ball fields, woods and wetlands, miniature golf, a restored carousel, a nature center, lovely nature trails, and even a miniature train ride in season. A colorful *Wizard of Oz*-themed playground with ruby-slipper slides and a yellow "brick" road recently replaced an older play area. With its appealing spectrum of offerings,

LOCATION
Largo, MD

RATING
Easy

DISTANCE
2.2 miles

ELEVATION GAIN
45 feet

ESTIMATED TIME
2.5 to 3 hours (including Watkins Nature Center and Old Maryland Farm)

MAPS
USGS Lanham; online: outdoors.pgparks.com/Sites/ Watkins_Regional_Park.htm

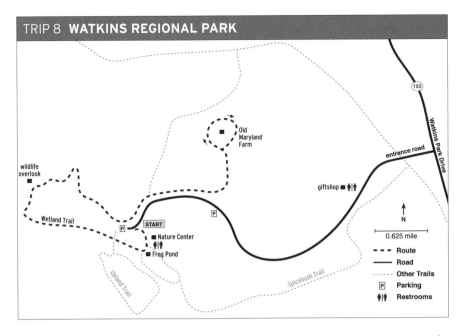

you could easily spend a whole day at Watkins Regional Park —and you might decide to do just that once you get here.

Created in 1964, the park is named in honor of Robert M. Watkins, a chairman of the Maryland-National Capital Park and Planning Commission who led efforts to establish open recreational space in Prince George's County.

Begin by walking from the parking lot across the bridge into the nature center, where several creatures are usually in residence, including owls, turtles, and snakes. Baby carriers and kid-friendly trail activity packs are available to borrow from the nature center (return them when you depart), as well as brochures on wildflowers and wildlife. Ask about Friday night bat hunts and Saturday morning hikes led by park naturalists.

Exit through the rear doors and cross over Frog Pond to the trailhead kiosk. At the kiosk, turn right and follow the yellow and blue trail markings for Wetland Trail and Spicebush Trail, which run together for a while. Pass a rustic amphitheater on the right and cross three small footbridges and the greenblazed Upland Trail. Follow the yellow-blazed Wetland Trail now as it curves away to the right and climbs a slope. Halfway up the slope, the trail veers left. Now you're on your way into the wetlands. Be prepared for mud if it has rained recently, even though trail maintainers have added gravel in some spots to assist with drainage and traction.

Take time to search for turtles and tadpoles, and the wildflowers of all kinds that thrive here. In spring, look for blue, cream, and yellow violets; wild ginger; and jacks-in-the-pulpit. In summer, watch for hyssop and strawberrylike cinquefoil. In late summer and fall, look for white boneset, mistflower, and Saint John's wort.

Cross the curving boardwalk of the wildlife lookout over the marsh, keeping an eye out for ospreys and eagles, as well as water critters. Beavers have been known to slap their flat tails for curious hikers. Among the ups and downs of this leg of the trail, look for the big, 125-year-old tulip poplars. Also watch for a split: The blue-blazed Spicebush Trail veers left, but you want to turn right to continue on the yellow-blazed Wetland Trail. The trail leads to its terminus at the western end of the nature center parking lot. Continue along the length of the parking area and, at the eastern end, look for the paved path leading alongside the entrance road to a crosswalk. Take this across the park road and turn right at the sign reading, "Trail to Park Facilities," following this paved sidewalk (also part of the park's paved Loop Trail) under a canopy of trees.

Cross a maintenance driveway then pass the seasonal snack bar and miniature golf course. The third paved path on the left after the driveway is the narrow Farm Path, which curves around to the right (east) of the miniature golf area. As you follow Farm Path, the big antique Chesapeake Carousel—believed to date from the turn of the twentieth century and attributed to respected carousel builder and carver Gustav Dentzel—appears on the left, as does the small-scale train ride. The carousel is considered quite a local gem, brought here and lovingly restored in the 1970s from the nearby bayside town of Chesapeake Beach, a popular summer resort destination in the early 1900s.

If you hear piercing, agonized-sounding cries as you move along Farm Path into the woods, fear not! Those are the calls of the half-dozen or so resident peacocks at Old Maryland Farm strutting

A curving boardwalk along Watkins Regional Park's Wetland Trail provides an inviting vantage point for observing beavers, waterfowl, and bald eagles.

their stuff. Flocks of turkeys and chickens also are vocal at times. In addition to fowl, the farm has llamas, rabbits, ponies, display gardens, agricultural exhibits and demonstrations, and the Barn Cat Gift Shop—with a very friendly gray cat in residence.

When you've finished taking in the sights and sounds at the farm, retrace your path back to the nature center parking lot.

Note: The latter segment of the trail, from the nature center to the Old Maryland Farm and back, is an easy-to-follow, paved asphalt path. If you are visiting with children young enough to be in a stroller, you might wish to skip the unpaved, rugged, and sometimes-muddy Wetland Trail loop portion of the hike (about 1.2 of the total 2.2 miles; its surface includes forest floor, tree roots, gravel, wood chips, and boardwalk), and stick to the nature center building and the out-and-back Farm Path, which is about 1 mile. The park's Loop Trail is also paved, if you want to stretch your legs a bit more.

MORE INFORMATION

Restrooms are located in the nature center, which is open Monday through Saturday from 8:30 A.M. to 5 P.M. and Sundays from 11 A.M. to 4 P.M. Old Maryland Farm is open Tuesday through Friday from 9 A.M. to 4 P.M., Saturdays 9 A.M. to 4:30 P.M., and Sundays and holidays 11:30 A.M. to 4:30 P.M.; closed on Mondays. Attractions are open in season: roughly Memorial Day to Labor Day, plus weekends in September; call ahead to make sure. For more information, visit outdoors.pgparks.com/sites/watkins_regional_park.htm or call 301-218-6700.

NEARBY

Six Flags America, just up the road, is a family-friendly draw for theme park enthusiasts, with nine major rollercoasters and plenty of other thrill rides, plus old-school amusements and a waterpark to boot. See sixflags.com/America for details. A few miles to the south in Upper Marlboro, the Show Place Arena at Prince Georges Equestrian Center offers year-round exhibits, shows, and events from jumping competitions to rodeo. Visit showplacearena.com for the latest information.

9

HARPERS FERRY TO MARYLAND HEIGHTS

This hike from downtown Harpers Ferry to Maryland Heights across the Potomac is as challenging as it is gorgeous.

DIRECTIONS

From the I-495 (Capital Beltway) inner loop, take Exit 38 (from the outer loop, take Exit 35) onto I-270 north toward Frederick. At Exit 32, take I-70 west, then immediately take Exit 52 for US 340 west (also US 15 south). Continue on US 340 west toward Charles Town, West Virginia. Cross one bridge over the Potomac River into Virginia, take the second bridge back over the river into West Virginia, then take the second right onto Union Street. Take a right onto Washington Street, a right onto Storer College Place (at the Appalachian Trail Conservancy headquarters), a right onto Fillmore Street, and an immediate left into the National Park Service visitor center parking lot. *GPS coordinates*: 39° 19.428′ N, 77° 44.492′ W.

TRAIL DESCRIPTION

Harpers Ferry, West Virginia, is the site of the abolitionist John Brown's infamous attempt to incite a slave insurrection. In October 1859, Brown and 21 men, including three of his sons, raided the U.S. arsenal located here, hoping to seize rifles and other firearms and distribute them to slaves and abolitionists, who could then fight for freedom. Robert E. Lee, representing the federal government he would soon disavow, led the U.S. reprisal. Ten of Brown's men were killed, five fled, and the rest were captured. The state of Virginia (West Virginia didn't come into being until 1863) tried and hanged the prisoners at nearby Charles Town. (See "John Brown and the Assault on Harpers Ferry," on page 44.)

LOCATION
Harpers Ferry, WV, via Maryland

RATING
Strenuous

DISTANCE
7.6 miles

ELEVATION GAIN
1,670 feet

ESTIMATED TIME
4 to 4.5 hours

MAPS
USGS Harpers Ferry; Potomac Appalachian Trail Club Map 7: Harpers Ferry to VA-7; National Park Service map available onsite; online: nps.gov/hafe/planyourvisit/hikes.htm

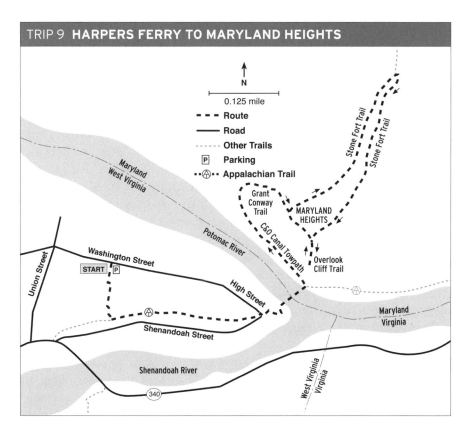

N
0.125 mile
- - - Route
—— Road
---- Other Trails
P Parking
Appalachian Trail

Maryland
West Virginia

Stone Fort Trail
Stone Fort Trail

Grant
Conway
Trail

MARYLAND
HEIGHTS

Potomac River

C&O Canal Towpath

Union Street

Washington Street

START P

High Street

Overlook
Cliff Trail

Shenandoah Street

Maryland
Virginia

Shenandoah River

340

West Virginia
Virginia

This 7.6-mile hike visits sites of both historical significance and pristine beauty, offering incomparable vistas. It starts at the National Park Service (NPS) parking lot near the US 340 bridge in West Virginia, descends into old-town Harpers Ferry and past John Brown's Fort, crosses the Baltimore & Ohio (B&O) railroad bridge into Maryland, follows the Chesapeake & Ohio (C&O) Canal towpath west, and ascends Maryland Heights to the ruins of a Union stone fort.

From the NPS parking lot, begin the hike by walking down the steps (in the direction of the Shenandoah River) to the white-blazed Appalachian Trail (AT). Take a left. At 0.3 mile pass an intersection with a blue-blazed trail and continue along the ridgeline with the Shenandoah River 200 feet below to the right. At 0.6 mile come to a short side trail that goes left to Harper Cemetery—a worthwhile stop to see where the town's namesake, Robert Harper, a Pennsylvania architect, set aside 4 hilltop acres in 1782. The next stop is Jefferson Rock, a beautiful overlook of the Potomac and Shenandoah rivers.

Pass the remnants of St. John's Episcopal Church, the earliest church in town, and drop down to the circa-1833, neo-Gothic St. Peter's Roman Catholic Church, which is open to visitors. Continue the descent down smooth stone steps carved from the hillside in the early 1800s and turn right at the bottom of the hill into downtown, going left on Shenandoah Street. Pass John Brown's

Fort on the right. This structure was the guardroom and fire engine house of the original river-powered United States Armory and Arsenal at Harpers Ferry, the building into which Brown and his cohorts retreated for their final stand. Continue over the B&O Railroad footbridge (the 1-mile mark), crossing the border into Maryland, and descend the spiraling steps to the C&O Canal towpath.

Turn left on the towpath and pass the stone remnants of lock 33, the old unloading point for goods bound for Harpers Ferry. Tread the preserved towpath where workers once struggled to maintain the water levels and keep the barges moving. The C&O Canal began operation in 1836, but after years of decline, a flood in 1924 spelled its end. (See "Centuries of Perseverance: The Chesapeake & Ohio Canal," on page 97.) Continue on the towpath for 0.25 mile, then turn right onto the green-blazed Grant Conway Trail to begin the tough ascent up the mountain called Maryland Heights.

Follow Grant Conway Trail uphill and to the right, away from the river. After about a half-mile, turn left onto the blue-blazed Stone Fort Trail, which leads to the Union stone fort atop 1,000-foot-high Maryland Heights. Proceed up a rather steep stretch—more than 500 feet of elevation gain in 0.5 mile.

Upon reaching the plateau, continue as the path winds through a level area, with circular earthen platforms that mark Civil War campsites. Stay to the right of a long stone-and-earth breastwork, one of two parallel rifle pits erected in June 1863. These fortifications were erected too late to prevent one of Lee's masterstrokes as a Confederate general—a three-pronged attack on Harpers Ferry in September 1862 that netted 10,000 prisoners.

The neo-Gothic spire of St. Peter's Roman Catholic Church at Harpers Ferry stands watch over the confluence of two celebrated rivers, the Shenandoah and the Potomac. In the distance, the US 340 bridge spans the Potomac, with Loudoun Heights rising on the opposite bank. Photo by Stephen Mauro.

The green Union defenders surrendered in droves, enabling the Confederate detachment to rejoin the main force just in time for the Battle of Antietam (see Trip 15: Antietam National Battlefield).

Follow the path uphill on log steps and cross a stone wall, turning left and continuing to the northwest corner of the interior fort. The parapet here is the largest earthwork constructed on Maryland Heights. Continue 250 feet, passing the northbound Elk Ridge Trail on the left (do not take this blue-blazed route), and turn right to follow the blue blazes on the rocks a short distance ahead into the stone fort. A row of large foundation stones offers an excellent view, especially in winter months.

Follow the blue blazes southward down the mountain on Stone Fort Trail. At 0.5 mile from the top, reach the former site of a giant Parrott rifle, which weighed 9,700 pounds and took 300 men to haul up the mountain. It was mounted on a 360-degree swivel and could hurl its 100-pound projectiles more than 2 miles toward the opposing high grounds of Loudoun Heights (in Virginia) and Bolivar Heights (in present-day West Virginia). Go left where the trail splits, and pass the pits of old, collapsed powder magazines. Walk on the spine of the rocky ridge downhill and take another left where the two trails become one again. Continue downhill and turn left onto the red-blazed Overlook Cliff Trail. Follow the path down a series of winding switchbacks to the cliff-top overlook above Harpers Ferry. It is a stupendous, worth-every-muscle-ache view of the two rivers, the railroad bridge, and the historic downtown. After enjoying the view, retrace your steps on Overlook Cliff Trail to Grant Conway Trail, the site of another gun emplacement. Turn left (downhill) and return to the gravel C&O towpath, and from there to Harpers Ferry.

MORE INFORMATION

The historic sites at Harpers Ferry are open daily (except Thanksgiving, Christmas, and New Year's Day), from 8 A.M. to 5 P.M. Visit nps.gov/hafe for an interactive map of Lower Town and a page devoted to the park's hiking trails, or call 304-535-6029.

NEARBY

Hiking all three of the heights—Bolivar, Loudoun, and Maryland—would make for an extremely ambitious day hike. For additional exciting adventures, check out whitewater river trips on the Shenandoah and Potomac rivers.

JOHN BROWN AND THE ASSAULT ON HARPERS FERRY

Born in 1800, the young John Brown found inspiration in the Bible and sought to enter the ministry. But after a failed stint at prep school, he went to work for his father, a respected tanner and one of the earliest known fugitive-slave helpers in Ohio. John preached antislavery and dabbled in Underground Railroad work himself. Still, he longed to do more.

Business failures hampered Brown as the years passed, and he found himself bankrupt in middle age. He decided to join five of his sons, who, in 1854 and 1855, had emigrated to Osawatomie, Kansas, where pro- and antislavery factions were fighting a bloody struggle over the future of that soon-to-be state. When proslavery men sacked the free-soil town of Lawrence in May 1856, Brown and several of his sons retaliated, routing five proslavery leaders from their beds one night near Pottawatomie and executing them posthaste with broadswords.

Other confrontations followed. One of Brown's sons, Frederick, was killed. But Brown gained national notoriety—and great credibility among black abolitionists—as a white man taking up arms to end slavery. "Old Brown" also managed to escape prosecution. These factors, plus Brown's gift for gaining the trust of strangers, opened doors to big-name financing in the North. Even with most of his donors, however, Brown was secretive about his next move. He had long plotted to launch a slave-revolt campaign at Harpers Ferry, Virginia (now West Virginia). Brown hoped to arm liberated slaves with weaponry looted from the town's federal armory and then strike southward, enticing more slaves to revolt against their masters and join his liberation army.

In the summer of 1859, Brown (using the name Isaac Smith, for operational security) rented a Maryland farmhouse 5 miles from Harpers Ferry where his group clandestinely gathered and trained. But neighbors grew inquisitive, finances dwindled, and Brown's friend Frederick Douglass—himself an escaped slave and a renowned abolitionist leader—refused to join the attack. Under pressure, Brown moved to strike, although he did not feel ready. On Sunday night, October 16, his band of sixteen white and five black men crossed the Potomac into Harpers Ferry, taking hostages and cutting telegraph wires. Raiders also captured the local planter Colonel Lewis Washington (George Washington's great-grandnephew), his slaves, and the first president's heirloom ceremonial sword, which Brown buckled reverently around his own waist.

The first casualty of Brown's campaign was a black man already free: a baggage porter who confronted raiders seizing a passing train. Unaccountably, Brown allowed the train to continue down the line, where crewmembers spread alarms about the attack. President James Buchanan quickly summoned a respected Virginia officer, Lieutenant Colonel Robert E. Lee, to lead U.S. troops to the scene.

The following day, Monday, went badly for Brown. Local militia (some reportedly drunk) swarmed the armory, firing on raiders, mutilating casualty corpses, surrounding buildings, and cutting off escape. Two of Brown's three raider sons lay dying in the village's brick firehouse, now known as "John Brown's Fort," to which the raiders had retreated with their hostages. Yet Brown remained determined.

As Tuesday dawned, Lee sent another Virginian and future Civil War icon, Lieutenant J.E.B. Stuart, to offer the mysterious "Smith" and his men fair treatment in exchange for peaceable surrender. From his own Kansas service days, Stuart recognized "Smith" as the infamous "Osawatomie Brown." When Brown refused to surrender, troops battered down the firehouse door. One Marine rushed Brown, slashing him with a dress sword. Brown and the surviving raiders were taken prisoner.

Savior? Terrorist? Fanatic? Fool? Brown has been called all of these things and many more, including prophet. In his determination to use violence for the abolitionist cause, Brown foreshadowed the long and bloody sectional war that erupted eighteen months after Harpers Ferry, as well as the end to slavery ultimately heralded by that war. Then again, friends both black and white warned Brown that he and his few men could not conquer the whole South and that many slaves would not take up arms against their masters. Douglass insisted that Brown was leading his men into a "steel trap" at Harpers Ferry. Brown's friends then, too, were reluctant but clear-eyed prophets of the age.

His Bible, Brown explained at his ensuing trial for treason, bade him "remember them that are in bonds as bound with [me]." Many held him as a martyr for this courageous, principled stance. Funereal bells tolled in many northern states, while southern slaveholders grimly gloated, as John Brown's body swung from a gallows a few weeks later, on December 2, 1859.

10
PATUXENT RESEARCH REFUGE

Grassy meadows and aquatic plants, hardwood forests and holly trees, Canada geese and bald eagles: You'll find all of these at the Patuxent Research Refuge, the only national wildlife refuge with a specific mission of wildlife research. Hands-on exhibits help hikers of all ages learn how scientists care for wild creatures.

DIRECTIONS

From I-95/I-495 (Capital Beltway), take Exit 22A and follow the Baltimore–Washington Parkway (MD 295) northbound toward Baltimore. Drive 3.5 miles on the parkway then take the Powder Mill Road/Beltsville exit and turn right (east) onto Powder Mill Road. Drive 1.8 miles and turn right onto Scarlet Tanager Loop, at the brown National Wildlife Visitor Center sign. Follow this one-way entrance road 1.4 miles to the parking lot. When departing, keep right to follow the one-way exit roadway. *GPS coordinates*: 39° 01.628′ N, 76° 47.944′ W.

TRAIL DESCRIPTION

Patuxent Research Refuge, named for nearby rivers in the Chesapeake Bay watershed and established in 1936 as an experiment station, is the only national wildlife refuge with a primary mission of wildlife research. Thanks largely to the refuge's leadership, the bald eagle has been brought back from the brink of extinction, and whooping crane populations have grown significantly; the latter's numbers had diminished precariously to 21 birds worldwide, but they now number more than 600. Before setting off on your hike, a stop in the National Wildlife Visitor Center is recommended. Say hello to the massive polar bear (taxidermic, of course) and other wild critters on display, a re-

LOCATION
Laurel, MD

RATING
Easy

DISTANCE
2.1 miles

ELEVATION GAIN
35 feet

ESTIMATED TIME
4.0 hours

MAPS
USGS Laurel; map available at the visitor center; online: fws.gov/refuge/patuxent/

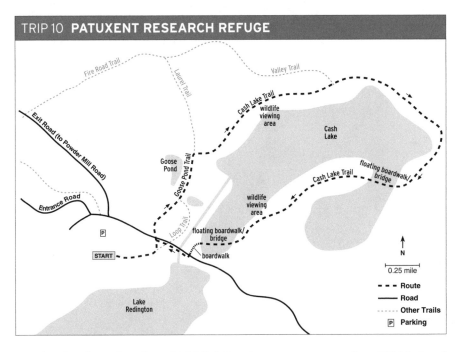

minder that the U.S. Fish and Wildlife Service manages more than 500 National Wildlife Refuge locations, representing very different climates and habitats. Enjoy the eight-minute introductory video then pop into the glass-walled viewing pod to try your hand with its scopes and radio tracking equipment. Check out the live-scale exhibit on habitats (good for kids), the endangered-species hall, and the Hollingsworth Gallery of wildlife art.

Exit the visitor center through the northeast doors and step onto the paved Loop Trail to begin the hike. You'll immediately see the first of numerous wayside signs focusing on aspects of wildlife management. This one discusses conservation landscaping and invites you into a small, wild garden; others farther along the trail explore utility-line right-of-way open spaces, meadow management, and habits of wild birds. Just past two benches, at the first fork, bear left to continue on Loop Trail and cross the tram roadway. At the next intersection, turn left onto Goose Pond Trail (which begins with a wood-chip surface and becomes rugged later on) and continue straight until you reach Goose Pond on the left. Look for nesting boxes atop poles, protected by conical predator guards to keep eggs and young birds safe. During nesting season, generally mid-March to mid-May, you can also see nesting baskets of straw-filled netting suspended over the water for use by Canada geese.

Just past the pond, turn right onto Cash Lake Trail, which veers into a forest predominantly made up of hardwoods. The tree trunks aren't blazed, but the pathway is well maintained and easily visible. Several good-size American holly trees grow in the understory along the trail here. Soon you'll reach the wildlife-viewing area for the near shore of Cash Lake, just

White-tailed deer enjoy the peace of Patuxent Research Refuge, where many species of wildlife thrive under benevolent management. Photo by Chesapeake Bay Program, Creative Commons on Flickr.

off the main trail to your right. Make a detour to enjoy this quiet spot by the water's edge, where aquatic plants abound. The lake, created in the late 1930s by President Franklin Roosevelt's Civilian Conservation Corps, is one of more than 40 impoundments, or artificial bodies of water, on the refuge. Scientists manage the water levels in the lake and in Goose Pond as needed to support wildlife populations. In just a bit, as you approach the fishing pier, you'll cross one of the spillways that drain water when needed. Look for beavers, bald eagles, great blue herons, ospreys, and the ubiquitous Canada geese.

Continuing along the trail, cross several footbridges, one of which was built as an Eagle Scout project with the support of local sponsors. After descending two sets of wooden-braced steps, reach a sign for Valley Trail to the left. Stay right to continue on Cash Lake Trail toward the fishing pier. A steel bridge takes you over the drainage spillway mentioned earlier, and a restroom is available on the pier. At this point, you can choose to take the boardwalk along the fishing pier or cross the concreted berm. In season, fishing enthusiasts pull largemouth bass, bluegill, black crappie, the colorful pumpkinseed, chain pickerel, and even American eel from the waters. Whichever route you chose, the two merge beyond the end of the berm. Follow the gravel path straight ahead (there's a service road off to your left, also gravel) to regain the trail as it winds back into the forest.

After a short woodland walk, with many varieties of moss and lichen beckoning, a floating boardwalk takes you over the calm waters onto a grassy meadow peninsula, edged by a wide variety of lush aquatic plants. Watch the marshy waters for beavers and turtles, listen for the bellowing of frogs, and be sure you've got some sun protection handy. Follow the trail back into the woods and to the south shore viewing area, a favorite haunt for raptors. When you rejoin the main trail after pausing to take in the view, it leads toward a second floating bridge. Cross this and proceed along the shore through more woods.

When you reach the paved road, turn right; Lake Redington is on the left. To the right, a boardwalk wildlife lookout offers a good view of Cash Lake. Cross the road bridge over the south spillway and take the first paved path on the left to finish your hike at the visitor center. Check out the wild garden, rest your legs for a few moments, and savor your visit to one of the largest forested areas—more than 12,800 acres on the north and south tracts—remaining today in the Mid-Atlantic states.

MORE INFORMATION

Trails and grounds are open daily (except for holidays) from sunrise to sunset. The National Wildlife Visitor Center building is closed Thursdays; otherwise, it's open daily (except holidays) 9 A.M. to 4:30 P.M. Call 301-497-5760 for details about the refuge's many special-interest programs and tram tour availability. Visit fws.gov/refuge/patuxent for more information.

To preserve the refuge's trails and its habitats, bicycles and skis are not allowed. Dogs must be kept on leashes no longer than 10 feet. Note that very few rest stops or benches are available along the lake portion of the trail. Fishing is by permit only, in season; call the refuge for details.

NEARBY

Just north of the Refuge, near the intersection of the Baltimore-Washington Parkway (Md. 295) and Md. Route 32, lies Fort George G. Meade, home of the National Security Agency. The NSA's public face is on display just outside the fort gates at the National Cryptological Museum, housing thousands of artifacts, including numerous working World War II German Enigma machines and a Navy Bombe used to break its codes. Displays, with some artifacts dating back to pre-Revolutionary War times, cover the history, people, machines, techniques, and locations of American cryptology. A research library and gift shop are also onsite, as is the outdoor Vigilance Park, displaying several reconnaissance aircraft. Fort Meade also offers a small museum devoted to post history and a collection of military vehicles such as Liberty and Sherman tanks and a Nike Ajax missile.

SAVING A LIVING SYMBOL: THE BALD EAGLE

Not long ago, and not far from the nation's capital, the bald eagle bounced back from the brink of extinction. In 1969, staff at the Patuxent Wildlife Research Refuge, located between Washington, D.C., and Baltimore, published data linking the pesticide DDT to thin eggshells among ducks living in the refuge. The research demonstrated that DDT was a major factor in population losses suffered by fish-eating birds, such as bald eagles. The majestic raptor's numbers had dropped to an estimated 487 breeding pairs nationwide in 1963. Thanks in part to Patuxent's work, the federal government banned DDT use in 1972.

Great harm had already been done, however, and human intervention was urgently required. Patuxent became involved in this phase, too, initiating a captive-breeding program to hatch each eagle pair's first clutch of eggs in an incubator. The parents usually produced a second clutch to raise naturally in their nests. This approach worked so well—124 eaglets were hatched at the refuge, earning it international attention—that Patuxent supplied eaglets to many states for their own recovery efforts.

States such as New York, using a technique called "hacking," placed incubator-hatched eaglets in elevated, isolated, human-made nests, where biologists fed them until they matured. Another conservation technique recognized that, while eagles can hatch up to three eggs per nest, only two eaglets are likely to survive. Some of these "surplus" hatchlings were transferred to foster-parent eagle pairs that readily adopted and raised them. Viability rates jumped for both eggs and live birds.

The Patuxent breeding program wound down in 1988, by which point eagle populations, and their reproduction in the wild, were clearly on the rebound. By 2006, breeding bald-eagle pairs were present in all 48 contiguous states, and total breeding pairs had increased twentyfold, to more than 9,700 nationally. The Chesapeake Bay area, in particular, enjoyed great success, increasing from 32 pairs and 18 annual young in 1977 to 151 pairs and 172 eaglets in 1993. In 2007, the bald eagle was taken off the federal list of endangered and threatened wildlife—a major milestone.

Bald eagles have survived, with a little help from their friends, but vigilance is needed for their continued protection. Clean water, habitat preservation, and the enforcement of laws against toxins and other threats will always be vital to the support of this noble national bird.

11

PISCATAWAY PARK

Accokeek Foundation's trails in Piscataway Park traverse a riverside forest with views of Mount Vernon and a Colonial tobacco farm.

DIRECTIONS

From the I-95/I-495 (Capital Beltway) outer loop, take Exit 2A (or from the inner loop, take Exit 3) onto MD 210 (Indian Head Highway). Travel about 9 miles. After you pass Farmington Road, take the next right onto Livingston Road (a B&J fast-food restaurant is on the corner). Drive one block and turn right onto Biddle Road. At the stop sign, turn left onto Bryan Point Road. Follow it 3.5 miles and turn right into the Accokeek Foundation parking lot. *GPS coordinates*: 38° 41.635′ N, 77° 03.946′ W.

TRAIL DESCRIPTION

Piscataway Park, named for the Piscataway American Indian inhabitants, is located in Prince George's County, Maryland, directly across the Potomac River from Mount Vernon. Congress founded the 5,000-acre park to preserve the view from that historic icon exactly as it had been in George Washington's time, when the first president boasted, "No estate in United America is more pleasantly situated than this." Piscataway stretches for 6 miles along the Potomac, from Piscataway Creek in the west to historic Marshall Hall in the east, but the entire park is not connected by a trail system. The Accokeek Foundation manages 200 acres jointly with the National Park Service (NPS), and the hike described here covers this complete area, which includes a historical Colonial farm, an experimental organic farm, a native-tree arboretum, and many fine views of Mount Vernon.

Begin the hike at the visitor center just north of the parking lot. Behind the center is a gravel path that splits north

LOCATION
Accokeek, MD

RATING
Easy

DISTANCE
4 miles

ELEVATION GAIN
Minimal

ESTIMATED TIME
1.5 to 2 hours

MAPS
USGS Upper Marlboro; NPS map onsite; online: nps.gov/pisc/planyourvisit/maps.htm

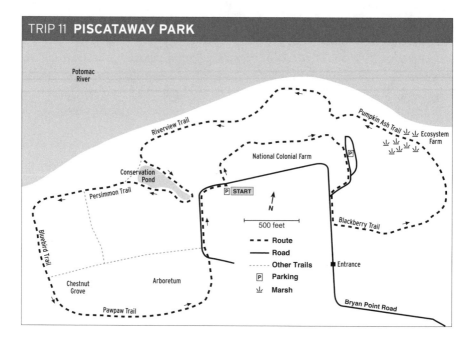

Map labels: Potomac River · Riverview Trail · Pumpkin Ash Trail · Ecosystem Farm · National Colonial Farm · Conservation Pond · Persimmon Trail · P START · N · 500 feet · Blackberry Trail · Bluebird Trail · Chestnut Grove · Arboretum · Pawpaw Trail · Bryan Point Road · Entrance

Legend:
- - - Route
—— Road
········ Other Trails
P Parking
⤭ Marsh
■ Entrance

and east. Follow the path north, turning left, to see a popular fishing pier with a view of Mount Vernon—a pleasant bonus while relaxing and reeling in catfish. Continue back to the split and turn right. Then, just before a line of evergreen cedars, turn right onto the 0.8-mile Riverview Trail. Follow the mowed swath of grass to a forested area along the Potomac River and travel westward along the forest's edge. This 6-acre riparian zone was planted between 1999 and 2002, and includes 60 species of trees and shrubs that protect 3 miles of Potomac shoreline from pollution, erosion, and nutrient runoff. Keep going, passing a side trail that leads to the boat dock. Farther on the left is National Colonial Farm's Museum Garden. Walk around to the front gate and enter for a look at Colonial-era crops native to the Americas (maize, beans, squash), Africa (sorghum, okra, yams), and Europe (potatoes, beets, cabbage).

The trail is unmarked in this area, so walk to the gravel road on the northern boundary of the Colonial Farm and turn right, passing in front of the caretaker's residence. A posted sign on the right points to where the trail returns to open fields. After a short distance, turn left onto the 0.4-mile Persimmon Trail, which encircles a small pond. After traveling the loop, turn right, back onto Riverview Trail, and enter a larger section of riparian forest. Cross a wooden bridge over a tributary and leave the trees, staying to the right where the trail branches and again where the trail branches a second time. This is now Bluebird Trail. Bluebird nesting sites line the path here: little habitats with entrances too small for competitors, such as starlings and house sparrows. These maintained nesting zones are responsible for helping to increase once-declining bluebird populations in the eastern states.

Continue, watching out for electrified fences on the left side. On the right is a grove of chestnuts, in the midst of which is an intersection. Leave Bluebird Trail where it forks left on a roadway, and turn right onto the 0.5-mile, white-blazed Pawpaw Trail. This trail winds uphill through the type of mature hardwood forest that dominated the Potomac watershed before the intensive introduction of European farming methods. Exiting the woods, the trail ends at the upper edge of the native-tree arboretum, where it reconnects with Bluebird Trail. You can see 128 documented tree species, all extant in the Chesapeake region in the eighteenth century, before continuing north on a paved road through the National Colonial Farm complex. Bluebird Trail officially ends near a barn that houses rare heritage breeds under conservation, such as Milking Red Devon cattle, Ossabaw Island hogs, and Spanish turkeys. Continue through the farm and pass an original Colonial tobacco barn before coming to a farmhouse, a kitchen, and a smokehouse. Guides in period garb provide historical interpretations to visitors on weekends in spring, summer, and fall.

Exit the farm between two zigzagged, split-rail fences and head south past the parking area along the access road that connects with Bryan Point Road. About 50 yards down, near a difficult-to-spot trail marker, turn left onto the 0.8-mile, purple-blazed Blackberry Trail. Follow this to the edge of the Robert Ware Straus Ecosystem Farm. Turn left along the fence line and continue

Visitors of all ages enjoy taking in the historic barns at Piscataway Park, which also offers stunning views of the Potomac River and Mount Vernon, as well as a working organic farm. Photo by Alliecat1881, Creative Commons on Flickr.

until the fence ends. Turn left onto the 0.5-mile, yellow-blazed Pumpkin Ash Trail and cross the open field, traversing a freshwater tideland area via a wooden boardwalk. Continue through a quiet patch of woodland to a picnic area and the parking lot.

MORE INFORMATION

Piscataway Park charges a $2 entrance fee. The visitor center has free self-guided education kits for children and birding kits (field guide, binoculars, spotting scope) on loan for adults. On Saturdays and Sundays, the foundation offers tours of the Robert Ware Straus Ecosystem Farm (11 A.M.) and Colonial Farm (1 P.M.). The park has a canoe and kayak launch point on the Potomac River, just to the east of the fishing pier. Historic Marshall Hall sits to the west of the park. Built in the early 1700s, it was the centerpiece of the Washington, D.C., area's first amusement park in the early 1900s. The park is a stop on the 27-mile-long Prince George's County Potomac Heritage Trail On-Road Bicycling Route.

NEARBY

Indian Head, to the south along MD 210 at the confluence of the Potomac and Mattawoman Creek, beckons visitors to explore its waters by kayak or stand-up paddleboard, which you can rent in the town. The nearby Indian Head Rail Trail, designed for walking and cycling, is a 13-mile paved trail 0.5 mile from the town's center.

Farther south near Port Tobacco (once Maryland's largest seaport), stands Saint Ignatius Church on the high bluff known as Chapel Point, with stunning views out to the Potomac. Founded in 1641 by Friar Andrew White, this church boasts a stained glass window depicting the baptism of Chief Kittamaquund (the "Great Beaver"), the first American Indian chief to be baptized in the Catholic Church. (See "Here All the While: The Piscataway People," on page 55.) The church's cemetery includes Piscataway Indian graves.

HERE ALL THE WHILE: THE PISCATAWAY PEOPLE

The Piscataway have no land reservations, no large numbers or renown, and no federal or—until just a few years ago—state tribal recognition. But hundreds of years ago, the Piscataway had power and population. They welcomed strangers to their native place. And they still have a story to tell of a proud people long ignored, marginalized, and mistreated.

When Captain John Smith arrived in Virginia in 1607, the great chiefdoms of the Piscataway and Powhatan—weakened by recent tribal wars but holding firmly to their lands—stewarded the Chesapeake Bay's western shores. The Piscataway, whose name is said to mean "where the waters meet," were mainly found north of the Potomac River in present-day Washington, D.C., and central Maryland, while the Powhatan lived to the south in Virginia's tidewater. Smith referred to the northern group by the name they gave their hereditary high chief's house: *Moyaons*. The high chief (*tayac*) was advised by local chiefs (*werowances*), wise elders, and shamans, and could demand tribute from villages or send their warriors into battle.

The Piscataway, descended from Algonquin peoples probably driven south by earlier periods of cooler climate, were cousins to the nearby Nacotchtank (Anacostans), Tauxenent (Dogue), Mattawoman, Nanjemoy, and Portobaco peoples, whose names also still appear throughout the region. In their palisaded villages, the Piscataway built longhouses shaped like loaves of bread, with sapling frames and bark or mat coverings. They cultivated the so-called three sisters (squash, maize, and beans), and they hunted, fished, and gathered. But even their rich diet couldn't promise immunity against unfamiliar diseases, such as smallpox, cholera, and measles.

British Catholic colonizers of Maryland, arriving in 1634, found the Piscataway to be willing allies. The *tayac*—Kittamaquund—who, with his wife, converted to Catholicism—offered the colonizers land to found St. Mary's City. The Piscataway hoped to benefit by using the settlers as a buffer against other tribes. But as the British population grew, relations between the colonizers and the native peoples deteriorated. By 1668, the Piscataway were confined to two small reservations. In 1675, Colonial leaders forced the Piscataway to permit rival Susquehannock, defeated in war by the Five Nations Iroquois (Haudenosaunee), to settle in these reservations as well. Conflict ensued. The Susquehannock headed north again and joined with the Iroquois against the Piscataway, making repeated incursions southward. The British offered no help. They, too, coveted what lands remained to the Piscataway.

In 1697, the Piscataway relocated across the Potomac to Fauquier County, but Virginia Colonists sought to send them back. In 1699 they moved again, to an island in the Potomac near Point of Rocks. By 1700, a chiefdom that likely had boasted 8,500 individuals a century earlier had dwindled—through war, disease, and loss of land and sustenance—to about 300. Some of the remaining tribal members moved north into Iroquois territory and eventually into New France (Quebec) and Ontario. Some may have moved south, joining the Meherrin.

Evidence indicates that a number of Piscataway remained on or returned to their ancestral lands. In the 1800s and early 1900s, however, the Piscataway, like black people, suffered widespread discrimination under Jim Crow-style laws. Their identity as a native tribal people was ignored, leaving them void of American Indian treaty protection. The Catholic Church, however, maintained records that more accurately described Piscataway families as native peoples. Anthropologists in the late 1800s also interviewed Piscataway who claimed descent from the chiefdom.

Phillip Sheridan Proctor began a Piscataway revival in the early twentieth century, claiming through his family lineage the title of Chief Turkey Tayac. In 1944 he invited Smithsonian scientists to examine an ancient carving of his peoples' revered forest guardian spirit above Piscataway Creek in Maryland. But in attempting to remove the stone for further study, researchers shattered the precious artifact.

After Turkey Tayac's death in 1978, the Piscataway fractured into three distinct communities: the Piscataway Indian nation and Tayac Territory, the Piscataway Conoy Confederacy and subtribes, and the Cedarville Band of Piscataway Indians. In the 1990s, a Maryland panel acknowledged the validity of Piscataway descent claims, but not until 2012 did Governor Martin O'Malley officially recognize the groups—some 4,100 people—as a native tribe.

"We were an unrecognized people," Natalie Standingontherock Proctor, a Piscataway leader, said in a 2013 Smithsonian blog interview. "But we were here all the while." Piscataway-hosted gatherings, such as the annual spring powwow and Awakening of Mother Earth ceremony, are helping to bring about the cultural revival Turkey Tayac sought.

12

GREENBELT PARK

Greenbelt Park, situated just inside the Beltway, offers an excellent loop hike traversing a secluded, second-growth forest.

DIRECTIONS

From I-95/I-495 (Capital Beltway), take Exit 23 to MD 201 (Kenilworth Avenue) south and exit immediately onto MD 193 (Greenbelt Road) east. Go 0.3 mile and turn right at a traffic light onto Walker Road, which enters Greenbelt Park. At the "T" intersection, turn right and then immediately left into the Sweetgum parking and picnicking area. *GPS coordinates*: 38° 59.637′ N, 76° 53.700′ W.

By Metrorail, take the Green Line to the final stop at Greenbelt Station. Then take Metrobus C2 for a short ride to the park entrance at the intersection of Greenbelt Road and Walker Drive.

TRAIL INFORMATION

Greenbelt Park is located just 12 miles northeast of the National Mall. This urban oasis is bounded by the Baltimore-Washington Parkway to the east, the Beltway to the north, and Kenilworth Avenue to the west. Once denuded for farming, the land has been recovering since the early 1900s and now supports a forest of mixed pine and deciduous trees. The small creeks in the park flow into the Anacostia River, which in turn feeds the Potomac River and Chesapeake Bay. The park was initially part of a never-finished "green belt" separating Greenbelt, Maryland—the first federally planned community—from Washington, D.C.

The 5.3-mile Perimeter Trail described here hugs the park boundaries, sometimes running close to the highways and dwellings but mostly cutting through green spaces and alongside gentle watercourses. The trail has

LOCATION
Greenbelt, MD

RATING
Moderate

DISTANCE
5.3 miles

ELEVATION GAIN
350 feet

ESTIMATED TIME
2 to 2.5 hours

MAPS
USGS Washington East; map in National Park Service brochure onsite; online: nps.gov/gree/planyourvisit/maps.htm

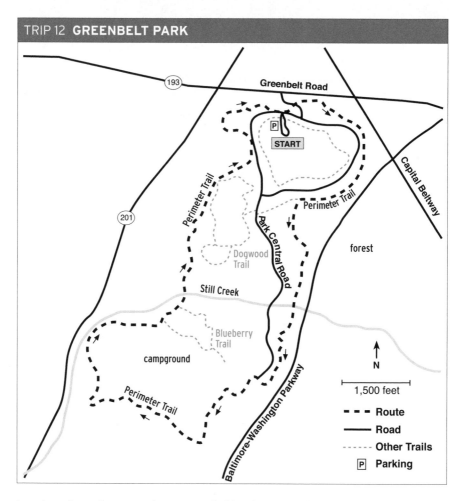

Greenbelt Road

193

201

START

P

Perimeter Trail

Park Central Road

Perimeter Trail

Capital Beltway

forest

Dogwood Trail

Still Creek

Blueberry Trail

campground

Perimeter Trail

Baltimore-Washington Parkway

N

1,500 feet

- - - Route
—— Road
- - - - Other Trails
P Parking

benches along the way at least every half-mile. From the Sweetgum Picnic Area, walk north past the start of Azalea Trail and across the road to the beginning of the yellow-blazed Perimeter Trail. Turn right to follow Perimeter Trail clockwise and note the first of many mile markers indicating distance traveled. In 50 yards, cross the road near the park entrance. Look for loblolly pines, whose developing cones glow yellow-green in spring. Continue past oak and beech trees, as well as maintenance sheds behind the park headquarters. At the 0.2-mile marker, head up a slight hill past a jumble of fallen pines. At the 0.4-mile marker, traffic comes into view on I-495 below and to the left.

Follow the trail along the shoulder of the park road, back into a wooded area of beech, laurel, and oak trees, and then downhill to an intersection. Turn left where a sign indicates Dogwood Trail parking area straight ahead, and double yellow blazes and a sign on the left mark Perimeter Trail heading left. Continue down the hill along the north branch of Still Creek, where large oaks grow near the streambed and large tulip trees, some with trunks 40 inches in diameter,

Greenbelt Park is home to more than half a dozen species of mushrooms, of both the stem-and-cap and polypore varieties. Photo by Stephen Mauro.

dot the area. During most of the year, more than a half-dozen species of colorful stem-and-cap and polypore mushrooms grow throughout the park. As the narrow trail crosses Still Creek, it comes within 25 yards of the Baltimore-Washington Parkway. Climb uphill to the right, where a secondary trail comes in. Continue to follow the yellow blazes to the left past the bench.

About 2 miles into the hike, cross the end of Park Central Road. To the left a paved bike trail begins, and straight across is a secondary road that leads to the ranger station and camping area. Take a quick side trip to read the kiosks at the ranger station describing the unique origin of the town of Greenbelt (just to the north) and how the park is helping to remove pollutants from Still Creek. Return to Perimeter Trail, following signs past large yellow poplars to the artificially developed wetland buffer area that slows water flow and filters pollution. Hike downhill through rugged terrain over exposed roots and past numerous holly trees. The trail turns into a boardwalk through the wooded, low wetlands. Cross Deep Creek. At the end of the boardwalk, turn right at the trail fork. Even though it flows intermittently, Deep Creek is responsible for significant erosion through this area.

After passing the point where the trail comes very close to the park's southern boundary fence, begin to traverse a relatively isolated portion, heavily wooded with more oaks and poplars but fewer evergreens. For 0.5 mile, hike just to the left of the gullies cut by Deep Creek then turn sharply to the right over both the creek and a maintained gravel path. Remain on the dirt trail as it wanders slightly uphill past oak, beech, and poplar trees. The mile markers that were scarce in the Deep Creek area return, here plotted every 0.2 mile.

Perimeter Trail follows the course of Still Creek (50 to 150 yards to the left), crosses a gravel road, and heads uphill along the side of a ridge. After passing two intersections that connect with the Blueberry Trail loop, cross Still Creek on an elevated wooden bridge. Continue uphill, past the intersection with the Dogwood Trail loop and adjacent to apartments along the park's boundary. Following the trail gets tricky as it passes between Park Central Road on the right and the apartment complex on the left. Look carefully for the yellow blazes after crossing the wooded bridge. Turn left past the bench then right up the hill past the parking garage. Cross two more wooden bridges over intermittent streams, hike past the park police station surrounded by willow oaks, and arrive back at the Sweetgum parking lot.

MORE INFORMATION

Greenbelt is administered by the National Park Service (NPS). There are no fees for hiking, horseback riding, bike riding, and picnicking, but there are fees for overnight camping. The NPS ranger station near the campground is open on weekdays and weekends but is sometimes unstaffed when rangers are on patrol. Facilities include bathrooms, picnic areas, a baseball field, and children's playgrounds. Other trails include the 1.1-mile Azalea Trail loop around the Sweetgum Picnic Area, located near the park entrance; the 1.4-mile Dogwood Trail in the center of the park; and the 1-mile Blueberry Trail, located near the campgrounds. For more information, visit nps.gov/gree or call 301-344-3944.

NEARBY

NASA's Goddard Space Flight Center, just a short distance east of Greenbelt Park, provides visitors a taste of the kinds of research and experimentation performed by America's space agency in the fields of Earth science, astrophysics, heliophysics, planetary science, engineering, communication and technology development. Onsite are a solarium, a lunar reconnaissance orbiter prototype, an outdoor rocket garden, a Gemini capsule model, child-sized space suits to try on, and more. More info is available at nasa.gov/goddard.

13

LAKE ARTEMESIA AND NORTHEAST BRANCH TRAIL

This peaceful, mostly level hike meanders through hardwood forests, wetlands, and the domains of birds both live and mechanical. A birding trail, fishing piers, and plenty of resting places at the lakeshore make this hike an enjoyable discovery for all ages.

DIRECTIONS

From I-95/I-495 (Capital Beltway), take Exit 23 for Kenilworth Avenue (MD 201) south. Drive 1.5 miles then turn right onto Paint Branch Parkway. Free parking is available at the Ellen E. Linson Swimming Pool/Herbert W. Wells Ice Rink at 5211 Paint Branch Parkway, on your left past the bridge over the Northeast Branch. *GPS coordinates: 38° 58.583' N, 76° 55.393' W.*

By Metrorail, take the Green Line to the College Park–U of MD station, then follow the walking directions below.

TRAIL DESCRIPTION

The full Northeast Branch Trail is a 3-mile-long leg of the Anacostia Tributary Trails network, reaching through northern Prince George's and eastern Montgomery counties in Maryland. On this hike, you'll travel a sampling of the trail along Northeast Branch Creek and around the College Park Airport runway, to its junction with the loop trail around Lake Artemesia. This hike is designed to be a Metro-friendly sojourn outside the boundaries of the city proper. If you're coming to College Park by car, start the hike from the Paint Branch Parkway crosswalk at 52nd Avenue.

From the top of the steps coming up from the College Park–U of MD Metro station, look to your left for the intersection of River Road and Paint Branch Parkway. Walk to the southeast corner of that intersection, standing

LOCATION
College Park and Berwyn Heights, MD

RATING
Easy

DISTANCE
3.5 miles

ELEVATION GAIN
20 feet

ESTIMATED TIME
2 hours

MAPS
USGS Washington East

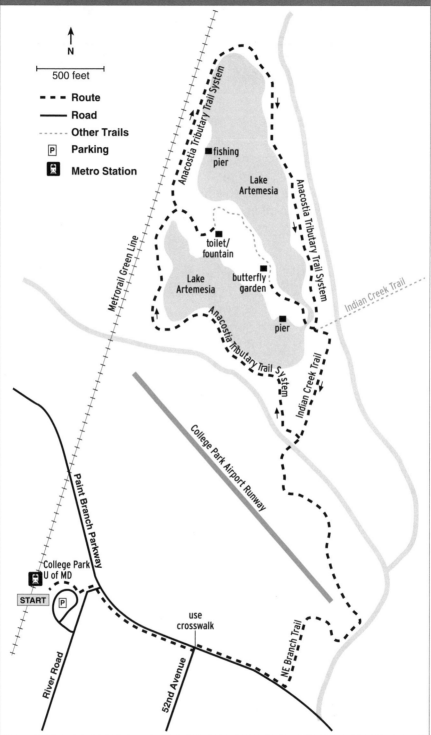

N

500 feet

- - - **Route**
———— **Road**
········· **Other Trails**
P **Parking**
🚇 **Metro Station**

Anacostia Tributary Trail System

fishing pier

Lake Artemesia

Anacostia Tributary Trail System

Metrorail Green Line

toilet/ fountain

Lake Artemesia

butterfly garden

Indian Creek Trail

pier

Anacostia Tributary Trail System

Indian Creek Trail

College Park Airport Runway

Paint Branch Parkway

College Park U of MD

START

P

River Road

52nd Avenue

use crosswalk

NE Branch Trail

in front of the U.S. Food and Drug Administration building (5100 Paint Branch Parkway), then follow Paint Branch Parkway east for two blocks.

Cross Paint Branch Parkway at the 52nd Avenue crosswalk (begin your hike here if you parked at the pool/rink) and continue walking east along the sidewalk on this side of the road. Pass the 94th Aero Squadron Restaurant sign, then watch for the pointed, wooden Northeast Branch trail marker, not much taller than the guardrail. Turn left down the trail entrance spur path, which is the steepest part of this hike.

At the bottom of the entrance path, continue straight ahead toward a chain-link fence in the distance. Along the trail here are a couple of large, lovely American holly trees. The trail and fence will bend around the end of the College Park Airport runway. This is a perfect spot from which to watch small craft landing on a pleasant day. (Bring a blanket if you plan to sit; no benches are provided.) Wilbur Wright trained the first military aviators at this airport, which celebrated its 100th anniversary in 2009 and was the site of the first controlled helicopter flight in 1924. You can also step up on the creek bank for a glimpse of Northeast Branch Creek running south to join with the Anacostia River, Washington, D.C.'s "forgotten river," since the Potomac is so well known. Named for the native peoples living along its banks when European colonists first settled here, the once-pristine Anacostia has long been the victim of pollution, and cleanup efforts progress slowly.

Continue along the trail through the oak woods, past the Anacostia Herring Restoration Area sign and over the wooden-decked steel bridge. By the far foot of the bridge, near the Northeast Branch Trail's 0-mile marker, a sign points to the left for Lake Artemesia. Look for deer tracks in this area. Pass the black-painted, chain-link fence and gate to enter the Lake Artemesia Natural Area. Turn left on the lake's loop trail and follow it along the lake's southern shore. Start watching for green and great blue herons, loons, and various ducks in the water. Check out the nesting boxes along the fence, home to swallows and eastern bluebirds year-round. Wayside signs describe local natural and human history.

This 38-acre lake was constructed in the 1980s, when the Washington Metropolitan Area Transit Authority needed sand and gravel to build up the nearby Green Line roadbed extension. In 1972, Artemesia N. Drefs, whose family had owned land hereabouts since the 1890s, donated some acreage—where a smaller lake also named Artemesia, for her mother and grandmother, already existed—to the county. The family had raised bass and goldfish in these waters. Following Mrs. Drefs's wish for a lasting natural area on this spot, Metro struck a deal: It would use the fill soils it dredged out locally to build its Green Line, thereby saving $10 million in material and transportation costs. In return, it would spend $8 million turning the resulting excavation into a green haven for wildlife and humans.

Turn right onto the peninsula path if you're in need of a pit stop; restrooms and a water fountain are available at the blue-roofed building. Then retrace your

Alongside the trail bearing its name, the northeast branch of the Anacostia River runs with snowmelt on a spring-thaw day. Its bank is a good vantage point for spotting small aircraft traveling into and out of the nearby College Park Airport.

steps back to the lake loop trail and turn right to continue following the western shore. A floating pier is on the right; local fishers say trout can be reeled in here. At the northern tip of the lake, a gazebo next to a copse of loblolly pines offers a good vantage point for watching the gulls, ducks (ruddy and ring-necked), and grebes (pied-billed and horned) on the water and in the vegetation along the shoreline. Keep following the lake loop trail around to the eastern shore, watching for woodpeckers, cardinals, nuthatches, and other small birds in the forested area on the left.

Turn right to cross the steel bridge onto the peninsula again. You'll see the covered octagonal pier with plenty of benches on the left; the right-hand path leads to a butterfly and wildflower garden on the northern edge of the peninsula. Walk back across the bridge and take the right-center path then take another right to follow Indian Creek Trail back toward the sleepy Northeast Branch. You might see deer or rabbit tracks here, or a black-crowned night heron along the creek. Continue for a short distance until Indian Creek Trail ends by the foot of the first steel bridge you crossed. Go straight over that bridge onto Northeast

Branch Trail, and you're on your way back around the runway to the parking lot or Metro station where you began.

MORE INFORMATION

Northeast Branch Trail and Lake Artemesia Natural Area are maintained by the Prince George's County Department of Parks and Recreation and the Maryland-National Capital Park and Planning Commission. The trails and natural area are open daily, sunrise to sunset. These are multiuse trails, so be aware of cyclists and other fast-moving users. Bicycles may be rented at the pool/rink facility. Leashed dogs are allowed. No alcoholic beverages are permitted. Fishing is allowed by permit; visit dnr.state.md.us/fisheries for information. For more information, visit outdoors.pgparks.com/sites/lake_artemesia_natural_area. htm or call 301-699-2255. In an emergency, call the park police at 301-459-3232.

Find birding information at the Prince George's Audubon Society website, pgaudubon.org/LGBirdingTrail.html. The Luther Goldman Birding Trail attracts both expert and novice bird-watchers hoping to glimpse finches, orioles, ibis, and other birds. The Prince George's Audubon Society hosts bird walks every first and third Thursday of the month.

NEARBY

The College Park Aviation Museum is a small but worthwhile Smithsonian-affiliated venue located on the grounds of College Park Airport. The museum's gallery displays historic and reproduction aircraft, many from the golden age of open-cockpit flight, and all associated with the history of the airfield, dating back to the Wright brothers. Hands-on activities and interpretive areas appeal to children of all ages. Visitors may bring a picnic lunch or snack to enjoy on the balcony looking out to the airfield. Check out collegeparkaviationmuseum.com for details.

14

CATOCTIN MOUNTAIN PARK AND CUNNINGHAM FALLS STATE PARK

Catoctin Mountain Park and Cunningham Falls State Park offer true mountain trails only an hour from Washington, D.C., with a pristine waterfall as the featured attraction.

DIRECTIONS

From the I-95/I-495 (Capital Beltway) inner loop, take Exit 38 (from the outer loop, take Exit 35) onto I-270 north to Frederick and merge onto US 15 north. Take US 15 approximately 18 miles north to Thurmont then take the exit for MD 77 west (east leads into town). Drive 2.5 miles, turn right onto Park Central Road in Catoctin Mountain Park, and then turn immediately right again into the visitor center parking lot. *GPS coordinates:* 39° 38.029′ N, 77° 26.980′ W.

TRAIL DESCRIPTION

Catoctin Mountain, the easternmost ridge of the Blue Ridge Mountains, offers serious mountain hiking only an hour from Washington, D.C. Two parks, each comprising roughly 5,000 acres, border each other on the range's northern stretch, near Frederick: Catoctin Mountain National Park to the north and Cunningham Falls State Park to the south. Highlights of the parks include 44-acre Hunting Creek Lake, 78-foot Cunningham Falls, trout-rich Big Hunting Creek, several overlooks, an old whiskey still, a nineteenth-century iron furnace, a historic arch bridge, and an aviary. The trail system is extensive, although the hike outlined here is the only way to complete a circuit between the two parks.

From the trailhead at the visitor center, begin a steep ascent on the trail leading toward Thurmont Vista through chestnut oak, hickory, spring-blooming dogwood, spicebush, mountain laurel, and rhododendron. At 0.6 mile, turn right (east), following the sign to Wolf Rock. Ascend

LOCATION
Thurmont, MD

RATING
Strenuous

DISTANCE
10.4 miles

ELEVATION GAIN
2,200 feet

ESTIMATED TIME
5.5 to 6 hours

MAPS
USGS Blue Ridge Summit, USGS Catoctin Furnace; free NPS map of Catoctin Mountain Park onsite; online: NPS map nps.gov/cato/planyourvisit/maps.htm, Cunningham Falls State Park trail guide dnr2.maryland.gov/publiclands/Pages/western/cunningham.aspx

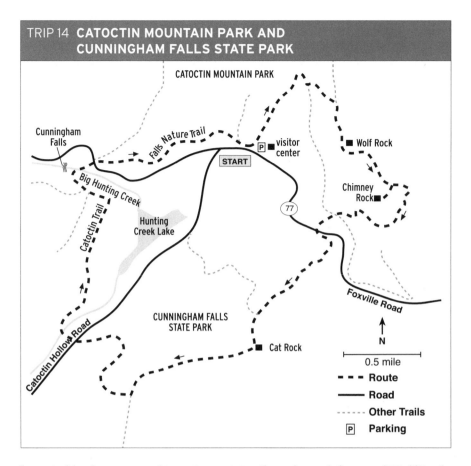

CATOCTIN MOUNTAIN PARK

Cunningham Falls

Falls Nature Trail

P visitor center

■ Wolf Rock

START

Big Hunting Creek

Chimney Rock ■

Catoctin Trail

77

Hunting Creek Lake

Foxville Road

CUNNINGHAM FALLS STATE PARK

Catoctin Hollow Road

■ Cat Rock

N

0.5 mile

- - - **Route**

——— **Road**

----- **Other Trails**

P **Parking**

by switchback to a second junction at 0.8 mile and turn left toward Wolf Rock. Begin a short, steep descent amid a field of huge boulders. At 1.1 miles, turn right at a "T" intersection, again toward Wolf Rock. Go downhill on log steps and continue on the rocky spine of the ridge. At 1.4 miles, reach 1,400-foot Wolf Rock—a large shelf of quartzite rocks, part of the Weverton Formation deposited 550 million years ago. The fissured rocks resemble giant fists punching into the sky. Climb atop them and head to the left for a great wintertime view. (Leaves mask the vantage in spring and summer.) Watch for poison oak and poison sumac growing between rocks.

Return to the trail and head south toward Chimney Rock, 0.5 mile away, accessible via a steep access trail that cuts right. Chimney Rock offers a year-round, awe-inspiring view of the mountains and valleys to the west, including the 1,500-foot Cat Rock peak to the southwest (the next major goal of this hike). There are several flat, exposed quartzite pedestals. After a strong dose of Catoctin Mountain beauty, return to the main trail and begin a steady descent under old-growth hickory and chestnut oaks. Turn right at 2.2 miles, away from a sign that points to Crow's Nest Campground (a 500-foot drop), and onto a westward trail that travels downhill over switchbacks, dropping 400 feet over a short 0.7 mile. At 2.7 miles, reach an intersection under a stand of young pines and go straight to descend to MD 77 and Big Hunting Creek (at 2.9 miles). Turn left along the road and travel a short distance, passing the entrance road to the National Park Service administration office, then cross the road (carefully) to a parking area at the trailhead to Cunningham Falls State Park.

Head into the woods on the yellow-blazed Cat Rock/Bob's Hill Trail and, on a rocky path through pines, begin an uphill climb that is among the most strenuous in this book—more than 700 feet in 1.3 miles to reach Cat Rock. At 3.7 miles, cross over Bear Branch, a rocky streambed tumbling down the mountainside. At 3.9 miles, the orange-blazed Old Misery Trail leaves to the right, offering access to Hunting Creek Lake. Soon after, note a sign that points right to Bob's Hill; continue straight here to Cat Rock, returning to this point after visiting the 1,500-foot, 360-degree overlook. Scrambling to the top of these rocks is more challenging (and fun) than Wolf Rock. Return to the main trail and turn left toward Bob's Hill, starting a well-deserved level stretch atop the ridge, where ferns, moss, and young saplings add diversity. At 5.9 miles (1.7 miles from Cat Rock), reach a "T" intersection and turn right onto the blue-blazed Catoctin Trail, a 27-mile trail that connects with the Appalachian Trail to the south at Gambrill State Park.

Proceed downhill, gradually at first then more steeply, on a winding dirt path through thick, old-growth forest. Clumps of deep-green ferns grow along the mountainside seepages. The trail becomes rocky in its final descent, crosses Catoctin Hollow Road, and reaches Hauver Branch (at 7.7 miles). Take care on the slick rock footholds across the branch. Proceed up a short, steep rock scramble then hike parallel to the ridgeline, crossing two feeder streams before reaching a clearing at the campground entrance. Cross the road and head back uphill, negotiating several ups and downs on wooden steps before reaching a "T"

The eponymous waterfall in Cunningham Falls State Park cascades 78 feet down the east slope of the Catoctin Mountains. Early homesteaders used the falls for baptisms. Photo by Stephen Mauro.

intersection with the yellow-blazed Cliff Trail. Turn left on a short stretch where Catoctin Trail and Cliff Trail run together then turn right at 8.8 miles, where a sign reads, "Return to Falls," and Cliff Trail turns to the right. Head down a dramatic cliffside with large granite boulders, following the sound of cascading water, and turn left again onto Lower Trail. The trail becomes a boardwalk and reaches the falls at the hike's 9-mile mark.

The largest cascading waterfall in Maryland, the 78-foot Cunningham Falls was named for a local photographer whose scenic shots popularized the location. Although sometimes crowded, the falls are a fitting climax to the hike. After a thorough rest, carefully pick your way across the rocky Big Hunting Creek to the boardwalk on the other side and follow it to cross MD 77 (carefully again—it's at a hairpin turn). Soon after reentering Catoctin Mountain Park, turn right onto Falls Nature Trail. Follow it 1.2 miles along the side of the ridge. A little wooden walkway over a small feeder stream is the last landmark you'll spot before returning to the visitor center at 10.4 miles.

MORE INFORMATION

Catoctin Mountain Park is open year-round, dawn to dusk; admission is free. Camping, picnicking, wildlife viewing, fly-fishing, and cross-country skiing are all available. Leashed pets are allowed on all trails. Visit nps.gov/cato or call 301-663-9388 for more information.

At Cunningham Falls State Park, swimming is permitted at Hunting Creek Lake between Memorial Day and Labor Day. No pets are allowed on the beach, although they are allowed on all trails. The park offers a number of interpretive programs. There is a fee, which changes depending on the season. Visit dnr2.maryland.gov/publiclands/pages/western/cunningham.aspx or call 301-271-7574 for more information.

NEARBY

At the south end of Cunningham Falls State Park, accessible by Catoctin Hollow Road, is a nineteenth-century furnace and the ruins of an ironmaster's house. The furnace, nicknamed Isabella, was built in the 1850s, but an earlier version, built in 1774, produced pig iron for the cannons of George Washington's Continental Army. North of the furnace, directly off Catoctin Furnace Road, is the Catoctin Wildlife Preserve Zoo, home to 450 animal species. South Mountain State Park, at a mountain pass important during the Civil War Battle of Antietam, is 10 miles west of Catoctin and Cunningham.

Also of note, but not open to the public, is Camp David, in the northern portion of Catoctin Mountain Park. The presidential retreat, first known as Shangri-La and later renamed for President Eisenhower's grandson, hosted the Camp David Accords, a 1978 agreement between Egypt and Israel, and is the site of Evergreen Chapel.

15

ANTIETAM NATIONAL BATTLEFIELD

Follow sleepy Antietam Creek along the quiet southern end of Antietam National Battlefield and across a series of ridges in beautiful farm country that belies the bloody contest waged here in 1862.

DIRECTIONS

From the I-495 (Capital Beltway) inner loop, take Exit 38 (from the outer loop, take Exit 35) onto I-270 north to Frederick. Take I-70 west. Take Exit 29 onto MD 65 south toward Sharpsburg. Travel 11 miles to downtown Sharpsburg and turn left onto MD 34 (Boonsboro Pike). Pass Antietam National Cemetery and turn right onto Rodman Avenue. At the "T" intersection, turn left onto Branch Avenue and follow it to its end at a 25-spot parking lot above Burnside Bridge. *GPS coordinates: 39° 27.029′ N, 77° 43.961′ W.*

TRAIL DESCRIPTIONS

In terms of human life lost, September 17, 1862, was the costliest day in American history. Two armies, composed of 40,000 Confederate and 75,000 Union soldiers, met in a ferocious series of clashes on the rolling Piedmont terrain of western Maryland. Before the battle, General George McClellan, commander of the Union Army of the Potomac, had trapped General Robert E. Lee's Army of Northern Virginia between the Potomac River and Antietam Creek, forcing the Confederates to trade blood for ground to survive.

Although McClellan had a large numerical superiority, he advanced his men piecemeal, first in the north at Miller Cornfield, West Woods, and Dunker Church; then in the center at Bloody Lane; and finally in the south at Burnside Bridge. This hike covers the southern portion of the

LOCATION
Sharpsburg, MD

RATING
Easy to moderate

DISTANCE
3.5 miles

ELEVATION GAIN
400 feet

ESTIMATED TIME
2 to 2.5 hours

MAPS
USGS Keedysville; National Park Service map, available free at visitor center, Battlefield America topographical map, available for purchase at visitor center; online: nps.gov/anti/planyourvisit/maps.htm

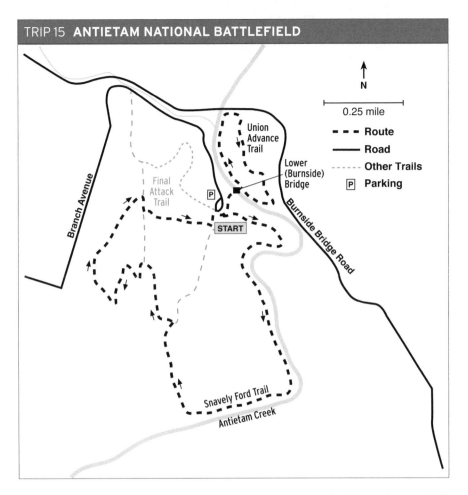

battlefield, upon which Lee's army was saved in the nick of time by Confederates arriving from Harpers Ferry. Today the area is much the same as it was before the 12-hour bloodletting: peaceful countryside with hills and farms and an unspoiled creek, now all protected by the National Park Service (NPS). The hike follows along Antietam Creek and over the hills south of Sharpsburg, and includes two interpretive trails: Union Advance Trail and Final Attack Trail.

From the parking circle on the west side of Antietam Creek, walk down the steps to Burnside Bridge, built in 1836 and recently restored stone by stone. The beautiful, two-trunked sycamore tree beside it was a sapling at the time of the battle. The Union needed to cross the triple-arched bridge, but they faced stiff resistance from Confederates entrenched on the opposite hillside. It took three separate attacks and 500 casualties to carry what today looks like a small span across a languid creek. Walk north along the stone wall, where fallen men were temporarily buried after the battle, and begin a 1-mile circle hike on Union Advance Trail, which enters the woods and climbs 60 feet to an overlook before circling past a monument to the 11th Connecticut Infantry and returning to

Shielded by a split-rail fence and overhanging hickories, hikers walk along the ridge at the south end of Antietam National Battlefield. Nearby Antietam Creek is a good place to spot rare, spiky-barked water locusts. Photo by Stephen Mauro.

the bridge. Go back up the hill and turn left where a sign points to Snavely Ford Trail. Follow Antietam Creek south to the ford where Union troops finally crossed and relieved the pressure on Burnside Bridge. Not far down the path is Georgian's Overlook, the 20th Georgia Regiment's lethal perch. Proceed downhill, dropping 130 feet in elevation over 0.25 mile to the river and continue to the right. (Benches are provided along the route.) The walk becomes prettier, quieter, and more secluded. Pass riverside pawpaws, sycamores, hickories, yellow poplars, black walnuts, black birches, and curiously spiky-barked water locusts.

At 2 miles into the hike, turn west along with the river, where steep cliffs rise on the opposite banks. Near Snavely's Ford (another 0.3 mile), turn north with the trail along the edge of the park and climb 40 feet in elevation over the next 0.25 mile. Turn left at the sign for Final Attack Trail.

Climb 40 more feet in elevation to an open area, where the trail becomes grassy and is lined with cedars and black locusts. A cornfield emerges on the right. Turn left at a "T" intersection underneath three conspicuous walnut trees onto historic Otto Lane. Union infantry and artillery stood on this ridge in preparation for the final attack intended as the knockout blow against the Rebels. Wind downhill to a small stream and then uphill 70 feet to the top of a hill bedecked with a majestic hackberry tree, beneath which is a welcoming bench. The stone wall behind it marks the park's boundary. The final Confederate attack came over this hill, with the men of General A.P. Hill's division marching from Harpers Ferry and crashing into the Union flank just in time to save the main Rebel force.

Follow the ridge off the hill and through high grass dotted with cotton thistle and Queen Anne's lace. Walk a straight stretch with cropland rising to the left and a row of trees on the right, passing the 16th Connecticut Infantry obelisk honoring its 43 men killed in action. Next go downhill among emerald-green cedars to the valley then turn right and go uphill, returning to Otto Lane at an opening in the fence. Take a left. Follow the lane north between split-rail fences and more hackberry trees. Cannons amassed on the ridge to the left mark the farthest point of advance for Union forces. At an intersection where the trail splits four ways, take either of the trails heading right (south), then swing left (north) on a path through a field at the top of the ridge. Ahead to the north, in the valley, note the Otto and Sherrick farms, both witnesses to the battle, and beyond them on the high ground, Antietam National Cemetery. Make a U-turn back to the south and follow more cedars, with South Mountain close enough that you can see individual trees set against the sky. Walk down, up, and downhill again, and then through a field back to the parking lot.

MORE INFORMATION

You can purchase three-day battlefield passes for $5 per person or $10 per vehicle. The pass includes admission to the battlefield, the museum and a movie, and ranger programs during your visit. Stop at the visitor center at the north end of the battlefield for interpretive maps on Union Advance Trail, Final Attack Trail, and other battlefield trails. For information on the fighting at West Woods and Bloody Lane, visit nps.gov/anti/index.htm or call 301-432-5124.

NEARBY

Antietam and the Sharpsburg area combine nicely as a weekend trip with Harpers Ferry (Trip 9), only ten or so miles to the south. Just across the Potomac from Antietam is the tiny, charming college town, arts hub, and alleged haunted village called Shepherdstown, W. Va., dating to 1762 and laying claim to the status of West Virginia's oldest town. Visit shepherdstown.info to learn more.

16

SUGARLOAF MOUNTAIN

Sugarloaf Mountain offers a challenging and popular hike close to D.C., with dozens of wildflower-rich trails.

DIRECTIONS

From the I-495 (Capital Beltway) inner loop, take Exit 38 (from the outer loop, take Exit 35) onto I-270 north toward Frederick. Take Exit 22 onto MD 109 south (Barnesville/ Hyattstown exit) and drive 3 miles to the intersection of Comus Road. Turn right onto Comus Road (west) and drive 2.5 miles to the base of Sugarloaf Mountain. Take the second right up the mountain road to the West View parking lot. *GPS coordinates*: 39° 15.092' N, 77° 23.611' W.

TRAIL DESCRIPTION

Sugarloaf Mountain is a monadnock, or a mountain that stands alone after the bedrock surrounding it has eroded away. The mountain is capped by 200-foot-thick, erosion-resistant quartzite that formed deep within the earth's crust 300 million years ago, when the North American and African continental plates collided to form Pangaea. A dominant, 150-foot-high quartzite cliff rises from Sugarloaf's western edge, with jumbles of talus rock split from the cliff by water freezing in joints and fissures scattered beneath it. The unique geologic history of the mountain is complemented by an unusually diverse ecosystem, where plants indigenous to the Mid-Atlantic coastal plain, Piedmont, and mountain region can all be found.

Obtain trail maps at the West View or East View parking lots, or at the wooden building just beyond the gated entrance at the base of the mountain. This hike starts from the West View lot. The recommended route to the summit begins with a sharp ascent from the West View lot and

LOCATION
Dickerson, MD

RATING
Moderate to strenuous

DISTANCE
5.3 miles

ELEVATION GAIN
1,375 feet

ESTIMATED TIME
3 to 3.5 hours

MAPS
USGS Buckeystown, USGS Urbana; free map at trailhead; online: sugarloafmd.com/ sl_trails.html

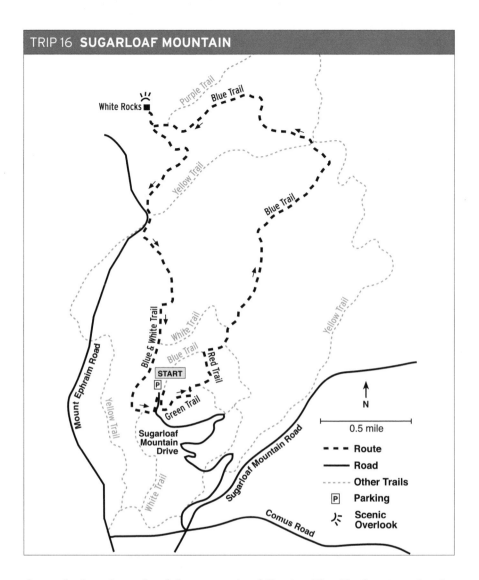

White Rocks ■

Purple Trail

Blue Trail

Yellow Trail

Blue Trail

Blue & White Trail

White Trail

Blue Trail

Red Trail

START

P

Green Trail

Sugarloaf
Mountain
Drive

Yellow Trail

Yellow Trail

White Trail

Mount Ephraim Road

Sugarloaf Mountain Road

Comus Road

N

0.5 mile

- - - Route

—— Road

- - - - Other Trails

P Parking

Scenic
Overlook

descends the other side of the mountain, following Blue Trail as it circles the northern ridge.

From the West View lot, locate Green Trail just beyond the covered wooden shelter. This trail rises 325 vertical feet over 0.25 mile. Begin a gradual climb and then a sharper ascent over granite rocks that lead to a series of steep stone steps toward the 1,282-foot summit, taking in the must-see view of Frederick Valley and the bluish Catoctin Mountains on the horizon. The Catoctin range abruptly ends to the south at Point of Rocks, where you can see the Potomac River and the circa-1833 Monocacy Aqueduct, the latter built largely from stone quarried at Sugarloaf. (See Trip 22: C&O Canal: Point of Rocks to Monocacy Aqueduct.) Start down the 0.25-mile Red Trail opposite the overlook. At the trailhead is a small forest of *Chionanthus*, or fringe trees, which are usually found in tropical or subtropical climates. Pass Orange Trail on the right and begin a steep descent via Red Trail. In spring, showy jack-in-the-pulpit, yellow corydalis, black cohosh, and wild geranium bloom on the forest floor. The high elevation also nurtures a unique canopy of black birch, red maple, tupelo, chestnut oak, and hickories. At 0.5 mile is a "T" intersection with Blue Trail and a northwesterly view on Bill Lambert overlook.

Blue Trail (also called Northern Peaks Trail) is a challenging 5-mile circuit that loops back to West View. Continue downhill and turn left where White Trail merges briefly. Turn right when Blue Trail leaves White Trail and passes a sign indicating 2 miles to White Rocks overlook. After a brief level stretch, climb steeply to the left and onto the crest of the northern ridge. Hike the narrow summit. In summer, watch for blueberry and huckleberry bushes (with edible berries) and deerberry bushes (with hard, inedible berries). Violets, cut-leafed toothwort, yellow corydalis, and the rare early saxifrage bloom in spring, followed by black cohosh in June. Continue downhill and onto level ground before climbing over moss-tinged granite rocks. This section is especially beautiful in early spring, when shadbushes unfurl creamy-white blossoms against the gray-pink rock.

Hikers savor the rugged terrain and pastoral views from Sugarloaf Mountain, a monadnock—or standalone mountain—that supports a unique blend of habitats. Photo by Alliecat1881, Creative Commons on Flickr.

At the peak of this small rise, climb the large pile of rocks for a view of the western wooded slopes. The trail then plunges downward 100 feet to a five-way intersection with the Blue, Yellow, and Purple trails. Continue ahead on Blue Trail, bearing left and meandering uphill before navigating a challenging set of switchbacks to a 1,015-foot-high summit—the highest point on the northern ridge and your approximate halfway mark. This is the most isolated portion of the trail. An ancient-looking cairn sits on the summit. Track downhill in the direction of White Rocks overlook, following the spine of the ridge. In spring, look for jack-in-the-pulpit and bulbous pink lady's slipper.

Pass Purple Trail as it comes in on the right and turn on a spur trail to White Rocks, where two overlooks offer views to the west of Lilypons Water Gardens; Adamstown, Buckeystown, and Frederick; and Catoctin and South mountains. When leaving White Rocks, ignore an incorrect sign that indicates West View parking is back toward the overlooks and instead go right on a trail that forms a U-turn with the one you came in on. The trail descends, ascends, and winds around to the left before reaching partially open meadows.

Reach Mount Ephraim Road at a valley and wade through a small, shallow tributary of Bear Branch. Pass a parking area and another stream flowing underneath the road; follow the road to the right. Turn left onto Blue Trail and begin a gradual ascent adjacent to the Bear Branch tributary. The deep, rocky streambed carves its right of way below a steep mountainside, bringing color in the form of cinnamon ferns, skunk cabbage, spicebush, Indian cucumber root, and the rare and beautiful whorled pogonia. American beeches and dogwoods are common on this stretch, as are resident birds, such as ovenbirds, wood thrushes, and red-eyed vireos. Turn abruptly to the right about 0.5 mile after Mount Ephraim Road and begin ascending. Turn right at a "T" intersection where White Trail again merges with Blue Trail. Stay fairly level alongside a boulder-strewn ridge before turning left (uphill) to the parking lot.

MORE INFORMATION

Sugarloaf Mountain is open to the public with no admission fee. Leashed dogs are permitted, and picnic areas are available. The mountain also offers bicycling and rock-climbing opportunities. The mountain's Strong Mansion is open to visitors and can be reserved for social events. Visit sugarloafmd.com or call 301-869-7846 for more information.

NEARBY

Lilypons Water Gardens (lilypons.com) has 300 acres of seasonally colorful aquatic plants and holds public events. Also nearby is Monocacy Natural Resources Management Area (dnr2.maryland.gov/publiclands/Pages/parkmaps/monocacy_map.aspx), which contains miles of wildflower-rich hiking trails.

17

BLACK HILL REGIONAL PARK

Black Hill Regional Park, surrounding the 500-acre Little Seneca Lake, is a butterfly hotspot with meadows that attract hundreds of monarchs during the insects' semiannual migrations in April and September.

DIRECTIONS

From the I-495 (Capital Beltway) inner loop, take Exit 38 (from the outer loop, take Exit 35) onto I-270 north toward Frederick. At Exit 16, go right on Father Hurley Boulevard, which becomes MD 27/Ridge Road. Turn left onto MD 355 (Frederick Road) and go 1 mile. Turn left onto West Old Baltimore Road and go 1.5 miles then turn left onto Lake Ridge Drive into the park. Follow Lake Ridge Drive 1.5 miles to the visitor center near Little Seneca Lake. *GPS coordinates*: 39° 12.025′ N, 77° 17.301′ W.

TRAIL DESCRIPTION

Black Hill Regional Park's 500-acre Little Seneca Lake was built by damming Little Seneca Creek to provide an emergency water supply for residents of the D.C. metro area. In the nineteenth century, the creek was used to power several lumber and grist mills, and the ruins of one are visible near where the creek enters the lake. The trails here traverse rolling terrain with lots of elevation change but little that is precipitous. Expect to encounter meadows, fields giving way to forest, thick deciduous woods, and stands of conifers. A dizzying number of monarch butterflies visits the park in late spring and early autumn during their migrations to and from Mexico.

Upon exiting the visitor center, turn left on the path through a wildflower meadow, then turn right onto the asphalt Black Hill Trail. The meadow is planted with milkweed, the larval host plant for monarch butterflies. Black

LOCATION
Boyds, MD

RATING
Moderate

DISTANCE
6.8 miles

ELEVATION GAIN
320 feet

ESTIMATED TIME
3 hours

MAPS
USGS Germantown; online: montgomeryparks.org/ parks-and-trails/black-hill -regional-park/

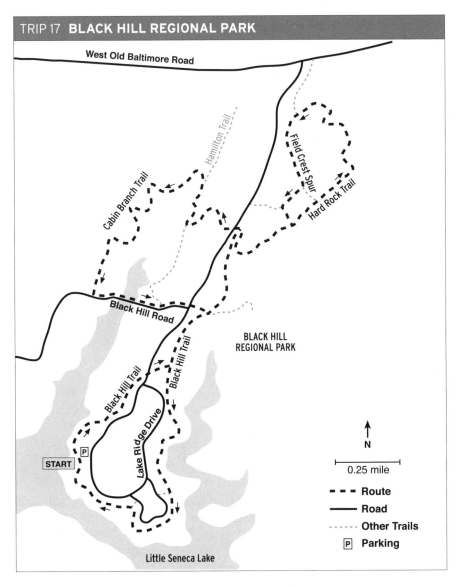

West Old Baltimore Road

Hamilton Trail

Cabin Branch Trail

Field Crest Spur

Hard Rock Trail

Black Hill Road

BLACK HILL
REGIONAL PARK

Black Hill Trail

Black Hill Trail

Lake Ridge Drive

P

START

N

0.25 mile

- - - Route
—— Road
· · · · Other Trails
P Parking

Little Seneca Lake

Hill Trail skirts Little Seneca Lake past wide-crowned Chinese elms, with picnic pavilions on the right. Where the trail reaches Lake Ridge Drive at 0.6 mile, stop at the park office on the left to see a circa-1850 mineshaft from the Black Hill Gold Mine. The local resident George Chadwick transformed the mine into a bomb shelter during the Cold War and used fieldstone from the mine to build the current park office.

Cross Lake Ridge Drive and follow a grassy clearing, visible between two thin strips of trees. Pass a greenhouse and reach the natural-surface Black Hill Trail where it splits in two, looping south around the tip of the peninsula. Turn left on the rocky trail through sycamores and yellow poplars and hike to a four-way intersection. Turn right for a quick side trip down a steep gravel road to a bridge over Little Seneca Creek. On a small side trail to the right, just beyond the bridge, are the remains of Water's Mill, built by Zachariah Water in 1810. The mill became one of the few in the area to press flaxseed into linseed oil before closing in 1895. The river power in this area was vital to the local farm economy until the railroad made it possible to bring in cheaper flour and cornmeal from the Midwest.

Return across the bridge and take the first right before the gravel trail then a second right to return to Black Hill Trail heading north. Cut across a pipeline clearing and walk parallel to a streambed on the right, almost reaching Lake Ridge Drive before making a U-turn and crossing the stream. Follow the stream south on the opposite slope and come back to the pipeline clearing before turning left and heading gradually uphill on a bed of loose, sprawling rocks. Pass two grass connector trails on the left and reenter the forest.

Here, begin a loop on Hard Rock Trail. Go between stone ruins and curve to the left. Exit the forest at a meadow, at the center of which is a group of bluebird nesting boxes. Stay straight on what is now the Field Crest Spur (although an erroneous sign indicates Field Crest Spur branches right) and enter another large meadow serving as a monarch way station, where milkweed provides opportunities for breeding and feeding. Pass a maintenance yard on the left and take the second left onto a connector trail, which leads back to Hard Rock Trail.

Turn right, and as the trail rises from the streambed at 3.3 miles, turn right again across Lake Ridge Drive, and start on Cabin Branch Trail. At the "T" intersection, turn right onto the combined Cabin Branch and Hamilton trails then turn left to cross a stream where Cabin Branch Trail goes its own way. Travel south parallel to the main stream and over a series of hills carved by small feeder streams. At 4.5 miles, reach a pipeline clearing and turn left, proceed over a third tributary stream, and immediately turn right. (Pay attention: The trail is unmarked.) Leave the forest as the trail cuts through a thickly-growing tunnel of shrubs before reaching a mowed swath near Black Hill Road.

Turn left onto Black Hill Road and cross a dammed causeway over the lake. Continue past the start of Hamilton Trail on the left and cross Lake Ridge Drive again, turning right onto Black Hill Trail. Pass the grass connector trail you previously took from the park office and tramp south, passing several side trails that lead to playgrounds and parking areas. Stay with the forested high ground above the lake. At 6.1 miles, the trail becomes asphalt and passes various exercise stands. Turn left at the "T" intersection just before the roadway, continuing past a grove of tall yellow poplars. Go by the boat-rental office and return uphill to the visitor center.

Black Hill Regional Park's diversity of wildflowers makes it a favorite destination for migrating and breeding butterflies, such as this clouded-sulphur (*Colias philodice*) variety. Photo by Domingo Mora, Creative Commons on Flickr.

MORE INFORMATION

The park is open year-round, sunrise to sunset. On the first Saturday of September, the park holds Monarch Fiesta Day, which includes guided exhibits and butterfly tagging by park naturalists. The boat rental facility near the visitor center offers pontoon boat tours Saturday and Sunday from May to September. Rent rowboats, canoes, paddleboards, pedal boats, and kayaks during the same period. For rates and information, visitmontgomeryparks.org/parks-and-trails/black-hill-regional-park or call 301-528-3480.

NEARBY

For more hiking options, continue on Black Hill Trail past the mill site, where the trail becomes asphalt and turns south for 2 miles along the eastern shore of Little Seneca Lake. End at Wisteria Drive and return to the park. Another good option is Hoyle's Mill Trail, which travels through South Germantown Recreational Park to Seneca Creek State Park. (See Trip 6: Seneca Creek State Park: Clopper Lake.)

18

MATTHEW HENSON TRAIL

This attractive and peaceful paved trail meanders along Turkey Branch through a state park and provides flora and fauna sightings uncommon in such a populated area.

DIRECTIONS

From I-495 (Capital Beltway), take Exit 33 for MD 185 (Connecticut Avenue). Drive about 3 miles and bear left onto Veirs Mill Road. Go about half a mile and turn left at the light onto Randolph Road. Take the third right (at a traffic light) onto Dewey Road. Drive approximately four blocks until you see Winding Creek Local Park on the left (before Dewey Road makes a sharp curve right), and park here. *GPS coordinates*: 39° 03.467′ N, 77° 05.523′ W.

Leaving a second vehicle at the trail's end is highly recommended; see the last paragraph of Trail Description. To do so, park on Alderton Road. *GPS coordinates*: 39° 05.169′ N, 77° 02.053′ W.

TRAIL DESCRIPTION

Well maintained, peaceful, wonderfully silent, and pleasantly hidden away, Matthew Henson Trail, which opened in 2009, is as yet a largely undiscovered gem, particularly along its northern reaches. Deer, cottontail rabbits, mallard ducks, cardinals and finches, and butterflies are plentiful along the path, keeping you company and providing enjoyment on your walk. The trail and the state park surrounding it are named in honor of the Maryland native Matthew Henson, the African-American Arctic explorer who was the first human being to reach the North Pole. (See "Matthew Henson and the Race to the North Pole," on page 86.)

Begin at the Winding Creek Local Park parking lot by looking for the white signs with green lettering pointing

LOCATION
Veirs Mill and Colesville, MD

RATING
Moderate

DISTANCE
4.5 miles (one-way hike)

ELEVATION GAIN
235 feet

ESTIMATED TIME
2.5 to 3 hours

MAPS
USGS Kensington; online: montgomeryparks.org/ PPSD/ParkTrails/trails_MAPS/ matthew_henson_trail.shtm

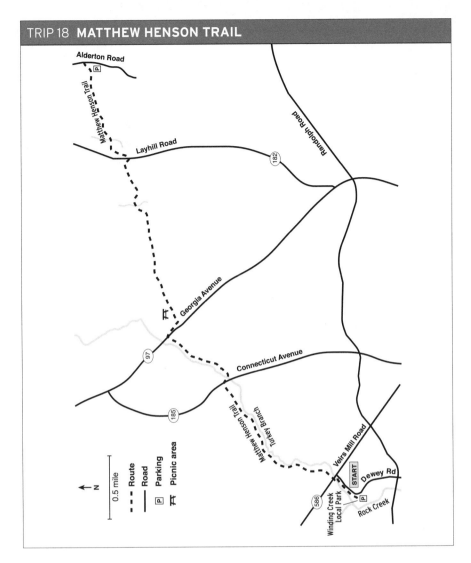

toward the trail. Start by heading northeast along the paved Matthew Henson Trail, following the extension of Dewey Road, and catch your first glimpse of babbling Turkey Branch. You'll soon see signs for the Veirs Mill Road crossing. The trail will jog left to cross an access road then make a quick right turn to cross the six-lane Veirs Mill Road itself. Watch for the black barred fences. Note that this crossing has neither a marked crosswalk nor a walk signal. On our visit, a signal button merely set off flashers to warn oncoming traffic. Traffic sometimes travels at high speeds here; use caution.

Honeysuckle spills over the fence just across Veirs Mill Road, and the easy-to-follow paved trail continues parallel to residential Turkey Branch Parkway on the left and alongside a forest renewal area to the right. The parks commission is working to remove invasive plant species and to restore a natural habitat

Lush ferns border the longest of Matthew Henson Trail's boardwalks as it runs downhill into a cool, shady marsh.

for plants and animals. Wild grapevines and bamboo can be seen along this segment of the hike. Just as you pass Grenoble Drive on the left, notice a grove of sycamores on the slope. Note the "10 mile" post. This and other markers indicate mileage for Matthew Henson Trail and the connecting Rock Creek Trail. Subtract 9 miles from each for an accurate guideline. You're now at the 1-mile point on Henson Trail.

Near the rows of planted American hollies is the first of several benches along the trail. Just past it is a large hemlock tree with honeysuckle vines entwined in its branches, sprawling 20 feet in the air. At mile 1.3 is an emergency call box (also located at mile 1.8 and mile 3.1). Now you're approaching the Connecticut Avenue overpass; connector trails lead up to this main road. Follow the main trail under the bridge, around to a curving boardwalk, and over a steel bridge. As the path meanders, look for a big, old, leaning willow tree to the right. Another steel bridge leads to the Georgia Avenue crossing. This one has no button to push but does provide a painted crosswalk.

The trail turns to the right, winds around a church, and begins to climb, The road crossing is at mile 2.1, and the trail inclines until about mile 2.8, where it descends to the long wooden boardwalk through wetlands. Pause for a break or a picnic at the benches behind the church or just a little farther on, at the shade pavilion and picnic tables. Moving on, come to a downslope and the start of the 0.6-mile boardwalk, which passes through a cattail marsh and crosses a couple of small streams. A horse farm is off to the right. At mile 3.7, cross Layhill Road, near another church. A crosswalk, push button, and walk signal make this one easier.

The last leg of the trail bears left into an open meadow area where deer are often seen. Flowering crabapple trees make a pretty picture in early spring. Cross the steel bridge and walk up a slope into a wide meadow, also frequented by whitetails. The final crosswalk of this hike takes you over the countrylike two-lane Sullivan Road and past the ball fields of Layhill Village Local Park. A last downslope leads to one more boardwalk, and soon you'll find the trail ending at a "T" intersection with Alderton Road.

Note: This is a one-way trail ending in a rather rural area. Leave a second car on Alderton Road, where street parking should not be a problem, or at Layhill Village Local Park if you're up for backtracking a bit. You are unlikely to find a taxi in the quiet Alderton Road neighborhood or along Layhill Road for the return to Winding Creek Local Park. (If you can't manage to leave a vehicle at trail's end, make sure you have at least two phone numbers for local cab companies before starting out.)

MORE INFORMATION

Matthew Henson Trail is maintained by the Montgomery Parks division of the Maryland-National Capital Park and Planning Commission. To report trail problems or suggest repairs, call 301-670-8080. Nonemergency park police can be reached at 301-949-8010. The only restroom available along this trail is a portable toilet at the starting point in Winding Creek Local Park. No trash receptacles are provided on the trail.

NEARBY

A short distance north along Georgia Avenue (Md. 97) is Olney Manor Recreation Park, where you'll find 61 acres of play space, from ballfields (including a lighted baseball park), basketball, handball, and lighted tennis courts, a playground, and a skate park for skateboarding and inline skating, and an indoor swim center to a one-acre fenced dog park. For more info, see montgomery-parks.org/parks-and-trails/olney-manor-recreational-park.

For the artistically inclined, the Mansion and Music Center at Strathmore, a few miles to the west in north Bethesda, is a set of unique venues showcasing performing and visual arts on a 16-acre scenic campus, with a café and dining hall onsite, and afternoon tea served several times weekly. Visit strathmore.org for information, schedules, and ticketing.

MATTHEW HENSON AND THE RACE TO THE NORTH POLE

Looking at an old photo of explorer Matthew Henson swathed in Arctic furs, with his dark skin and large, kind eyes, you might well wonder: What led this black man to the North Pole, of all places?

Henson was born in 1866 on a southern Maryland farm to sharecropper parents who had been free people of color prior to the American Civil War. Soon after his birth, they moved to Washington, D.C., in hopes of better opportunities. Orphaned by age 12, Henson sought adventure as a merchant-ship cabin boy, sailing the world and learning about mathematics, navigation, and cultures around the globe. When his captain and mentor died, Henson returned to Washington, D.C., and found work in an outfitter shop. There he met the Naval officer Robert Peary, who was determined to reach the North Pole but meanwhile had military orders to lead a surveying expedition to Nicaragua. Peary hired Henson as his assistant and, impressed by the young man's abilities, later took him on an 1891 expedition to Greenland, seeking paths to the Pole. When Peary warned him of Arctic hardships, Henson retorted, "I'll go north with you, sir, and I think I'll stand it as well as any man."

And he did. Peary insisted Henson join every attempt Peary made to reach the Pole. It would take eight brutal and deadly treks across the crevasses of the Arctic icepack. The explorers befriended and learned from the Inuit natives. Some, including Henson and Peary, fathered children with Inuit women. But only Henson learned the Inuit language.

Peary chose Henson as the only non-Inuit to accompany him on his final push to the Pole, in April 1909. A weakened Peary rode in a dogsled while Henson, nearly losing his life in a crevasse, forged ahead to plant the U.S. flag at the top of the world. By then, Henson no longer felt like anyone's servant. But Peary saw things differently.

Upon their return to the United States, Peary downplayed Henson's achievement as the first to set foot at 90 degrees north latitude (although the claim is still disputed today). Henson received only an obscure federal clerk's job in New York, while Peary and Frederick Cook (a physician on the 1891 Greenland expedition who falsely claimed to have reached the Pole a year earlier than Peary) were showered with glory, medals, and cash. Not until age 70 was Henson accepted into the exclusive Explorers Club. Today, however, his remains rest adjacent to Peary's in Arlington National Cemetery, and his Inuit descendants still speak of him as *Maripahluk*, or "Matthew, the Kind One."

19

CAPITAL CRESCENT TRAIL

Popular with local commuters, this shady, gently descending paved rail-trail travels through historic areas in Maryland and Washington, D.C., offering views of the Chesapeake & Ohio Canal, the Potomac River, and several attractive old railway crossings.

DIRECTIONS

From I-495 (Capital Beltway), take Exit 34 (Wisconsin Avenue/Bethesda/Rockville) and follow MD 355 (Rockville Pike/Wisconsin Avenue) south 2.8 miles. Turn left onto Willow Lane. Elm Street Park is one block ahead on your left. Paid public parking is available in several garages and metered lots nearby. *GPS coordinates:* 38° 58.948′ N, 77° 05.522′ W.

By train, take Metrorail's Red Line to the Bethesda station. Exit the station near a yellow abstract sculpture along Wisconsin Avenue at the intersection with East-West Highway. Cross to the eastern side of Wisconsin Avenue and walk south three blocks to Elm Street (not signed for southbound traffic), just past the Air Rights Building. Turn left onto Elm and walk one block straight into Elm Street Park, the official address for which is 4601 Willow Lane.

TRAIL DESCRIPTION

Capital Crescent Trail is a local rails-to-trails creation that follows the roadbed of the Baltimore & Ohio (B&O) Railroad's old Georgetown Branch line. This line began in the 1880s when the B&O's competitor, the Pennsylvania Railroad, refused to allow other rail companies access to its Potomac River bridges in and around Washington, D.C. The B&O planned instead to build a new river crossing near present-day Chain Bridge, connect-

LOCATION
Bethesda, MD, and Washington, D.C.

RATING
Moderate

DISTANCE
8 miles (one-way hike)

ELEVATION GAIN
-310 feet downslope

ESTIMATED TIME
3 hours

MAPS
USGS Washington West; online: cctrail.org/CCT_Maps.htm

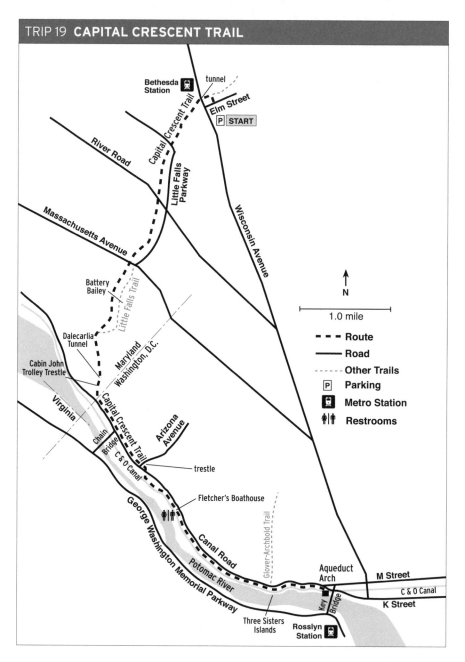

ing Baltimore and Washington with the South. By the early 1900s, rail companies were working more cooperatively, and the B&O's trans-Potomac connection north of Washington, D.C., was never built. The Georgetown Branch line did operate from Georgetown to Silver Spring, mainly as a freight route, until 1985. Local efforts created the present-day trail, popular with commuters, athletes, and leisure-seekers.

From Elm Street Park, look north between two jungle gyms for the path leading into the Wisconsin Avenue tunnel. Turn left into the tunnel to begin this hike. At first, the trail signs read, "Georgetown Branch Trail," in honor of the old rail line now re-created as a hike-bike trail. Note that you're beginning the hike at approximately the 3-mile marker (the mile count begins at the Lyttonsville–Silver Spring end), so subtract 3 miles from the numbers on the mileposts to get a rough idea of your progress. Travel through the 855-foot tunnel beneath Wisconsin Avenue and two office buildings constructed using the air rights over the old roadbed. When you emerge, follow the yellow markers to the corner of Bethesda and Woodmont avenues. Turn right on the sidewalk to the Bethesda Avenue crosswalk; a sign points toward Capital Crescent Trail. Cross Woodmont and bear right to reach the brown trailhead sign. Turn onto the paved trail. A water fountain and benches are available just down the path, by the wayside sign on trail history.

You might not realize as you walk that the trail slopes gently downhill. Montgomery County Parks Department has done a good job in the past several years clearing snow from the trail after winter storms, but do use caution if weather necessitates. The first road crossing comes just before the 1-mile point: a crosswalk at Little Falls Parkway, which is a major artery. A quarter of a mile farther, past a small park on the right with lovely white pines, comes the crossing at Dorset Avenue, a more residential road. At milepost 4.5 (your 1.6-mile point) is another rest and water stop by the inclined bridge over busy River Road.

You'll soon come to the marker for Loughborough Mill, built around 1830 by the local businessman and federal office seeker Nathan Loughborough. The mill was closed in the early 1860s when the Loughborough family, Virginians by birth and inclination, moved south to support the Confederacy.

At milepost 5.5 (your 2.6) is a brief reference to and glimpse of Battery Bailey, a nearby Civil War fortification built to protect Washington, D.C.'s water reservoir from Confederate attack. At mile 5.9 (your 3), look for a majestic old oak tree on the right.

Moving along, cross what locals call the "bridge over nothing" at Little Falls Trail that protected the water conduits below from the railway's weight and vibrations. Those conduits allow water to flow from the Potomac River into the Dalecarlia Reservoir now visible on the left. Just ahead is the 341-foot-long brick Dalecarlia Tunnel, built in 1910—one of the trail's jewels. Walking through its cool, dim passage, note the arched "step-backs" or "duck-ins" intended to protect track workers from passing trains.

At milepost 6.5 (your 3.7) is another rest and water stop, just before the Cabin John Trolley Trestle, which passes over an old streetcar route popular with summer visitors traveling to the historic Glen Echo amusement park. Look right and see crabapple trees blooming in early spring; look left to the Washington Aqueduct water tower, established in 1853. Now cross the boundary into the District of Columbia at your mile 3.9. (Be advised: Except at Fletcher's Cove and Boathouse, there are no resting places along the Washington, D.C., leg of the trail.)

The Chesapeake & Ohio (C&O) Canal is just below the trail at this point, and the Potomac River and many elegant cliff-side homes are visible. Look above you to get a sense of the Potomac's erosive power over time. The landscape is wilder now, and invasive kudzu spills over the branches of large trees. Wild strawberries and blackberries appear at trail's edge in late spring and summer. At milepost 7.2 (your 4.4), if the flora isn't too overgrown, you might glimpse historic Chain Bridge at river level. Vines also grow up and over the Arizona Avenue Trestle, another trail showpiece you'll cross 0.5 mile ahead, built around 1910 from pieces salvaged from other structures.

From here, the trail parallels the C&O Canal and its towpath. Half a mile more brings you to Fletcher's Cove and Boathouse at your mile 5.6. Portable toilets, a seasonal snack bar and boathouse, picnic tables, and water fountains are found here in a shady riverside park. Pale-yellow columbines grow here, as well. At your mile 6.7, the stone wall of the canal berm is exposed, near some rough steps leading up to the towpath.

This leg of the trail has some spectacular vistas over the Potomac River. One, in particular, looks out on Three Sisters Islands, which mark the northernmost navigable point on the river for large craft. The water often smells brackish, as the Potomac is a tidal river all the way up to Great Falls. At your mile 7.5, in the woods, is a stone and concrete bridge connecting the trail to Foxhall Road and Glover Archbold Hiking Trail. Next pass the green-painted Washington Canoe Club before reaching the stone Aqueduct Arch. The arch is actually

Capital Crescent Trail's Arizona Avenue trestle was built in 1910 of metal salvaged from three older bridges. Decking for bicycles was added in the 1990s.

an old abutment from a highly advanced canal bridge, built in 1843, that carried canal barges and mules across the Potomac River to connect with the Alexandria Canal. After the Civil War, the Aqueduct Bridge was revamped with two decks to carry both water and road traffic.

At this point, climb the wooden steps on the left up to the towpath, turn right, and cross under one overpass to the steps leading up to M Street. To find a Metrorail station, walk across Key Bridge into Virginia and proceed about four blocks to the Rosslyn station (Blue/Orange Lines). Or hail a cab on M Street to the Dupont Circle station (Red Line) near 20th and P streets NW or to the Foggy Bottom station (Blue/Orange Lines) at 23rd and Eye (I) streets NW.

MORE INFORMATION

For a free, full-color trail brochure with a map and historical points of interest, write ahead to: Coalition for the Capital Crescent Trail, P.O. Box 30703, Bethesda, MD 20824; include a self-addressed stamped envelope. For recorded information, call 202-234-4874. An all-volunteer network supports and promotes the trail, which is maintained by a public-private partnership between Montgomery County Parks and the National Park Service. For information on Metrorail schedules, routes, and fares, call 202-637-7000 or visit wmata.com. Parking is free on weekends and holidays at Montgomery County's Waverly Garage, about three blocks from this hike's starting point in Bethesda, on Montgomery Avenue between Waverly and Pearl (*GPS coordinates:* 38° 59.038′ N, 77° 05.487′ W).

NEARBY

Restaurants and taxis are plentiful along M Street. The famous iron stairs from the film *The Exorcist* lead up toward the Georgetown University campus on the western side of the brick, clock-towered Car Barn, an old trolley storage and repair facility. (The film's screenplay was written by a Georgetown alumnus.) Just east of the Key Bridge is a park dedicated to Francis Scott Key, the Georgetown resident and lawyer best known for penning "The Star-Spangled Banner."

20

BILLY GOAT TRAIL AT GREAT FALLS

Billy Goat Trail at Great Falls is one of the metro region's most popular—and most spectacular—hikes, tracing the top of the 50-foot-high Mather Gorge above the Potomac River.

DIRECTIONS

From I-495 (Capital Beltway) near the American Legion Bridge, take Exit 41 (Carderock/Glen Echo) onto Clara Barton Parkway and drive west to a "T" intersection. Turn left onto MacArthur Boulevard. Go 2.5 miles to the intersection with Falls Road. Turn left into the Chesapeake & Ohio Canal National Historical Park entrance. *GPS coordinates*: 39° 0.149′ N, 77° 14.809′ W.

TRAIL DESCRIPTION

Billy Goat Trail is actually three separate trails, all linked by the Chesapeake & Ohio (C&O) Canal towpath on the Maryland side of the beautiful Potomac River's Great Falls. (There's also good hiking on the Virginia side of Great Falls; see Trip 39: Riverbend Park and Great Falls Park.) This hike proceeds downriver on sections A and B—the first, a difficult rock scramble; the second, somewhat easier—and returns via less-used forest trails. The C&O Canal towpath offers flat ground between the challenging sections. The land here falls within the Potomac Gorge, a biologically diverse 15-mile stretch located at the fall line. Surprisingly for a metropolitan region, this is one of the continent's most intact fall lines, unaffected by dams and riverfront development. At Great Falls, the river drops 60 feet in less than 1 mile. Rare plant species (Indian grass, rough rush grass, and bluestem—the latter more common to midwest prairies) survive here, deposited during periods of intense flood scouring. Threatening these species

LOCATION
Great Falls, MD

RATING
Strenuous

DISTANCE
8.2 miles

ELEVATION GAIN
650 feet

ESTIMATED TIME
4 to 4.5 hours

MAPS
USGS Falls Church; Potomac Appalachian Trail Club Map D: Potomac Gorge Area; free NPS map of C&O Canal at visitor center; online: nps.gov/choh/planyourvisit/maps.htm

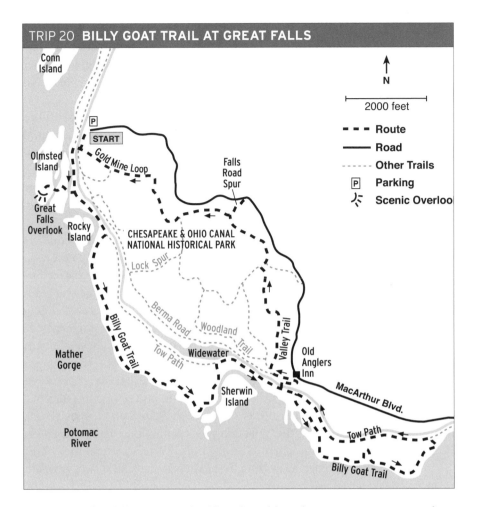

Conn
Island

Olmsted
Island

Great
Falls
Overlook Rocky
Island

START

Gold Mine Loop

Falls
Road
Spur

N

2000 feet

- - - **Route**
—— **Road**
----- **Other Trails**
P   **Parking**
⼃   **Scenic Overloo**

**CHESAPEAKE & OHIO CANAL
NATIONAL HISTORICAL PARK**

Lock Spur

Berma Road   Woodland Trail

Billy Goat Trail

Tow Path   Widewater

Valley Trail

Old
Anglers
Inn

Mather
Gorge

Sherwin
Island

MacArthur Blvd.

Potomac
River

Tow Path

Billy Goat Trail

are human footfalls (stay on the blazed trails) and nonnative species, such as
Japanese honeysuckle, kudzu, and garlic mustard.

From the large parking lot, head past the circa-1850s Washington Aqueduct
gatehouse to the Great Falls Tavern Visitor Center, which has in-depth exhibits
on the ill-fated C&O Canal. The canal took decades to build and was quickly
usurped as a transportation corridor by the B&O Railroad (see "Centuries of
Perseverance: The Chesapeake & Ohio Canal," on page 97). The visitor center
building was constructed in 1828 as a lock house, and in 1831 the lock tender
added a three-story north wing as a hotel and tavern for weary barge workers.
From the tavern, cross the canal on the footbridge at lock 20 and turn left (downstream) on the towpath past locks 19 and 18. Turn right (just before lock 17) for a
0.1-mile side trip over the pedestrian bridge to Great Falls Overlook on Olmsted
Island. The overlook offers a tremendous view of Great Falls. The island landscape here, a jumble of flat boulders crisscrossed by deep crevices, was once the
Potomac riverbed. Swirling, sediment-filled river eddies carved out the crevices

and potholes over time. (See "Far Away in Time: The Geology of Great Falls," on page 197.) An ecologically unique bedrock-terrace forest, featuring white oak, northern red oak, hickory, Virginia pine, and federally endangered wildflower species, such as wispy yellow nailwort and hardy rock skullcap, thrives here and on Bear Island to the south.

Return to the towpath and continue past lock 17. At 0.8 mile, 30 yards before a footbridge and a stop lock (the point where the canal enters Widewater, a natural channel left dry when the river shifted course), turn right onto the blue-blazed Billy Goat Trail A. The 1.7-mile Trail A follows the eastern edge of Bear Island, another ancient riverbed, atop the Mather Gorge. Overuse is threatening the more than 50 rare plant and animal species on the island, so do not stray from the path. American hornbeam has been replanted in several damaged areas.

Start on the rocky Billy Goat Trail A through the woods, to a shelf of boulders over the gorge. To the right, level rocks at the cliff's edge make a nice picnic spot. Carefully scramble atop the narrow-edged boulders, following the blazes forward, before swinging behind an escarpment at the edge of the gorge and gradually descending toward the river. Next, call on reserve energy for a challenging 50-foot climb along a sloping cliff face, the most difficult portion of this hike.

Continue as the trail snakes along the edge of the gorge, passing several ponds and rocky hills. Descend to a point of rocks above a large channel of the Potomac River. A seashell-filled landing, shaded by sycamores, is accessible at low water. The hill just to the left is Sherwin Island. Beyond it, on the opposite heights, is the conspicuous brick auditorium of the Madeira School, an all-girls private boarding school. Continue as the trail curves back toward the canal at the end of Bear Island, following a large channel on the right. Traverse several rocky hills cut by streams then head left away from the channel to the C&O Canal towpath at the end of Widewater, at 2.5 miles.

Turn right onto the towpath and head past the entrance to a bridge over the canal that leads back to Old Angler's Inn and connections to other trails (to which this hike returns). Continue 160 yards to the start of Billy Goat Trail B. This area, another bulge of land in the Potomac's watercourse, is a floodplain forest dominated by sycamore, ash, and elm trees. Follow the narrow path 80 yards into the woods. Swing left with the blue blazes and follow the crest of the bluff before descending to the river. Proceed downstream, at one point veering sharply inland around a gully and then returning to river's edge. Opposite a large island, turn left away from the river and climb back to the C&O towpath, at 4.5 miles.

Turn left, keeping the canal on the right, for a 0.9-mile return trip to the bridge that leads to Old Angler's Inn; an interpretive sign marks the intersection. Cross the bridge and head uphill. At the Cropley parking lot, make a hairpin turn up and to the left onto a wide path, Berma Road, that runs atop the Washington Aqueduct on the east side of Widewater. Near a small power station, turn right onto the yellow-blazed Valley Trail.

Follow Valley Trail for 0.6 mile to the "T" intersection at 6.3 miles with the blue-blazed Gold Mine Loop. Turn right onto Gold Mine Loop and head uphill on an old woods road, passing a yellow-blazed spur to Rockwood School. At a point where the main trail veers 90 degrees to the left, take the spur trail to the ruins of the Maryland Mine.

Gold fever began at Great Falls when a Union soldier discovered specks of gold while washing skillets in a stream. Following the war, investors swarmed the area and built several 100-foot-deep mineshafts. Profits were minimal, however, and pits, shafts, trenches, and tunnels came and went. The rusty ruins here were part of the Maryland Mine, which even in its heyday was a rickety contraption of sheds and shanties stuck together on stilts at different levels.

Turn right back onto Gold Mine Loop and ascend a draw, where the path follows an old prospecting trench. Reach a "Y" intersection at 7.2 miles where the loop closes, and turn slightly right to descend to an old roadbed. This was once the Washington and Great Falls Railroad, which ran trolleys to the area. Turn right onto the roadbed and ascend slightly, passing through dense hardwood forest. After 200 yards, turn left off the raised roadbed and continue downhill 300 yards to the trailhead, near Great Falls Tavern, at 8.2 miles.

MORE INFORMATION

Three-day park passes for C&O Canal NHP are $10 per vehicle. Mule-drawn canal-boat rides are offered three times daily, Thursday to Sunday, April through October. Purchase tickets at the Great Falls Tavern Visitor Center; call 301-767-3714; or visit nps.gov/choh. The National Park Service also offers ranger-guided hiking tours of Great Falls, biking tours on the C&O Canal, and overnight stays (by advance reservation) at Riley's Lockhouse.

Dogs are prohibited on Olmsted Island and Billy Goat Trail A. Swimming at Great Falls is prohibited due to dangerous underwater currents. To learn more about human pressures on the Potomac Gorge and what can be done to lessen them, consult the Nature Conservancy's *Good Neighbor Handbook: Tips and Tools for River Friendly Living in the Middle Potomac Region* (2005).

NEARBY

Glen Echo Park (the site of a restored amusement park that once attracted crowds of Washingtonians), the Clara Barton House, and Cabin John Trail are all worthwhile visits on the Maryland side of the Potomac Gorge.

CENTURIES OF PERSEVERANCE: THE CHESAPEAKE & OHIO CANAL

The dream of a transportation route to the Ohio River began in Colonial days—and contributed to the horror of the French and Indian (Seven Years') War. But the founders didn't quit. Thomas Jefferson advocated development of waterways to the West. George Washington, envisioning a growing nation, selected sites for the new capital and a federal armory along the Potomac. The Patowmack Company, organized by Washington himself in 1785, dredged river shallows near Washington, D.C., and blasted locks around Great Falls. But progress seemed elusive. Skilled canal labor, for instance, was mostly nonexistent in the new nation; slaves and indentured servants had to do much of the work.

A new organization, the Chesapeake & Ohio Company—with the Erie Canal's former chief engineer on board—pushed westward from D.C. in 1828 through the Potomac Valley's rugged terrain. But by the time the canal reached Cumberland, Maryland—184.5 miles upstream—in 1850, the upstart Baltimore & Ohio Railroad had beaten it there (and beyond) by eight years. This complication limited the canal mainly to local traffic—coal for Georgetown's foundries and breweries, produce for city markets. By 1860, decades of legal battles and loan interest left the canal company facing massive deficits. The C&O would never come within 100 miles of the Ohio River.

Postbellum growth put investors into the black at last. But in 1889, with railroads enjoying ever-greater transportation dominance, a hurricane caused flooding that shoved barges and lockhouses into the nearby Potomac. Repairs were prohibitively expensive, so the B&O Railroad took over the beleaguered waterway in 1890 and kept it going. By 1924, when another major flood hit, canal operations were halted. Nature's bad moods likewise stumped New Deal efforts to reinvent the canal as a recreation area.

Following World War II, Congress introduced plans for a scenic parkway along the C&O, but the avid outdoorsman and Supreme Court Justice William O. Douglas insisted people couldn't truly enjoy the canal from inside an automobile. He invited *Washington Post* editors, who advocated the parkway plan, to hike the entire 184.5-mile C&O towpath with him. Douglas easily completed the eight-day trek (it seems the editors made it only partway), raising strong public—and editorial—support for a towpath recreation area. In 1971, the C&O was designated a National Historic Park at last.

Perseverance continues today. In early 2010, meltwater from the "Snowpocalypse" storm left Great Falls Tavern marooned and broke through part of Lock 5, a few miles upstream from D.C. Alarms went out to Georgetown businesspeople and residents, in case the lock's other half couldn't hold. On another happy note, it could, and did.

21

GWYNNS FALLS AND LEAKIN PARK

Many non-locals heard of this park for the first time while listening to the haunting podcast *Serial* or watching the gritty TV show *The Wire*. In reality, the park is a charming hodgepodge of historic remains, modern art, and plant life in a wild setting.

DIRECTIONS

From I-495 (Capital Beltway), take US-29 North/Columbia Pike. Take Exit 25A to merge onto I-70 east toward Baltimore. Take Exit 94 from I-70 east and merge onto Security Boulevard. After 0.2 mile, take a slight right onto Ingleside Avenue. Turn right onto Dogwood Avenue then continue on Franklintown Road for 1.3 miles. The parking lot is on the left, marked with a sign for Gwynns Falls Trail. *GPS Coordinates*: 39° 18.274′ N, 76° 41.635′ W.

TRAIL DESCRIPTION

Baltimore's Leakin Park and Gwynns Falls Park span 1,216 acres in Baltimore City. The City Department of Recreation and Parks operates them as a single park; combined, they make up the city's largest. Scenes for the 1999 horror film *The Blair Witch Project* were filmed in the park, and outside of Baltimore, it's best known for dark mentions on the HBO show *The Wire* and in the *Serial* podcast. Contrary to its reputation, Leakin Park is a hidden gem packed with rich history, local art, and forests of red oak, yellow poplar, and American beech. In contrast to other Baltimore parks, the area remains mostly in its naturally wild state, punctuated with mowed lawns. Leakin Park lies on the land that was once Thomas Winans's Crimea estate, named in honor of the Ukrainian peninsula. Winans, who was born in New Jersey, gained his wealth as a chief engineer of the Russian Railway between St. Petersburg and Moscow after

LOCATION
Baltimore, MD

RATING
Easy to moderate

DISTANCE
2.5 miles

ELEVATION GAIN
217 feet

ESTIMATED TIME
1.5 hours

MAPS
USGS Baltimore West; Map available at trailhead. Online: friendsofgwynnsfalls leakinpark.org/docs/ GwynnsFallsLeakin ParkTrailMap.pdf

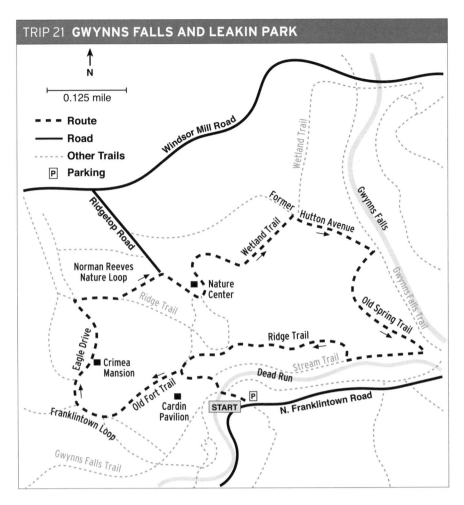

traveling there at his father's behest. He later returned to the United States with his Russian-born wife. Today, their 1850s summer home, the Orianda mansion, and other estate buildings still stand in Leakin Park.

This 2.5-mile loop hike brings you past many of the park's diverse features with minimal elevation change. On quiet days, you're likely to see white-tailed deer crossing the path in forested areas. From the parking lot, pass the restrooms and the informational sign and cross the paved hike-bike bridge over Dead Run. At the first intersection, go right, heading toward the Cardin Pavilion. At the pavilion, take another right to cross a tributary stream on a wooden footbridge to a grassy dip where a stone wall opens via a door into the side of the hill. This is the old Crimea Estate's ice house and root cellar. Continue straight with the root cellar on your right and take the splinter trail a couple of hundred yards up into the forest to see the ruins of what was once the estate caretaker's home.

Return to the field and pass over the root cellar, heading into the forest. Go straight on Ravine Trail when Stream Trail departs to the right. Ravine Trail passes above Stream Trail, climbing to a switchback. Go left on the switchback, following yellow blazes and signs for Old Fort Trail and the mansion.

As you climb, pass a stone cistern on the right, where a short boardwalk elevates the trail over muddy ground. Immediately following, pass an old mock-fort rampart on the left, offering a view out over the park's tall trees. The path curves right after the mock fort, still climbing gently. An unmarked trail departs to the right; continue straight on Old Fort Trail. Shortly, pass the remains of a brick circle, on the left. Climb steeply to the "T" intersection and turn right. After another 100 yards, an intersection points left to the meadow and right to the mansion. Turn right, following orange and blue blazes toward the mansion.

Continue climbing on the now rocky trail, soon arriving at a sign pointing left to the Franklintown Loop. Once again, turn right and proceed toward the mansion; on your left, you may notice the Outward Bound climbing wall peeking through the trees. Soon after, emerge at a parking area intersecting a paved road. Head right on this road toward the historic Orianda Mansion, noted on park maps as the Crimea Mansion. Pass a yellow buckeye bush immediately before the mansion. In late spring, this bush swarms with yellow and black eastern tiger swallowtail butterflies—and possibly bees.

Pass the nineteenth-century Russian Imperial-style mansion, pausing to note its distinctive high ceilings and porches, as you walk on the paved road that curves toward the picnic pavilion. As you pass the "Park Rules" sign, pause for a detour onto the lawn on the right to walk the stone labyrinth. The labyrinth, created by Antonio Carpenter, is a permanent installation, offering visitors the opportunity to reflect or meditate as they walk its paths.

Continuing on the road, turn right when you reach Group Picnic Area 2. Pass the pavilion and approach the trunk of an old tree capped with a small, pointed roof. Within the hollowed-out center of this trunk is a sign describing the "Nature Art in the Park" exhibit, the bulk of which lies along Norman Reeves Nature Loop. This installation features works by local artists—sculptural pieces, fiber arts, pottery—inspired by the natural setting. Ten new pieces are added each spring, and any artwork that has disintegrated is removed on a yearly basis.

Continue to Norman Reeves Nature Loop, just past the pavilion and the hollowed-out tree, and turn right onto the loop, passing the first art pieces. Walk through a tunnel of low-leaning trees then immediately turn left to continue on the orange- and white-blazed Norman Reeves Nature Loop, toward the Carrie Murray Nature Center, as Ridge Trail exits to the right. Norman Reeves Nature Loop tracks a stone wall through the woods, passing several more art installations. As the loop leaves the trees, turn right onto a paved road toward the pavilion and the Nature Center.

Pass the E Meadow, where more hardy and permanent nature-related statues stand, on your left as you approach the nature center. You also may notice the hum of bees coming from bee boxes on the right.

The walk to the root cellar showcases Leakin Park's rich greenery. Photo by Annie Eddy.

Immediately before the white-painted nature center, turn left. Pass along the side of the building and through its backyard and gardens toward the sign for Wetlands Trail. Enter the forest on Wetlands Trail; at the unmarked "Y" intersection, go right. The trail slopes down gradually. At both the second and third unmarked intersections, go right again, following orange and white blazes. The narrow, grassy trail winds around the nature center at a distance then descends to a section of wooden boardwalks as a splinter trail joins from the left. Use caution; the wood surface may be slippery after rain. The boardwalk descends in steps before turning left then curving right.

Emerge on the former Hutton Avenue (the "former" is noted on some maps) and turn right on this paved road. Descend gently down the forested slope as the road crosses a creek. Soon after, emerge from the trees at a "T" intersection with the paved hike-bike Gwynns Falls Trail, which parallels its namesake waterway. Make a hairpin turn to the right to head back toward the trees through the small Greenway Meadow, toward the sign for Spring Trail. As you pass through the meadow, watch for swallowtail and monarch butterflies and purple finches among the milkweed and goldenrod. Queen Anne's lace also blooms here in early August. Enter the forest on the blue- and orange-blazed Spring Trail, which immediately turns left and climbs gently, parallel to Gwynns Falls Trail below, before turning right into the forest and climbing the ridge. A short boardwalk elevates the trail over a muddy area, and rocks line the trail as you continue to climb.

Cresting the ridge, the trail descends steeply to the intersection with Ridge Trail. Take a right onto the white-blazed Ridge Trail, looking and listening for running water below to your left. At the 2-mile point, the trail hairpins to the left, crossing over a dip in the slope, and soon after begins to climb log stairs. This steep stretch is brief. Soon the trail levels out as it curves to the right and passes the sculptural stairs that descend from the back end of the nature center. Take a left to descend on narrower stairs, quite steeply at first. At the bottom of the stairs, a cliff overlook is visible through the trees to the left; it is not easily reached from the trail, and is best viewed from a distance. Here, the trail turns right, crossing a narrow stream on a broad boardwalk that rests on stone trestles. Hang left after the bridge and cross another, smaller bog bridge. Emerge back at the "Y" intersection with Old Fort Trail and turn left to head back toward the Cardin Pavilion. Descend as the trail opens up, offering a view of the field above the root cellar framed with towering trees. Turn left to pass over the footbridge and left again to cross the hike-bike bridge and return to the parking lot.

MORE INFORMATION

The clash of urban reality and wilderness notwithstanding, Gwynns Falls and Leakin parks are a huge and beautiful property within Baltimore's city limits. In the past decade, park advocates have worked hard to enhance park trails and safety, closing off isolated, dead-end access roads from high-crime neighborhoods and creating a bike trail around the park's perimeter. The Friends of Gwynns Falls/Leakin Park offer customized tours by appointment and can be reached at fogflp@gmail.com; for more information, see their website at friendsofgwynnsfallsleakinpark.org.

NEARBY

Leakin Park and Gwynns Falls Park offer several other options for hikes. For a shorter walk, the Franklintown Loop Trail is a 45-minute ramble through a forest of tall beech trees in the western portion of the park. Reach the Franklintown Loop from the same parking area as our featured hike or from the parking area off Windsor Mill Rd at 1920 Eagle Drive.

The Gwynns Falls Trail spans 14 miles from the end of Interstate 70 on the west side of Baltimore to the Inner Harbor. A section of the trail follows the Gwynns Falls Stream on its east bank. Maps of the Gwynns Falls Trail are available at trailheads.

22

C&O CANAL: POINT OF ROCKS TO MONOCACY AQUEDUCT

This 12.2-mile meander along the gently graded C&O Canal towpath terminates at the canal's largest aqueduct, at the intersection of the Monocacy and Potomac rivers.

DIRECTIONS

From I-495 (Capital Beltway), take I-270 Spur north to I-270 north. After 23.3 miles, take Exit 26 for MD 80. Turn right onto MD 80 west. Continue 5 miles then turn left on MD 85 south. After 4.6 miles, turn left on MD 28 west and continue 4.5 miles. Turn left on Monroe Street then immediately turn right as Monroe Street becomes Commerce Street. After 400 feet, turn left on Canal Road. The parking area is located above the boat launch at 3707 Canal Road. *GPS Coordinates:* 39° 16.393′ N, 77° 32.403′ W.

TRAIL DESCRIPTION

The Chesapeake and Ohio (C&O) Canal towpath stretches 184 miles beside the Potomac River through Pennsylvania, Maryland, West Virginia, Virginia, and Washington, D.C. This hike along the towpath, flanked by the railroad tracks on one side and the river on the other, offers several vistas of the Potomac's shores and islands on the way to Monocacy Aqueduct, the largest of C&O's eleven original aqueducts. The out-and-back hike clocks in at a lengthy 12.2 miles, but due to the lack of elevation change, it is possible to complete the route in four or five hours. Views of the Potomac are more extensive in winter and spring when the foliage is sparse, but the shaded forest tunnel of the towpath and its gradual, easy pace make it a good option for hotter weather as well. Expect to see other hikers and bikers regularly on this well-traveled route. Restrooms and water sources abound along the trail; dogs are allowed, but must be leashed.

LOCATION
Point of Rocks, MD

RATING
Moderate

DISTANCE
12.2 miles

ELEVATION GAIN
50 feet

ESTIMATED TIME
4 to 5 hours

MAPS
USGS Point of Rocks; online: nps.gov/choh/planyourvisit/upload/CHOHmap-full-140922-v7.pdf

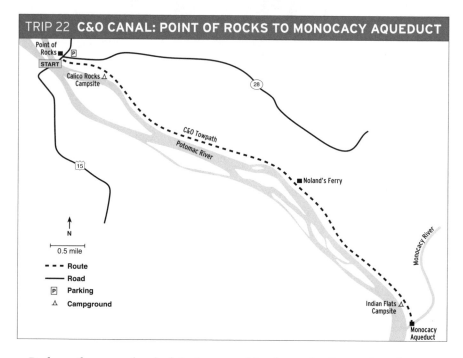

Point of
Rocks P
START
Calico Rocks △
Campsite
28
C&O Towpath
Potomac River
15
Noland's Ferry
Monocacy River
N
0.5 mile
- - - Route
—— Road
P Parking
△ Campground
Indian Flats △
Campsite
Monocacy
Aqueduct

Park on the upper level of the large parking lot at the Point of Rocks access point. The lower level is reserved for vehicles using the boat launch. Turn right to see the bridge that carries US 15 over the Potomac. Proceed to the left, toward the sign that reads, "Point of Rocks Access Point/Mile 48.2," and pass through the gate to begin your hike on the wide gravel towpath. The tall forest creates a tunnel-like feeling, and ivy and vines blanket the trees. On the left, the still, shallow canal parallels the trail, while the Potomac flows by on the right, coming in and out of view through the trees. Look for bright-red cardinals and white-tailed deer crossing the path as you proceed south toward the aqueduct.

The path crosses above a winding stream. Soon after, pass the short post marking mile 48 on your right. The trail emerges into a sunny copse as it intersects another tributary on the right then quickly returns to shade. Shortly, you will see the sign for Calico Rocks Hike/Bike Campsite on the right, which is named for the region's multicolored composite rocks. This site features a portable toilet and an iodine-treated water pump. As you continue along the towpath, the old canal on the left is nearly dry. Beyond its muddy bed, the railroad tracks are now visible through the trees. Unlike the canal, these tracks are still in use today, and you may even see a freight train or two passing. On the right, the river comes into better view through the trees. The towpath intersects with a narrow metal boat launch on the right, which slopes down through a small open field that offers a pleasant view of the Potomac.

Soon after, pass mile marker 47 on the right. Thorns fringe the trail as the river remains visible through the trees. Look to the left for a large cliff draped with ivy and blanketed with moss. The trail curves gently to the left as the railroad tracks and the river continue to flank the path. After mile marker 46, the towpath departs slightly from the Potomac. Open patches occasionally offer obscured views of the water; listen for ducks. After mile marker 45, the edge of the trail rises to the right. After 0.4 mile from mile marker 45, pass a large stone building on the right with a red door as you approach the Noland's Ferry access point; you are now 2.5 miles from Monocacy Aqueduct. Continue straight, crossing the road and keeping left of the Noland's Ferry sign and the stone retainer wall, continuing on the towpath. You will emerge in an open area as the path passes a small parking lot, restrooms, and picnic tables.

At mile marker 44, the towpath crosses a stone trestle bridge. For a pleasant view of the Potomac River and its small islands, turn right immediately after crossing the bridge and descend a short, steep slope. At the base of the bridge, the brown waters of the small tributary open into the river, and the muddy plain allows you to walk to the water's edge. Return to the towpath and continue south along a peaceful section of the trail.

After an open area populated with dead trees, you will reach mile marker 43. Shortly after, pass over another tributary. Immediately on the right is the Indian Flats hike-bike campsite with its picnic area and water pump. The Monocacy Aqueduct emerges in sight far in the distance. The path is very straight here and offers visibility nearly 0.5 mile ahead. Arrive at the aqueduct, a tenth of a mile before the towpath's mile 42 marker. For a nice view of the west side of the aqueduct from below, descend to the grassy area on the right before crossing.

Monocacy Aqueduct, the largest aqueduct on the C&O Canal, spans the Monocacy River just east of where it joins the Potomac.

The aqueduct spans the Monocacy River just northeast of where this tributary joins with the Potomac. When operational, the waters of the canal flowed through the depression in the middle of the aqueduct, allowing one water source to cross another, while horses walked on the elevated parapet wall. With the aqueduct dry for many years, both hikers and bikers may cross in either the depressed waterway or on the downstream side of the towpath parapet wall, which is 8 feet wide and has a railing. Although signs warn bikers to walk their bikes across, many do not comply, so use caution when crossing the aqueduct on foot. As you reach the middle of the aqueduct, turn left to see a railroad bridge spanning the Monocacy River upstream.

After crossing the aqueduct, continue on a gravel path that curves to the left, toward the parking lot and a pleasant picnic area by the river's east bank. Informational placards present the area's rich history. During the Civil War, Confederate troops considered destroying the Monocacy Aqueduct, which the Union often used to transport materials or troops. Canal employee Thomas Walter convinced Confederate General D. H. Hill that his troops would have greater success draining the canal instead. Initially falling under suspicion of collaborating with the enemy, Walter was later thanked by the C&O Canal company, having saved them thousands of dollars in repairs. A later attempt by Confederate troops to blow up the aqueduct with gunpowder charges was also unsuccessful due to inadequate ammunition, and the aqueduct survived the war. Suffering from the stresses of time and weather, the marvel of engineering was restored to its original condition and formally rededicated in 2005.

When you have finished viewing the aqueduct, cross back over to the north and retrace your steps the 6.1 miles to the Point of Rocks parking lot.

MORE INFORMATION

If you would like to keep the mileage to a more manageable 6.1 miles, simply park a second car at the Monocacy Aqueduct access point. If you lack two vehicles but wish to keep the distance to 5 miles, begin at the Noland's Ferry access point (the parking lot there is small, so make sure to arrive early) and hike the 2.5 miles to the aqueduct before retracing your steps to your car. Parking is free at all parking lots mentioned in this section. For more information about Monocacy Aqueduct, visit nps.gov/choh/learn/historyculture/themonocacyaqueduct .htm or contact the National Parks Service at 301-739-4200, Monday through Friday from 8 A.M. to 4 P.M.

NEARBY

The tiny, unincorporated community of Point of Rocks, which runs parallel to the canal and railroad tracks, is named for a rock outcrop on Catoctin Mountain, visible from the Potomac River. Its Victorian-era passenger railway station was built by the B&O Railroad Company and now services the MARC (Maryland Area Regional Commuter) train's Brunswick Line, which runs only on weekdays.

23

PATAPSCO VALLEY STATE PARK

Cascade Falls, on the ridge east of the Patapsco River, highlights this hike.

DIRECTIONS

From I-95/I-495 (Capital Beltway), go north on I-95 to Exit 47 (BWI Airport) and go east on I-195. Take Exit 3 to Elkridge and turn right at the stoplight onto US 1 south. Take the next right onto South Street then an immediate left into Patapsco Valley Park. Pass through the contact station ($2 per vehicle fee for in-state residents; $4 per vehicle for out-of-state; on weekends April through October, fees are $3 per person in-state and $5 per person out-of-state). Travel under the Thomas Viaduct and turn left at the "T" intersection with Gun Road. Park at the far end of the first lot. *GPS coordinates*: 39° 13.595′ N, 76° 43.463′ W.

TRAIL DESCRIPTION

Patapsco Valley State Park extends along nearly 35 miles of the Patapsco River in Maryland, from Elkridge in the east to Woodbine in the west. The river valley encompasses more than 14,500 acres and is divided into multiple recreation areas. This hike explores the eastern section, known as the Avalon, Hilton, Glen Artney, and Orange Grove areas, all named for long-gone mill towns.

Although the mills are no longer here, the river valley remains a transportation corridor. Maryland Area Regional Commuter (MARC) trains rumble across the breathtaking, 704-foot Thomas Viaduct, which was the largest bridge in the nation at the time of its completion in 1835 and remains the oldest stone arch railroad bridge still in use.

This hike starts from the Avalon area parking lot on the southern side of the Patapsco River and encompasses five major south-side trails. Leave the lot and hike north on River Road, turning left onto the orange-blazed Ridge

LOCATION
Elkridge, MD

RATING
Strenuous

DISTANCE
6.9 miles

ELEVATION GAIN
1,300 feet

ESTIMATED TIME
3 hours

MAPS
USGS Relay; Waterproof Maryland Park Service trail maps available at Avalon Visitor Center; online: dnr2.maryland.gov/publiclands/Pages/central/patapsco.aspx

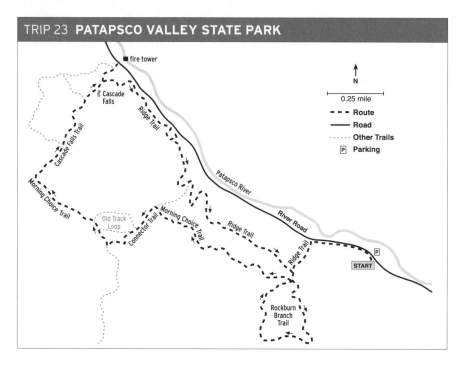

Trail. After a bracing climb up 180 feet, turn slightly left at the intersection at the top, where the Rockburn Branch loop and Morning Choice Trail diverge. Turn left and hike the 1.2-mile, purple-blazed Rockburn Branch loop, enjoying the mature open forest and pleasant views into stream valleys. Return to the start of the loop and begin a leisurely stroll uphill on the yellow-blazed Morning Choice Trail, heading northwest. Pass through big-leafed pawpaw thickets, reach a large open field, and travel along the edge of the woods. Come back under tree cover beneath a large shagbark hickory. Just ahead are the remains of two old two-story houses and a connector trail to Ridge Trail.

Continue on Morning Choice Trail to another open field that marks the edge of the Belmont Conference Center lands; the center is just visible uphill to the left. Reenter the woods and, after a slight uphill climb, plunge down across the source of a creek then up a second draw (small valley sloping toward a stream-bed) to a series of wide curves. On the left is an open area with a large climbing wall. Turn sharply left and pass the Old Track Loop on the right. Continue underneath a massive grove of tulip trees and come to a "T" intersection; both branches are Morning Choice Trail. Turn right to pass a bamboo thicket at the link-up of Old Track Loop and Norris Lane. Take time to admire the old, squat, burly maple tree, then go downhill to the "Y" intersection, bearing right onto the blue-blazed Cascade Falls Trail.

At the "T" intersection, turn right again and look for the Cascade Falls stream on the left. During the Great Depression of the 1930s, families were allowed to camp out for the entire summer in this park, and many of the campsites were

Cascade Falls, which once must have attracted the valley's mill workers just as it attracts today's sightseers, is the perfect spot to stop for lunch. Along with the Thomas Viaduct, Bloedes Dam, and the old suspension bridge, it is one of the best-known sites in the park. Photo by Stephen Mauro.

located along Cascade Falls and its tributaries. Follow the stream, crossing it twice on small bridges. Then cross a tributary and the main stream two more times. Notice the dramatic cliffs on the opposite bank. Climb a rocky ridge above the water to reach the falls themselves, where the stream course is strewn with large boulders and the water drops 15 feet into a pool. Follow a spur of Cascades Trail northeast as it crosses the stream just below the waterfall and makes its way to River Road and the site of Swinging Bridge, a metal-and-wire structure that shortened the distance workers had to travel between the mill towns. The bridge itself was destroyed by Hurricane Agnes in 1972.

Go south on River Road and take the first left heading back uphill onto Ridge Trail for a challenging 1.3-mile ridge run that undulates down and up the sides of steep draws and turns back on itself in tight switchbacks. Mountain laurel, dogwood, and pawpaw crowd the trail. After passing the connector trail on the right, take the second left past twin dogwood gatekeepers to continue on Ridge Trail. Wind down along the side of two draws and then crest a hill before running along the side of a steep ridge to the left. Finally, drop to the right via a series of switchbacks, through patches of pawpaw, and return to River Road. Turn right back to the parking lot.

MORE INFORMATION

Besides hiking, Patapsco Valley State Park is perfect for road biking (paved trails extend along either side of the river), mountain biking (especially on Rockburn Branch Trail), swimming and fishing (at numerous points on the Patapsco River), and photography (Ilchester Rocks Trail and the Thomas Viaduct provide excellent vantages for photographing trains). Dogs are welcome on all the trails. Additional use fees may apply. Visit dnr2.maryland.gov/publiclands/Pages/central/patapsco.aspx or call 410-461-5005 for more information.

NEARBY

Historic Ellicott City, county seat of Howard County, lies to the southeast along the banks of the Patapsco. This former mill town, dating to pre-Revolutionary days, offers a range of attractive homes, shops, and public buildings, and even a ghost tour of the village, which has been called one of the most haunted small towns on the East Coast. The circa 1833 hilltop mansion Mount Ida, home to the Historic Ellicott City nonprofit and the Patapsco Female Institute, is open for public tours one Saturday per month, June to November, for a small fee. Severe flash flooding in the summer of 2016 caused extensive damage to the historic district; rebuilding efforts are well underway. The paved Trolley Line #9 Trail follows a shady 1.25-mile segment of the now-defunct trolley right-of-way that shuttled passengers from Ellicott City to Baltimore from the 1890s until its decommissioning in the 1950s. See visitellicottcity.com/tourism-center and visithowardcounty.com for more information.

24

GREENWELL STATE PARK

Hike diverse terrain—pine forests, agricultural fields, tidal creeks, sandy beaches—at this idyllic state park on the banks of the Patuxent River.

DIRECTIONS

From I-95/I-495 (Capital Beltway), take Exit 11 onto MD 4 east (Pennsylvania Avenue) in the direction of Upper Marlboro. MD 4 becomes MD 4/MD 2. Drive approximately 50 miles then cross the Patuxent River Bridge. At the traffic light after the bridge, turn right onto MD 235 north. At the third traffic light, turn right onto MD 245 (Slotterley Road). Travel approximately 3 miles and turn right onto Steer Horn Neck Road. Travel 0.8 mile and turn left into the park, which is open year-round. *GPS coordinates*: 38° 21.933' N, 76° 31.502' W.

TRAIL DESCRIPTION

In 1971, the Greenwell family donated 600 acres on the Patuxent River in St. Mary's County to the state of Maryland, providing recreational facilities for the public and for people with disabilities, in particular. The ten color-coded dirt trails, including two shoreline trails, loop through the park for a total of 10 miles and are fairly level, wide, and well marked. This hike offers spectacular views of the broad Patuxent River with a bonus: historic tobacco barns.

From the parking lot near the circa-1880 Rosedale Manor, cross the access road and follow River Trail to the right side of the white rail fences surrounding the horse pastures. Turn right at the revetment, or piled rocks that prevent erosion, along the small cove, and follow the trail around the point to the right. Continue along River Trail past the fishing pier and the ranger station on the right to the sandy swimming beach. Pick up the trail on the other side of the beach and follow it 1,000 yards between the

LOCATION
Hollywood, MD

RATING
Moderate

DISTANCE
4.5 miles

ELEVATION GAIN
290 feet

ESTIMATED TIME
2.5 to 3 hours

MAPS
USGS Hollywood; Maryland Trail Guide (dnr.maryland.gov/publiclands); online: dnr2.maryland.gov/publiclands/Pages/parkmaps/greenwellmap.aspx, greenwellfoundation.org

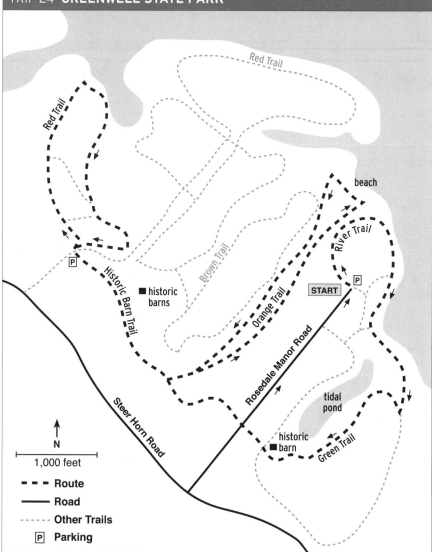

shoreline and the trees to a path on the right that leads away from the water. Follow the path uphill through the woods where it intersects Green Trail along the edge of a large field. Turn right and follow Green Trail as it curves left and skirts the edge of the field. Follow the woods' edge and the contours of the terrain through the middle of the field to a tidal pond. Leave the edge of the field and enter the woods for about 150 yards. Upon reemerging from the woods, turn right, but instead of following the trail as it reenters the woods, continue left along the forest edge for 100 yards to the first of four historic tobacco barns. These barns are some of the oldest in tidewater Maryland. Go back to where the trail enters the woods to the left, hike 200 yards to the edge of a new field, and continue on to the park's gravel access road.

Cross the road and turn left down the gravel Gray Trail, following it between the fields to a small parking lot with a kiosk. Walk past the kiosk and turn left on the other side of the line of barrier trees. Follow marker posts to the edge of the field around to the right, then turn left onto Barn Trail through a break in the trees. Travel 150 yards straight along the forest edge to the second historic barn and then, farther on, a third, designated as the oldest of its type in tidewater Maryland. Continue to the gravel road and follow it to the left. Where the road turns 90 degrees left, Yellow Trail starts to the left and Red Trail to the right.

Continue on Red Trail to the fourth historic barn. Then enter the woods and travel through a mostly deciduous forest with occasional tall pines. Hike up a slight incline; follow the trail along the top of a ridge, past locust, white oak, holly, and red maple trees; and go down the left side of the ridge. A creek runs at the bottom of a deep ravine to the left. Continue downhill over a log into a field. Turn left and follow Red Trail along the edge of the field. Leave the path and walk through the trees past large oaks and beeches to the point of land above the river. With luck, you can spot beavers, otters, or muskrats in Hog Neck Creek below. Continue along Red Trail as it follows the field's irregular boundaries. Below to the left, through the trees, the river cove gives way to a marshy tidal area.

Young hikers scamper near the banks of the Patuxent River on Maryland's western shore. Photo by Alliecat1881, Creative Commons on Flickr.

At the end of the field, a marker post leads to the left back to Gray Trail. Continue through the trees for 200 yards then cross the gravel road. Follow Gray Trail straight ahead past the sign for Blue Trail on the right. At the end of the field, turn left, walk through the break in the trees, and go right along the woods' edge. Follow the forest edge as it curves left. Turn right back to the small parking lot with a kiosk for the Orange Trail trailhead.

Orange Trail is a slightly more rugged loop around a deep, wooded ravine and down to a small beach. Turn left from Gray Trail onto Orange Trail and enter the woods, following the right-hand path of Orange Trail where it forms a Y. Hike past the large wild cherry tree. Coming out of the woods, the trail bears left to meander along a short beach, a pleasant spot for a rest. Cross a small wooden bridge and head uphill back into the ravine. At the large beech tree near the lip of the ravine, turn left off Orange Trail and walk to the immense oak tree on the bluff for another spectacular view of the Patuxent River. Follow Orange Trail back to the Y intersection with Gray Trail and turn left onto the access gravel road, past the fenced horse pastures to the parking lot.

MORE INFORMATION

Greenwell State Park's use fee is $3 per in-state vehicle, $5 per out-of-state vehicle, run on an honor system. Leashed dogs are permitted in the park. Other activities at the park include fishing and crabbing from the pier, swimming at two beaches (no lifeguard on duty), kayaking and canoeing, horseback riding, bicycling, picnicking, and hunting (hikers should wear bright clothing during hunting season). On weekends, hobbyists fly model aircraft from a landing strip inside the Yellow Trail loop. The nonprofit Greenwell Foundation provides children's nature programs, recreational and therapeutic horseback riding, guided kayak trips and lessons, and weekend vacations for military service members recovering from post-traumatic stress disorder. For more information, visit dnr2.maryland.gov/publiclands/Pages/southern/greenwell.aspx and greenwellfoundation.org or call 301-872-5688.

NEARBY

A dozen or so miles to the south lies historic St. Mary's City, an outdoor living history museum interpreting the seventeenth-century life of Maryland's first European settlers. Make a weekend of it and continue south another ten miles or so to Point Lookout State Park, the very southern tip of Maryland's western shore where the Potomac River flows into the Chesapeake Bay. A former Civil War-era prison camp to over 50,000 Confederate soldiers, the park still offers camping today, and the beaches are appealing. For information, visit dnr2.maryland.gov/publiclands/Pages/southern/pointlookout.aspx.

WASHINGTON, D.C.

Many of us who have come to D.C. from elsewhere—as visitors or for a longer stay—are surprised to learn how many green spaces the city offers, where hikers can escape the stress of the nation's power centers and enjoy the solace of woods, rivers, canals, and creeks. These retreats

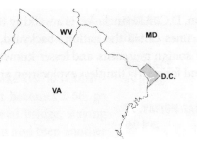

include large forested areas such as the 1,754-acre Rock Creek Park (more than twice the size of Central Park in New York City), Kenilworth Park and Aquatic Gardens, and Theodore Roosevelt Island, as well as narrower strips of buffer land tucked between neighborhood streets and the city's embassies, monuments, museums, bridges, and historic structures. D.C.'s longstanding moratorium on building any downtown structure reaching higher than the dome of the U.S. Capitol (enacted after the Washington Monument had been built) has created a sprawling skyline that encourages distinctive enclaves: the National Mall; unique neighborhoods such as Georgetown, Adams Morgan, Dupont Circle, Columbia Heights, Anacostia, and Brookland; and the green spaces that draw hikers, bikers, ballplayers, horseback riders, and inline skaters.

Rock Creek Park comprises a significant portion of northwest Washington, D.C., and contains Civil War-era fortifications, historical structures, horse stables, and even a planetarium. Rock Creek Trail follows its namesake creek through the park and beyond, from the Potomac River at Foggy Bottom in the south to Lake Needwood, near Rockville, Maryland, in the north. East–west trails etch their way through the park's river valleys and rolling hills, offering creative hiking combinations. Two subsections of Rock Creek Park, Dumbarton Oaks Park and Montrose Park, are included in Trip 29: Around Georgetown. These leafy corridors link to Chesapeake & Ohio (C&O) Canal Trail, which parallels the Potomac on the Georgetown waterfront as it begins its journey to Cumberland, Maryland, 184.5 miles northwest.

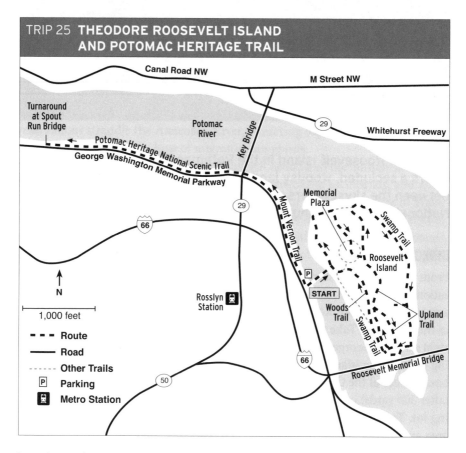

Canal Road NW

M Street NW

Turnaround at Spout Run Bridge

Potomac River

Key Bridge

29

Whitehurst Freeway

Potomac Heritage National Scenic Trail

George Washington Memorial Parkway

29

66

Memorial Plaza

Swamp Trail

Roosevelt Island

Mount Vernon Trail

N

1,000 feet

P

START

Rosslyn Station

Woods Trail

Swamp Trail

Upland Trail

- - - Route

—— Road

- - - - - Other Trails

P Parking

Metro Station

66

50

Roosevelt Memorial Bridge

lawn beneath stately oak and linden trees. In 1833, John was forced to relinquish his island as collateral for unpaid loans, but the family story held that the Masons moved because the mosquitoes had gotten too bad.

In 1931, the Theodore Roosevelt Memorial Association purchased the 88.5-acre island and donated it to the federal government as a tribute to the former president. The Theodore Roosevelt Memorial, officially dedicated in 1967, stands upon this island, which was planned as a bird and wildlife sanctuary—nearly 200 species of birds pass through here in the course of a year—to honor the naturalist president.

This hike includes a circuit around Theodore Roosevelt Island and a straight out-and-back on the rugged Potomac Heritage National Scenic Trail to the Three Sisters: three legendary rocks in the Potomac. From the parking lot on the west bank of the Potomac River, head a short distance south to the long, wide footbridge that crosses the Potomac, which is called Little River in this section. While crossing, look north to Francis Scott Key Bridge (locally known as Key Bridge) and Georgetown, and south to Roosevelt Memorial Bridge and beyond to Arlington Memorial Bridge. As you step onto the island, you'll see a kiosk displaying a map of the island's well-maintained trails. Turn left onto Swamp

WASHINGTON, D.C.

Many of us who have come to D.C. from elsewhere—as visitors or for a longer stay—are surprised to learn how many green spaces the city offers, where hikers can escape the stress of the nation's power centers and enjoy the solace of woods, rivers, canals, and creeks. These retreats

include large forested areas such as the 1,754-acre Rock Creek Park (more than twice the size of Central Park in New York City), Kenilworth Park and Aquatic Gardens, and Theodore Roosevelt Island, as well as narrower strips of buffer land tucked between neighborhood streets and the city's embassies, monuments, museums, bridges, and historic structures. D.C.'s longstanding moratorium on building any downtown structure reaching higher than the dome of the U.S. Capitol (enacted after the Washington Monument had been built) has created a sprawling skyline that encourages distinctive enclaves: the National Mall; unique neighborhoods such as Georgetown, Adams Morgan, Dupont Circle, Columbia Heights, Anacostia, and Brookland; and the green spaces that draw hikers, bikers, ballplayers, horseback riders, and inline skaters.

Rock Creek Park comprises a significant portion of northwest Washington, D.C., and contains Civil War-era fortifications, historical structures, horse stables, and even a planetarium. Rock Creek Trail follows its namesake creek through the park and beyond, from the Potomac River at Foggy Bottom in the south to Lake Needwood, near Rockville, Maryland, in the north. East–west trails etch their way through the park's river valleys and rolling hills, offering creative hiking combinations. Two subsections of Rock Creek Park, Dumbarton Oaks Park and Montrose Park, are included in Trip 29: Around Georgetown. These leafy corridors link to Chesapeake & Ohio (C&O) Canal Trail, which parallels the Potomac on the Georgetown waterfront as it begins its journey to Cumberland, Maryland, 184.5 miles northwest.

Complementing the relative wilds of Rock Creek Park are the meticulously planned and engineered yet naturally lovely green spaces of the National Arboretum and Kenilworth Aquatic Gardens. The arboretum is a haven for tree lovers, featuring rare dwarf conifers, ancient bonsai, and once-thought-extinct dawn redwoods. Kenilworth Aquatic Gardens is fragrant with brilliant-flowered lotuses and waterlilies sustained within a marsh habitat. Both of these nature reservations straddle the Anacostia River, attracting ospreys, great blue herons, egrets, bald eagles, and a host of migratory songbirds.

Two islands, the natural Theodore Roosevelt Island and the human-made East Potomac Park, offer secluded walks, thought-provoking memorials, and alluring flora, such as cherry blossoms in season, within the busy borders of Washington, D.C. Also included is a walking tour of the ever-popular National Mall, sometimes called the nation's backyard, which, with its famous monuments, Smithsonian museums, and lesser-known garden spots, serves as a perfect playground for nearly limitless exploration and enjoyment.

25

THEODORE ROOSEVELT ISLAND AND POTOMAC HERITAGE TRAIL

Theodore Roosevelt Island in the Potomac River offers a secluded, woodsy landmass to explore between the skyscrapers of Arlington and the National Mall in Washington, D.C.

DIRECTIONS

From downtown Washington, D.C., take US 50 (Constitution Avenue) west. Continuing as it becomes I-66, go across the Theodore Roosevelt Memorial Bridge, staying in the right lane. Take the first right exit and then another right onto the George Washington Memorial Parkway going north. (The island is accessible only from the northbound lanes of the GW Parkway.) Take the first right turn (after 300 yards) into the Theodore Roosevelt Island parking lot. To return to Washington, D.C., exit the parking area and drive 0.8 mile north on the GW Parkway. Take the first left exit onto Spout Run Parkway, then take the first left exit onto the southbound GW Parkway. *GPS coordinates*: 38° 53.745′ N, 77° 4.010′ W.

By Metrorail, take the Blue or Orange Line to Rosslyn station and walk 0.8 mile to the trailhead. Hike north downhill on North Moore Street, cross Nineteenth Street, turn right onto Lee Highway, cross North Lynn Street, and turn left down it. At the far corner, turn right onto Mount Vernon Trail, following it south to the trailhead.

TRAIL DESCRIPTION

In the early 1800s, the island later designated Theodore Roosevelt Island was the summer home of John Mason, son of the Virginia statesman George Mason. John erected an elegant brick mansion on the highest point of land, providing views across the Potomac River to the White House and the U.S. Capitol. Georgetown's wealthy elite would gather for dinners and dances on the Masons' manicured

LOCATION
Arlington, VA, and Washington, D.C.

RATING
Easy

DISTANCE
4.7 miles

ELEVATION GAIN
160 feet

ESTIMATED TIME
2 to 2.5 hours

MAPS
USGS Washington West; online: nps.gov/this and nps.gov/pohe/planyourvisit/maps.htm

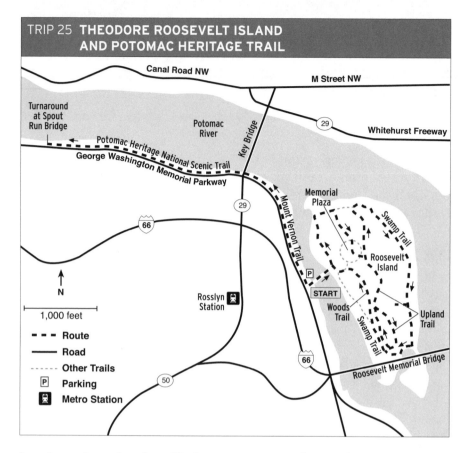

TRIP 25 THEODORE ROOSEVELT ISLAND AND POTOMAC HERITAGE TRAIL

Canal Road NW

M Street NW

Turnaround at Spout Run Bridge

Potomac River

Key Bridge

29

Whitehurst Freeway

Potomac Heritage National Scenic Trail

George Washington Memorial Parkway

29

66

Mount Vernon Trail

Memorial Plaza

Swamp Trail

Roosevelt Island

N

1,000 feet

Rosslyn Station

P

START

Woods Trail

Upland Trail

Swamp Trail

- - - Route
— Road
----- Other Trails
P Parking
Metro Station

66

50

Roosevelt Memorial Bridge

lawn beneath stately oak and linden trees. In 1833, John was forced to relinquish his island as collateral for unpaid loans, but the family story held that the Masons moved because the mosquitoes had gotten too bad.

In 1931, the Theodore Roosevelt Memorial Association purchased the 88.5-acre island and donated it to the federal government as a tribute to the former president. The Theodore Roosevelt Memorial, officially dedicated in 1967, stands upon this island, which was planned as a bird and wildlife sanctuary—nearly 200 species of birds pass through here in the course of a year—to honor the naturalist president.

This hike includes a circuit around Theodore Roosevelt Island and a straight out-and-back on the rugged Potomac Heritage National Scenic Trail to the Three Sisters: three legendary rocks in the Potomac. From the parking lot on the west bank of the Potomac River, head a short distance south to the long, wide footbridge that crosses the Potomac, which is called Little River in this section. While crossing, look north to Francis Scott Key Bridge (locally known as Key Bridge) and Georgetown, and south to Roosevelt Memorial Bridge and beyond to Arlington Memorial Bridge. As you step onto the island, you'll see a kiosk displaying a map of the island's well-maintained trails. Turn left onto Swamp

The conservationist and president Theodore Roosevelt's 17-foot-tall likeness greets visitors to his namesake Potomac River island, which is both a memorial and a bird sanctuary. Photo by Ted, Creative Commons on Flickr.

Trail and follow the broad path along the west shore. Tree diversity here enriches the hike; expect to see sycamore, yellow poplar, beech, elm, holly, ash, hophorn-beam, black walnut, young maples, and large pin oak trees.

A sign along the trail describes the causeway built in 1805 between the northern end of the island and Virginia. The causeway was built both for foot traffic and to serve as a dam to flush out the accumulated sediment on the north end of the island, allowing ships to reach Georgetown. The causeway was not completely removed until 1979.

At the intersection near the sign, go straight a few dozen steps to discover a small, thorny deciduous tree peculiar for this area: the Osage orange, which flowers in June and bears distinctive fruit in the fall. The softball-sized, yellow-green fruit has a bumpy surface and a milky juice that smells faintly of oranges, but it isn't generally considered edible for humans.

Retrace the few dozen steps and take the trail now to the left, climbing up the gentle ridge that runs the length of the island. At the second intersection, post 5, turn right near the water fountain and walk down the broad Woods Trail to the Theodore Roosevelt Memorial. It is startling to find such an elaborate memorial in the middle of the woods. A moat flanked by large willow oaks encircles four 21-foot-tall granite tablets and a 17-foot-tall bronze statue. At the center of the structure, turn left and exit across one of the stone bridges.

At the "T" intersection marked by post 7, turn right onto Upland Trail. Hike along the low ridge of the island and turn left at the fork marked by post 8. In winter, look through the trees to the left to see marshland below and the Watergate Hotel and Kennedy Center across the water. Hike around the trail loop, past a sign about the Mason estate near post 9, to an intersection with a short trail on the right that connects with Swamp Trail below. Take the right fork to the second sign that marks the spot of the Mason mansion. All that remains are a few bricks.

The trail continues back to intersection 8. Head back down Upland Trail past intersection 7 near the Theodore Roosevelt Memorial to the "T" intersection at post 6. Turn right onto Swamp Trail, which becomes a wide elevated boardwalk that runs 800 yards through the swampy portion of the island. Extending to the right off the main trail is a short section of boardwalk with views of a tidal marsh.

Turn right along the southeast end of the island near the Theodore Roosevelt Memorial Bridge. Under the bridge is Little Island. The boardwalk ends, and the trail continues on dry land up a short hill then curves to the right, past a large oak tree with a trunk 5 feet in diameter. Most of the trees on the island are younger than 100 years, as much of the land was cleared for farming and gardens in the late 1800s, but in this area, the trees are older and larger.

To reach Upland Trail, hike past the connector trail on the right and a small brown building housing public restrooms, also on the right. About 200 yards beyond the restrooms, the trail splits; the narrow Swamp Trail heads downhill to the left, and the wide Woods Trail heads to the right. Take Woods Trail and walk 300 yards to the next intersection. Stay to the left and head toward the water to the "T" intersection at post 2. Turn right onto Swamp Trail then turn left back over the footbridge to the parking lot.

Follow Mount Vernon Trail north past the two parking lots and go to the right along the river at the Potomac Heritage Trail sign near the bottom of the ramp. The narrow, light-green-blazed trail squeezes between the George Washington Memorial Parkway on the left and the Potomac River on the right. Head through a small meadow, past ivy-covered trees, and under the arches of Key Bridge. Along the way are great views of the Georgetown waterfront, Key Bridge, and Georgetown University. The trail follows the shoulder of the GW Parkway for about 150 yards, but the traffic sounds seem to fade with steady hiking.

Near the Three Sisters, a trio of bare stones jutting out of the Potomac River, the trail narrows as it runs between the parkway retaining wall and a post-and-rail fence at the top of the steep riverbank. The three rocky islets have long been said to mark the spot where three Algonquian sisters drowned while crossing the Potomac in an attempt to secure the release of three young boys captured from their tribe by another. A Victorian ballad about the legend concludes:

Three rocks, spired and gloomy,
Gray as a stormy sky,
Sprang from the depth of the whirlpool,
Where the Indian sisters lie.

Ever at night they ring,
Like a sad cathedral bell,
Echoing far on the waters,
They sound the warning knell.

Hike 150 yards farther to reach the point where Spout Run joins the Potomac River. Turn around here and head east along the same Potomac Heritage Trail to the Theodore Roosevelt Island parking lots.

MORE INFORMATION

The park is open daily from 6 A.M. to 10 P.M. There are no fees, but parking is limited and tends to fill on weekends. There are restrooms but no visitor center per se. During spring and summer, park rangers lead guided tours. Visit nps.gov/this.

NEARBY

An alternate circle around the island is available via boat; rent one at Thompson Boat Center or the former Jack's Boats (now Key Bridge Boathouse) underneath Key Bridge on the Georgetown bank. Also visit the nearby memorial to Theodore's fifth cousin, Franklin D. Roosevelt, along the Tidal Basin in southwest Washington, D.C.; you will also find a statue of Theodore's niece, Eleanor. (See Trip 30: East Potomac Park and Hains Point.)

26

NATIONAL ARBORETUM

The National Arboretum offers an ever-changing hike of rich discovery, thanks to its many special collections containing flora and fauna from around the world.

DIRECTIONS

From downtown Washington, D.C., take US 50 (New York Avenue NW, which becomes NE at North Capitol Street) heading east. Drive 3.5 miles and turn right onto Bladensburg Road. After 0.4 mile, turn left onto R Street and drive 1.2 miles to reach the arboretum's main entrance. To get back onto New York Avenue for the return trip via R Street, turn right onto Bladensburg Road then turn left onto Montana Avenue, which intersects New York Avenue. *GPS coordinates: 38° 54.388′ N, 76° 58.141′ W.*

Via public transportation, take Metrorail's Orange or Blue Line to Stadium-Armory station and transfer to the northbound Metrobus B2. Exit the bus at Bladensburg Road and R Street and walk 0.2 mile east on R Street to the arboretum.

TRAIL DESCRIPTION

Founded in 1927, the National Arboretum in northeast Washington, D.C., is a 446-acre living museum dedicated to plant research and education. The goal of this hike is to see the entire grounds while stopping to study or admire the various collections. Driving and biking are speedier ways to view the arboretum, but traversing its wonders on foot helps put each new collection into perspective and offers an intimate look at the diverse plant life.

From the Administration Building parking lot, walk past the tram kiosk and proceed beyond the koi pond to the National Bonsai & Penjing Museum, a complex of structures reached through a Japanese garden. The museum houses trees maintained in miniature, and the

LOCATION
Northeast
Washington, D.C.

RATING
Easy to moderate

DISTANCE
8.2 miles

ELEVATION GAIN
800 feet

ESTIMATED TIME
4.5 to 5 hours

MAPS
USGS Washington East; map available free in arboretum brochure; online: usna.usda.gov/Information/arbormap.html

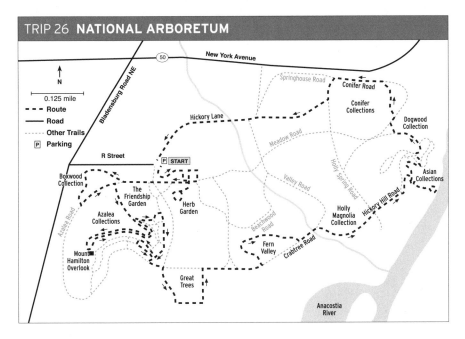

Japanese Pavilion has a must-see white pine that survived the Hiroshima atomic blast in 1945 (see "Peace and Long Life: Spirit Within a Tree," on page 126) and was one of 53 bonsai given to the United States by the Japanese government to commemorate the 1976 bicentennial. The American Pavilion contains *Goshin*, a famous bonsai work by John Naka.

Exit the museum to the south onto Meadow Road, where a right turn leads immediately to the 2.5-acre National Herb Garden. Enter beneath a hanging garden, follow a cul-de-sac path lined with hundreds of herb species—more than 50 types of peppers alone—and proceed to a rose garden with historical varieties once widely cultivated across Europe. Return to Meadow Road, which will become Azalea Road, and turn left. Continue past the intersection with Eagle Nest Road and turn right down the path that leads past the National Boxwood Collection and the beds of perennials that bloom from late February through July.

From Azalea Road, turn left then take the first right just before the entrance to the Boxwood Collection. Walk past a parking area to a mulch path that ascends Mount Hamilton. This 40-acre section of high ground is adorned with the arboretum's stunning Azalea Collection, which showcases its colors best in April and May. Proceed to the overlook by turning right at the first fork and traveling 0.25 mile to where the path ends in a cul-de-sac, affording fine views of the U.S. Capitol 2 miles to the southwest.

Returning from the overlook, turn right at the fork and stay left past a second fork, then left again at a third fork to loop around Lee Garden. As you go around the north side of the pond, turn right at a "T" intersection to head south then turn left at the four-way intersection to arrive at a tended avenue

One of the National Arboretum's signature attractions is this forest of Corinthian columns that once graced the East Front of the U.S. Capitol, watching over presidential inauguration ceremonies from the 1820s to the 1950s. Photo by Simon, Creative Commons on Flickr.

known as Henry Mitchell Walk. At its end is the Morrison Garden, a squared-off structure of bricks housing 15,000 Glenn Dale hybrid azaleas arranged in overlapping colors and bloom times.

Exit the garden at the south end and turn right onto the circle, take another right, and then an immediate left to join a steep mulch path on the south side of Mount Hamilton. Travel this path for a short distance and take the first right, followed by another right. When you return to the circle, turn right to link up with the paved Azalea Road.

Turn left onto Azalea Road. Walk 100 yards and turn right onto Eagle Nest Road, along the left side of the National Grove of State Trees. Turn left into the parking lot area and take another left at a marble semicircular display etched with the leaf of each state's tree. When leaving the grove, gravitate toward its eastern side, turn left onto a roadway lined with scarlet oaks (the official tree of Washington, D.C.), then take a right back onto Crabtree Road.

Follow Crabtree Road to a left turn onto Ellipse Road, which leads to the National Capitol Columns. After viewing them, return south on Ellipse Road and turn right onto Crabtree Road, passing the arboretum's Youth Garden on the right and two small side trails on the left before taking a left into the main entrance to Fern Valley. This area is planted with ferns, wildflowers, shrubs, and trees native to the eastern United States and is a prime spot for bird-watching. At a central intersection near a shed, turn left and circle around to the north.

Proceed through Fern Valley, a microcosm of the natural ecology of the eastern forests. Just after the path crosses the stream, arrive back at Crabtree Road.

Turn left onto Crabtree Road, then quickly right onto Hickory Hill Road, passing the Holly and Magnolia Collection on the left. Continue past the intersection with Holly Spring Road and trek uphill to the arboretum's Asian Collections. Take the first right and follow a sharp descent that wraps around China Valley. Return on the path and turn right up steep stone steps to the pagoda. Turn left and then make the first right to skirt the edge of Asian Valley. Turn right at the "T" intersection and travel around a circle, taking another right at its opposite end to dip down into the Japanese Woodland. Turn left at an alcove at the southern end, go straight past a three-way fork, and continue north to a parking area on Hickey Hill Road.

Hickey Hill Road makes a U-turn back to the west, passing the Dogwood Collection on the right. Take the first right past a stand of dawn redwoods onto Conifer Road. Beyond them, turn left into the maze of the 7-acre Gotelli Dwarf and Slow-Growing Conifer Collection, making your way generally north through 1,400 firs, cedars, pines, yews, and spruces. After navigating the trees, return to Conifer Road at the northern edge of the arboretum, near New York Avenue. From here, return to the Administration Building parking lot via a 1.25-mile walk, first turning left onto Holly Spring Road then quickly right onto Hickory Lane, which drops into the parking lot from the north.

MORE INFORMATION

The National Arboretum is open daily (except December 25) from 8 A.M. to 5 P.M. Admission is free. Tram tours run on weekend and holiday afternoons in season. Purchase tickets at the information desk in the Administration Building. Tram tours last 35 minutes and cost $4 for adults and $2 for children ages 4 to 6; children under 4 are free. Trams depart from the Arbor House gift shop near the Friendship Garden. For more information, visit usna.usda.gov or call 202-245-2726.

NEARBY

While in Northeast Washington, D.C., consider a visit to two other sites of great beauty and spiritual uplift. The Basilica of the National Shrine of the Immaculate Conception, on the campus of Catholic University, is one of the ten largest churches, and one of the most stunning displays of mosaic art, in the world. See nationalshrine.com for details and directions.

Just a few blocks away from the Basilica, the Franciscan Monastery of the Holy Land in America's building and stunning gardens evoke St. Francis of Assisi's deep love of birds, flowers, and all creatures, along with a number of holy shrines from around the world. Visit myfranciscan.org for more information.

PEACE AND LONG LIFE: SPIRIT WITHIN A TREE

They live quiet, highly restricted, sometimes very long lives—often outlasting their caretakers—in cramped quarters. Grown usually from standard-size stock or seed, they are kept artificially small, their appendages bound by fired clay, rope, and wire. They undergo frequent pruning and root reductions, performed with reverence and patience by skilled masters using the tools of an ancient art. Perhaps surprisingly, under such constant attention they thrive and tend to live longer than their wild counterparts.

In the Japanese tradition, they are known as *bonsai* ("tree in pot") and grown in shallow, plain, ceramic trays to showcase the beauty of the plants. Chinese growers call them *penjing* ("scene in pot") and cultivate them in deeper, more decorative containers, sometimes adding whimsical animal and human figurines. For centuries, both cultures have honored these miniature giants, a captured landscape symbolizing the inner forest.

Maintained as a symbol of spiritual simplicity, tranquility, and depth—allowed to grow and flower according to their natures, yet deliberately refined to a standard of minimalistic, truth-enhancing beauty—they are a sort of Buddhist "middle path" in high horticultural art. Western interest in bonsai blossomed in the 1950s and 1960s, when the Allies occupied Japan and Asian thought came into vogue in the United States, thanks partly to the literary Beat Generation. Sadly, by that time, many centuries-old bonsai in the ancient and renowned Japanese Imperial collection and elsewhere had become casualties of World War II bombings.

"Further limitations release deeper powers," wrote the poet May Sarton. She could have been speaking of one bonsai in particular in the National Arboretum's National Bonsai & Penjing Museum: a prized Japanese white pine standing about 3.5 feet tall and 4 feet wide. When the United States dropped the atomic bomb on Hiroshima on August 6, 1945, this bonsai at the Yamaki Bonsai Nursery, just 2 miles away, survived. Concrete walls surrounding the nursery saved this bonsai and others nearby from devastation.

The tiny tree was donated to the United States in 1976 as part of a bicentennial peace-and-reconciliation gift by the bonsai master Masaru Yamaki, a descendant of the grower who began training the little evergreen nearly 400 years ago, in 1625. Generations of the Yamaki family had cared for it ever since; they, too, survived the 1945 blast. This lush, healthy, venerable old tree's branches form successively rising, green, soft steps—as if the plant itself is happily beckoning visitors to keep growing, to flourish, to overcome, and to seek peace in simplicity.

A bicentennial gift to the United States from Japan, this nearly 400-year-old white pine bonsai survived the 1945 atomic blast at Hiroshima.

27

KENILWORTH PARK & AQUATIC GARDENS

This easygoing hike visits ponds teeming with summer-blooming waterlilies and lotuses, as well as the last remaining preserved tidal marshland on the Anacostia River.

DIRECTIONS

From downtown Washington, D.C., take US 50 (New York Avenue NW, which becomes NE at North Capitol Street) east, then take I-295 (Kenilworth Avenue) south to the Quarles Street/Eastern Avenue exit. Go straight through the light at the top of the ramp then turn right onto Douglas Street. Turn right onto Anacostia Avenue. The park is on the left. *GPS coordinates: 38° 54.778′ N, 76° 56.412′ W.*

By Metrorail, take the Orange Line to Deanwood station then walk across the pedestrian overpass to Douglas Street. Walk north on Douglas to Anacostia Avenue and turn right into the park entrance (0.4-mile walk). You also can take the V7 bus toward the Bureau of Engraving to the corner of Kenilworth Avenue and Douglas Street.

TRAIL DESCRIPTION

Kenilworth Aquatic Gardens, at the northern end of the 11-mile-long Anacostia Park, protects the last remaining tidal marshland in the District of Columbia. Located on the east side of the Anacostia River 8 miles north of its confluence with the Potomac, Kenilworth Aquatic Gardens has a unique history rooted in the commercial production of water lilies and lotuses. In the 1920s, L. Helen Fowler, the owner of W. B. Shaw Lily Pond, imported lilies and lotuses from Asia, Egypt, and South America and built a greenhouse and sales office (today's visitor center). The spot was a favorite of outdoorsy Washingtonians, including President Calvin Coolidge. In the 1930s, when a misguided U.S. Army Corps of Engineers project to fill in

LOCATION
Northeast Washington, D.C.

RATING
Easy

DISTANCE
2.5 miles

ELEVATION GAIN
Minimal

ESTIMATED TIME
1.5 to 2 hours

MAPS
USGS Washington East; map of the aquatic gardens (but not River Trail) available for free in the visitor center; online: nps.gov/keaq/planyourvisit/maps.htm

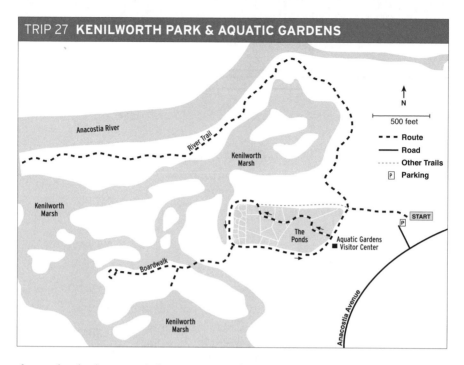

the wetlands threatened the aquatic gardens, the National Park Service (NPS) stepped in and purchased the land for $15,000, renaming the site Kenilworth for the nearby farm community.

Today, the site has 75 acres of freshwater tidal marsh and 45 ponds filled with tropical and hardy water lilies, lotuses, and other aquatic species. The best time of year to see these blooming water plants begins in late May, peaks in July, and ends in mid-September. The best time of day to view the surreal spectacle of night bloomers closing and day bloomers opening is the early morning. Afternoon heat and sun cause the day bloomers to close. In general, the hardy lilies are located in the central ponds, the tropical lilies (including the giant, platterlike *Victoria amazonica*) in the western ponds farthest from the visitor center, and the lotuses in the large pond in front of the visitor center and the southern ponds.

To begin the hike from the parking lot, follow the gravel path past the greenhouses to the left, go through a gate, and reach a sign marking points of interest. Take the second right to begin the 1.5-mile out-and-back on River Trail. This trail runs along an artificial spit and borders a marsh on the left that the NPS constructed in 1992. At 0.2 mile, at the concrete ruins of an old tower on the left, reach the Anacostia River and follow it to the left. Wintertime affords views of the river and the stone Corps of Engineers sea wall on the opposite shore. In spring and summer, blackjack and northern red oak, red and silver maple, willow, tupelo, sycamore, black locust, black birch, holly, black walnut, sweetgum, and yellow poplar make up the view to the right.

A pink East Indian lotus, India's national flower, blossoms in Kenilworth Aquatic Gardens, offering nectar to bees and other insects. Photo by Stephen Mauro.

Hike 100 yards farther to reach a bench on the left with wide-open views of the wetlands: vibrant and almost tropical in summer, and silent and peaceful in winter. At 0.75 mile, reach the end of River Trail, where a bench sits underneath a dual-trunked sycamore tree on the right. Take the path leading down to the riverbank and the inlet where tidal waters reach the marsh. A stone wall to the left ends abruptly in broken shards; the wall once blocked the very water that now feeds this natural ecosystem. Return to River Trail and head back to the aquatic gardens via the same route.

Back at the entrance sign, continue along the southern edge of the ponds. Pass several distinctive trees (an American bald cypress, a large magnolia, a few hollies) and a wooden greenhouse (built in 1913) before reaching the visitor center. Stop in to pick up a hand-drawn map of the ponds and to see interesting relics, such as Helen Fowler's 1936 book on growing water lilies, complete with her pastel drawings. The center also has information on particular plant species found at the gardens, including the pink-flowered East India lotus. This lotus, the offspring of 600-year-old seeds discovered in Manchuria and planted in 1951, thrives in the pond behind the center.

From the visitor center, step around back if visiting in summer to see the East India lotuses then head straight onto the dike between a giant pond of lotuses on the left and a pond of yellow-flowered spatterdock on the right.

Come to the next pond, turn left, then take the first right and stay left at the fork, heading through the heart of the winter-hardy water lily collection. Head toward the tropical lilies by crossing a wooden walkway, turning right at the next "T" intersection, and going left around the outside edge of the *Victoria amazonica*. This tropical lily is the most dramatic in the park. Discovered in the deep, wide lagoons of South America, its leaves can grow 7 feet wide, and its edges turn up to form a platterlike rim. The flowers open at dusk and remain open all night in August and September.

Continue south on the gravel road between the tropical lilies and the marsh, and turn right onto the boardwalk at the sign reading, "Boardwalk Closed at 4 P.M." Walk onto the zigzagging walkway past a few unique paperbark maple trees and continue straight to the far platform. Take in the ecological bounty of this mid-marsh zone, including native cattails, buttonbush, wild rice, arrow arum, pickerelweed, and two wild varieties of flowering aquatic plant: the spatterdock and the American lotus. Also look for great blue herons, great egrets, belted kingfishers, and raptors.

On the way back, detour to the right to visit a second platform then return to the gardens and turn right, walking along the southern rim past more East India lotuses. Walk past the front of the visitor center and turn right to return to the parking lot.

MORE INFORMATION

Kenilworth Aquatic Gardens is open daily 9 A.M. to 5 P.M. April through October and 8 A.M. to 4 P.M. November through March and is closed January 1, Thanksgiving Day, and December 25. Dogs are allowed in the gardens but must be on a leash. Visit nps.gov/keaq or call 202-692-6080. The adjacent Kenilworth Park is open 8 A.M. to dusk.

NEARBY

Directly across the Anacostia River from Kenilworth is the National Arboretum (see Trip 26: National Arboretum). Also visit the Frederick Douglass National Historic Site, the Center for African-American History and Culture, and the Anacostia Historic District, all in southern Anacostia. The 10-mile Fort Circle Trail is another excellent Anacostia hiking option; it follows a chain of forested parks on heights that were fortified during the Civil War.

28

ROCK CREEK PARK

Rock Creek Park is a natural oasis in the heart of the nation's capital: 1,754 hilly, wooded acres containing the surprisingly turbulent Rock Creek, historic sites, and miles of challenging trails.

DIRECTIONS

From downtown Washington, D.C., take Connecticut Avenue NW north to Nebraska Avenue NW. Turn right onto Nebraska Avenue for 0.4 mile. Turn right onto Military Road and drive east 0.7 mile. Then turn right onto Glover Road to enter Rock Creek Park, driving 0.4 mile and taking the first left into the parking lot for the Rock Creek Park Nature Center and Planetarium. *GPS coordinates:* 38° 57.537′ N, 77° 3.080′ W.

For the Metrorail and Metrobus, from either the Friendship Heights Metro station (Red Line) or the Fort Totten station (Red, Yellow, and Green lines), take Metrobus E2 or E3 down Military Road. Exit at Oregon Avenue opposite Glover Road. From the southeast side of the intersection, walk uphill a short distance to reach the nature center.

TRAIL DESCRIPTION

Rock Creek Park is a national park that covers 1,754 acres, more than twice the area of Central Park in New York City, and reaches from the northern tip of Washington, D.C., all the way south to the Potomac River at Foggy Bottom and Georgetown. Rock Creek Park was established by an act of Congress and signed into law by President Benjamin Harrison on September 27, 1890, the same year Yosemite became a national park. The park's two major trails are the blue-blazed Valley Trail along the east side of the creek and the green-blazed Western Rim Trail that follows the park's western ridge. This hike centers on the

LOCATION
Northwest Washington, D.C.

RATING
Moderate

DISTANCE
6 miles

ELEVATION GAIN
840 feet

ESTIMATED TIME
2.5 to 3 hours

MAPS
USGS Washington West; Potomac Appalachian Trail Club Map N; NPS brochure map available at the nature center; online: nps.gov/rocr/planyourvisit/maps.htm

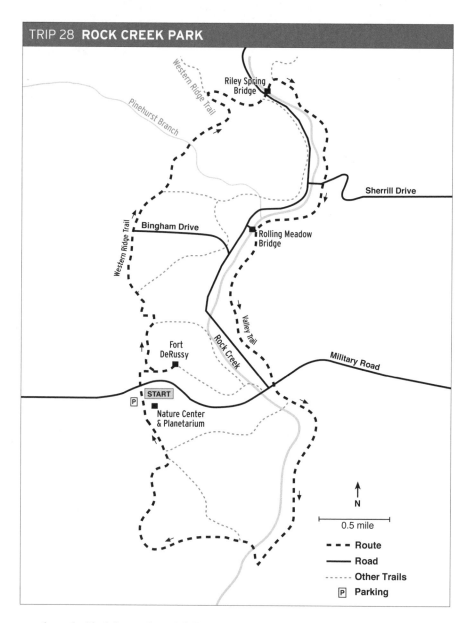

Riley Spring
Bridge

Western Ridge Trail

Pinehurst Branch

Sherrill Drive

Western Ridge Trail

Bingham Drive

Rolling Meadow
Bridge

Valley Trail

Rock Creek

Military Road

Fort
DeRussy

P

START

P

Nature Center
& Planetarium

N

0.5 mile

- - - **Route**

——— **Road**

------- **Other Trails**

P **Parking**

northern half of the park and follows Western Rim Trail north, cuts east across
the wooded hills, and returns south on Valley Trail.

From the nature center, walk straight out the front door to the blacktop Western Rim Trail that parallels Glover Road. Follow signs to Fort DeRussy, crossing
Military Road and proceeding uphill. When you reach the NPS sign relaying the
history of Fort DeRussy, turn right and follow the green blazes. Stay straight on
the dirt trail and continue past where the green-blazed Western Rim Trail goes
north. Look for a sign, a plaque, and a spur trail on the left that leads over the
fort's 150-year-old, dirt-covered fortifications.

After visiting the fort, return to the intersection with the green-blazed Western Rim Trail and turn right. Head downhill on a series of gradual, easygoing switchbacks. At 0.7 mile into the hike, where a sign points straight ahead for Milkhouse Ford, turn left and stay on Western Rim Trail. Next cross a small creek and make a right, traveling between the park police horse stables and garden plots. Turn left at the "T" intersection with the service road and follow the green-blazed blacktop trail to the right. Cross Bingham Drive and turn right into the woods on a dirt trail. Head uphill through thickets of viburnum shrubs rich with red berries through autumn and cut to the left at the "Y" intersection. Go downhill, bending to the right at the valley, then turn immediately left to cross Pinehurst Branch Trail. Ford the stream and head uphill through beeches and oaks. At the top of the hill, the trail passes through a narrow section then takes a right turn (unmarked) in the direction of the Riley Spring Bridge. Head downhill to the "Y" intersection and go left toward Beach Road and the bridge.

At 2.7 miles, cross the bridge over Rock Creek and turn right onto the blue-blazed Valley Trail, where a sign indicates a distance of 1.6 miles to Military Road. Here Rock Creek is gentle and meandering, but farther south it gets rocky and turbulent. Pass through an area of gnarled black birches and under the Sherrill Drive Bridge before fording a small feeder stream. Pass Rolling Meadow Bridge on the right and cross a wooden walkway over another stream. Just after crossing the stream, make sure to cut left at the "Y" intersection. Go uphill to the

Recreators explore the hillsides for which Rock Creek, and the park stretching for miles along its banks in the midst of D.C.'s bustle, are named. Photo by Dion Hinchcliffe, Creative Commons on Flickr.

edge of the public golf course, descend to Beach Drive, and edge back uphill at a blue-blazed black birch tree. After scaling the precipitous ridge, drop back down to Beach Drive and cross under Military Road.

Here the trail follows Beach Drive south to the park police station. Just after, at a blue-blazed oak tree at the foot of a steep ridge, cut left up the ridge and away from Rock Creek. Cross several large boulders and proceed uphill again to a wooden bridge spanning a small ravine. Turn right immediately after the bridge to stay on the blue-blazed Valley Trail.

Go back downhill over more rocky terrain, following Rock Creek on the right. At the Rapids Bridge, leave Valley Trail to cross the creek. Rapids Bridge offers perhaps the best view in the entire park of Rock Creek, with water slamming over, under, and around large boulders to the north and south. Turn left at the "T" intersection at the end of the bridge, walk approximately 75 yards, and turn right onto an unmarked trail. Go steeply uphill, staying to the left at the "Y" intersection over Ross Drive. Cross Glover Road at 5.7 miles and go straight ahead to the green-blazed Western Rim Trail; turn right. Go around a hill to the right, cutting sharply left to stay on the trail just before reaching Grant Road. Cross and return to the nature center.

MORE INFORMATION

Be sure to pick up a park map and brochure at the nature center before you start your hike. The amenities at Rock Creek Park include 29 picnic areas, a large recreation field, 25 tennis courts, a public golf course, a 1.5-mile exercise course, bicycle routes, 13 miles of bridle trails, an equestrian field, and a horse center. In season, the Carter Barron Amphitheatre offers a wide variety of staged events. Find more information at nps.gov/rocr or by calling 202-895-6000.

NEARBY

After all this hiking, you'll likely have a good appetite. Head to the funky, colorful, culturally diverse Adams Morgan neighborhood, centered at 18th Street and Columbia Road NW, where you can chow down on cuisines ranging from South American to Middle Eastern to Ethiopian. Brewpubs and salsa clubs also await the brave, thirsty, and energetic. See washington.org/dc-neighborhoods/adams-morgan for ideas.

To work off your meal, stroll over to Meridian Hill Park along 16th Street between W and Euclid Streets NW, a noncontiguous section of Rock Creek Park. Here you can enjoy a unique cascading waterfall of 13 successive basins and join the regular Sunday afternoon drum circle and dancing in the park's northern section—a tradition here since the 1950s.

AROUND GEORGETOWN

Follow woodsy avenues on each side of Georgetown for a secluded circuit hike around the leafy heart of northwest Washington, D.C., and through the southern section of Rock Creek Park.

DIRECTIONS

Take Metrorail's Red Line to the Woodley Park-Zoo/ Adams Morgan station on Connecticut Avenue. Public parking is very limited in availability and duration, so driving is discouraged for this hike. *GPS coordinates: 38° 55.499' N, 77° 3.141' W.*

TRAIL DESCRIPTION

Rock Creek Park includes not only the wide swath of forest along the Rock Creek valley in northwest Washington, D.C., but also several narrow strips of parkland circling Georgetown: Montrose, Dumbarton Oaks, Whitehaven, and Glover-Archbold. This circuit hike takes advantage of these green avenues in the midst of an urban landscape. Sights include the Connecticut Avenue Bridge, Holy Rood Cemetery, an abandoned railway to Glen Echo Amusement Park, canal locks, Key Bridge, and Mount Zion Cemetery.

From the Woodley Park-Zoo/Adams Morgan Metro station, head downhill on 24th Street and cross Calvert Street. At the bottom of the hill, south of the Connecticut Avenue Bridge and its famed Roland Hinton Perry lion sculptures, turn right onto the paved Rock Creek Trail. Continue on, and just before the bridge across Rock Creek, turn right on the gravel Parkway Trail (unmarked) that follows the west bank downstream. Take this leafy route past Normanstone Trail on the right. Just before going under the ivy-covered Massachusetts Avenue Bridge, notice the

LOCATION
Northwest Washington, D.C.

RATING
Moderate

DISTANCE
6.9 miles

ELEVATION GAIN
800 feet

ESTIMATED TIME
3.5 hours

MAPS
USGS Washington West

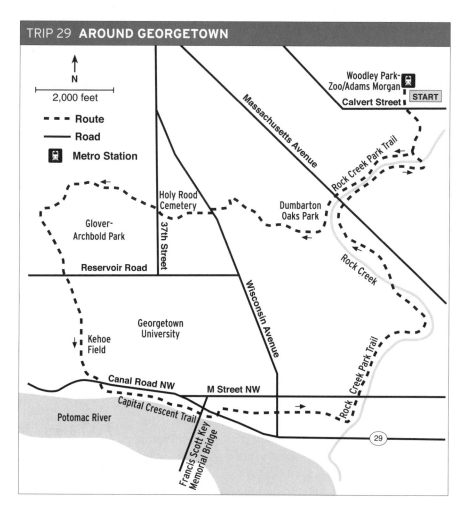

N

2,000 feet

--- Route
— Road
🚇 Metro Station

Woodley Park-
Zoo/Adams Morgan
Calvert Street | START

Massachusetts Avenue

Rock Creek Park Trail

Holy Rood
Cemetery

Dumbarton
Oaks Park

Glover-
Archbold Park

37th Street

Rock Creek

Reservoir Road

Wisconsin Avenue

Georgetown
University

Kehoe
Field

Rock Creek Park Trail

Canal Road NW

M Street NW

Capital Crescent Trail

Potomac River

Rock Creek Park Trail

Francis Scott Key Memorial Bridge

29

remains of a quarry visible on the right. Workers at this quarry mined norite stone, a type of sea-bottom basalt that underlies much of Georgetown and that was used to construct the buildings at Dumbarton Oaks.

At 0.7 mile, cut away from Rock Creek and follow the dirt trail uphill along a rocky tributary, skirting the north end of Montrose Park and eventually reaching a "T" intersection with Lovers' Lane and the entrance to Dumbarton Oaks Park. The park's namesake, Dumbarton Oaks, is the former private estate and gardens of Mildred and Robert Woods Bliss. Now a research library under the auspices of Harvard University, the institute's museum collections, gardens, and music room are open to the public most afternoons with an admission fee. When the Blisses donated their estate to Harvard, they also turned over much of the estate's land to the American people, and the National Park Service began to administer it as Dumbarton Oaks Park. Cross the lane, enter the park, and proceed on a dirt trail along the left side of the creek. This "in-between" landscape—rich in sugar maples, American beech, tulip trees, flowering dogwoods, oaks, and hickories—was originally part of the private Dumbarton Oaks estate, serving as a buffer between the formal gardens and the wilds of Rock Creek Park.

Hike past a stone bridge and crumbling stone chimney, with hornbeams and dogwoods arching overhead, then head uphill. Enter a small, bowl-shaped field with wildflowers, then pass through wild shrubbery and a swampy section before climbing a dirt switchback on the far side of the bowl. Upon reaching Whitehaven Street NW, turn left toward Wisconsin Avenue.

Cross Wisconsin Avenue, turn right, and walk a block for a short detour to Holy Rood Cemetery, one of the highest points in the District of Columbia. This cemetery was established in 1832 by Georgetown's Holy Trinity Catholic Church, about a mile to the south. (President John F. Kennedy attended this church when he lived in Georgetown during his Senate years and later, when he moved into the White House.) The cemetery has gravestones in various states of disrepair, a proximity to the arterial bustle of Wisconsin Avenue, and a tree-framed view of the Washington Monument that together create a uniquely Washington, D.C., atmosphere. After strolling around the cemetery, return south down Wisconsin Avenue.

Take the next right onto 35th Street. Just before Whitehaven Parkway, make a right onto a yellow-blazed trail and ascend the wooden steps up the ridge. Level off and descend the steps to 37th Street. Cross the street and enter

A busy thoroughfare from a quiet spot: The Francis Scott Key Bridge connects Rosslyn, VA, as seen from the C&O Canal towpath in Washington, D.C. Photo by Stephen Mauro.

Whitehaven Park, following a line of maple trees and passing a dog park. Return to the brush and follow the yellow blazes past a community garden on the left and a rope climb on the right to reach a "T" intersection at a row of town homes. Turn right here, still following the yellow blazes. At the "Y" intersection, take the left-hand path through hornbeams and beeches. Upon reaching the "T" intersection, turn left onto Glover-Archbold Trail.

Heading south toward the water, cross Foundry Branch and hike uphill through a maple-rich forest. Cross Reservoir Road, turn left past a bus stop, and turn right downhill on a barely discernible dirt trail. Walk beneath several large tulip trees and past black walnuts to the right. Continue straight to reenter the woods, passing a trail that comes in from the right. Go under an abandoned, rusted railroad bridge (the remains of a trolley that once took Washingtonians to Glen Echo Amusement Park) and come to Foxhall Road. Turn left onto Foxhall Road, then take another left onto a path going downhill to reach a pedestrian tunnel beneath the Chesapeake & Ohio (C&O) Canal. Go through the tunnel and come out onto Capital Crescent Trail. Take the signed side trail to the left to immediately connect with the gravel/clay C&O Canal National Historical Park towpath.

Continue east on the towpath. Just after you pass the arched Key Bridge, cross over to the north side of the canal. Continue east through Georgetown. The path becomes brick, passing a series of lift locks, the NPS visitor center, and a bust of Supreme Court Justice William O. Douglas (see "Centuries of Perseverance: The Chesapeake & Ohio Canal," in Section 1, page 97) before reaching Rock Creek Trail. Bend left and follow the trail as it parallels busy Rock Creek Parkway. Follow the trail left into the woods and cross the bridge over Rock Creek, with Mount Zion Cemetery on the left and a clearing where old Lyons Mill once stood on the right.

Proceed beneath the Massachusetts Avenue Bridge, on the opposite bank from the first section of the hike. Follow the creekside trail as it meanders for nearly a half-mile, then cross a footbridge, and return to the exercise area just before the Connecticut Avenue Bridge. Turn left uphill along Shoreham Drive, cross Calvert Street, and return to the Woodley Park-Zoo/Adams Morgan Metro station.

MORE INFORMATION

There is no fee for this hike, and dogs are permitted.

NEARBY

Well worth a visit, Dumbarton Oaks estate's pre-Columbian and Byzantine collections and its gardens are open to the public most afternoons. Visit doaks.org for details.

30

EAST POTOMAC PARK AND HAINS POINT

Mostly level, and filled with architectural and natural beauty, this scenic loop route takes in four memorials to revered Americans, four bodies of water, and dozens of cherry trees.

DIRECTIONS

This hike is designed to be a Metrorail-friendly sojourn within the city. Take the Blue/Silver/Orange Lines to the Smithsonian station and use the Independence Avenue exit.

If you wish to drive, begin your hike at a different point along the route (see text of Trail Description). Be advised that parking can be hard to find and traffic at a near-standstill during cherry blossom season in early spring. From downtown Washington, D.C., take US 50 (Constitution Avenue) west. Turn left at 15th Street SW (becomes Raoul Wallenberg Place at Independence Avenue SW). Turn left at Maine Avenue SW and immediately turn right onto East Basin Drive SW. Turn left onto Ohio Drive SW. Continue past the park police headquarters to the stop sign at Buckeye Drive and turn right. Go to the next stop sign, at Ohio Drive, and make another right. Drive under the railroad bridge; you'll see three free parking lots on your right (C, B, and A) for the founders' memorials. Park here and begin your hike as indicated later in the Trail Description. *GPS coordinates (Parking Lot C):* 38° 52.645′ N, 77° 02.198′ W.

TRAIL DESCRIPTION

East Potomac Park is one of Washington, D.C.'s larger and better-known green spaces, but even in the busy spring tourist season, there is room to stretch out and recreate. The park offers multiple leisure facilities and impressive groves of ornamental cherry trees that put their energy into flowering rather than fruiting. East Potomac Park is a

LOCATION
Southwest Washington, D.C.

RATING
Easy to moderate

DISTANCE
6.6 miles

ELEVATION GAIN
30 feet

ESTIMATED TIME
3 to 4 hours

MAPS
USGS Alexandria; online: nps.gov/nama/planyourvisit/maps.htm

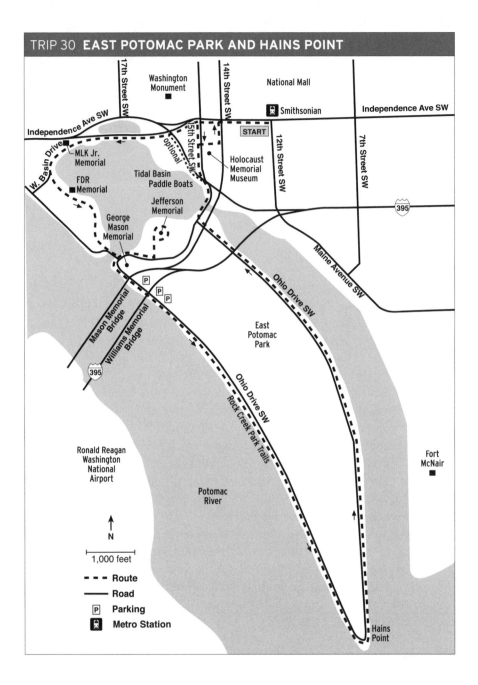

TRIP 30 EAST POTOMAC PARK AND HAINS POINT

perennial favorite for enjoying the beauty of several varieties of cherry blossoms in season, usually late March to late April.

From the Independence Avenue exit of the Smithsonian Metrorail station, turn left (west) on Independence Avenue, crossing 14th and 15th (Raoul Wallenberg Place) streets SW and passing the brick U.S. Forest Service headquarters. Pause to view the obelisk of the Washington Monument through the trees on your right. (See Trip 31: National Mall.) Continue westward, past the planting beds of the Floral Library and across the Kutz Bridge, a low span that carries Independence Avenue over the Tidal Basin. This basin was constructed in the early 1900s to help drain the lowlands roundabout by taking in the overflow when the Potomac's water levels rise with the Chesapeake Bay tides. Despite this effort, many structures near the Tidal Basin "float" upon mucky soil—including the round-topped Jefferson Memorial across the water to your left, which was recently renovated to improve its seawall and pilings. Proceed along the sidewalk for the time being, noting on your left the satiny bark of the Yoshino ornamental cherry trees and the small stone Japanese lantern marking the spot where the first of these iconic trees was planted in 1912. (See "For the Love of Cherry Trees," on page 145.)

Turn left onto the path leading to the Martin Luther King Jr. Memorial, the capital's newest major memorial and its first honoring a black man. This much-anticipated outdoor plaza was dedicated in 2011 to the civil rights leader. Its centerpiece, a standing statue of King carved upon a "stone of hope" liberated from the "mountain of despair," references lines from his 1963 "I Have a Dream" speech (delivered from the Lincoln Memorial steps, where Trip 31 concludes). Note that the memorial is located along a line between the Jefferson Memorial and the Lincoln Memorial, symbolically tying King's legacy of equal rights with the assertion in the Declaration of Independence that "all men are created equal" and the Great Emancipator's urging that Americans might reunite "with malice toward none."

Proceed along the Martin Luther King Jr. memorial's wall to West Basin Drive. Turn left then take the next left into the Franklin Delano Roosevelt Memorial, dedicated in 1997. As you enter the plaza, observe the life-sized bronze sculpture of FDR sitting in a wheelchair—a testament to his life after polio struck in his 20s. Because FDR was elected four times to the presidency, and because those years were eventful for Americans, this memorial was designed with an open-air "room" representing each four-year term. The quotations, sculptural works, and waterfalls in each room symbolize the mood of that term. In the first room, for instance, look for inspiring speech excerpts such as, "The only thing we have to fear is fear itself." In the second room, note the sculptures of Great Depression-era hardship scenes.

In the third room, you find a larger statue of the president, wearing his signature Inverness cape and sitting in a straight-backed chair with casters visible at a close look. The lack of an obvious wheelchair in this statue, even though FDR himself avoided drawing attention to his disability, was at the center of the controversy that led to the creation of the second, smaller statue you saw earlier. Next to FDR sits his beloved Scottish terrier, Fala. As you move into the "world stage" of the fourth and final room, take in the statue honoring FDR's wife, Eleanor, who was a U.S. delegate to the United Nations following World War II.

Continue along the Tidal Basin by either path; both lead to the Thomas Jefferson Memorial, this hike's next landmark. Watch out for low-hanging tree limbs, standing water, and buckled pavement on the walkways. Cross the low stone bridge at Ohio Drive. Take the nearest accessible path along the water's edge to your left and follow it until you emerge onto the plaza, beneath the domed marble edifice. Look up at the north façade of this beautiful neoclassical structure, reminiscent of the third president's own designs for Monticello and the University of Virginia rotunda. Notice the frieze above the columns. Young Jefferson, age 33, stands before the other members of the committee assigned to draft the Declaration of Independence: John Adams and Benjamin Franklin, most notably. Climb the steps, if you like; be sure to turn around at the top and enjoy the view across the water to the White House, a mile away. The memorial's interior is both inspiring and cool on a warm day. You also might enjoy the exhibit in the lower level juxtaposing Jefferson's many accomplishments with world events of the era.

Walk back to Ohio Drive/East Basin Drive along the large square lawn, turning right just past the hexagonal snack bar. Proceed to the stop sign near the stone bridge then cross to your left to enter the George Mason Memorial circular garden. You might not have heard much about Mason, sometimes called the "forgotten founder," but you're probably familiar with many of his principles. His beliefs strongly influenced both Jefferson's draft of the Declaration of

Spotted through the hanging boughs of one of East Potomac Park's Weeping Higan cherry trees, a pleasure boat cruises the Potomac on a bright spring day. Photo by Alan Kotok, Creative Commons on Flickr.

Independence and the Bill of Rights, drafted by James Madison to spell out clear Constitutional limits on the new federal government's power over individuals and states. In spring the garden here blooms with daffodils and flowering shrubs. Turn left when leaving this memorial park, proceed around a curve, and walk under the bridges toward the memorial parking lots.

If arriving by car, start your hike here. Cross Ohio Drive and turn left to begin your walk along the riverside path, passing the intersection with Buckeye Drive. You might notice some flowering cherry trees with flexible branches resembling willows; this weeping Higan variety bears small pink-purple flowers usually in early to mid-April. Soon you'll see the first of the park's several restroom buildings across the road, among a grove of Kwanzan cherry trees whose ruffled pink blossoms appear around mid-April. Continue on a long straightaway, where locals like to fish along the riverbank. Look across the Potomac River to catch a glimpse of the limestone Pentagon, headquarters of the U.S. Department of Defense, and the three curving, soaring spires of the Air Force Memorial. Farther downriver are the towers of the Crystal City neighborhood in Arlington, Virginia. Also notice the yellow-arched terminal at Ronald Reagan Washington National Airport, designed by the architect Cesar Pelli. (The curving, northern aerial approach to the airport over the Potomac, known as the River Visual, is one of the more interesting and challenging for pilots nationwide.)

Walk past the playground and picnic area. As you approach Hains Point, East Potomac Park's southern tip, you'll see Old Town Alexandria and the Woodrow Wilson Memorial Bridge several miles to the south. Major General Peter Conover Hains—a member of the Army Corps of Engineers and a veteran of the Civil War, the Spanish-American War, and World War I—designed the Tidal Basin. His Corps built the artificial island underfoot largely from soil dredged to create that artificial lake. Hains Point marks the confluence of the Anacostia and Potomac rivers. Named for the native peoples living along its banks when European colonists first settled here, the once-pristine Anacostia has long been the victim of pollution, and cleanup efforts progress slowly.

Carved from a portion of the "stone of hope" liberated from the "mountain of despair" behind it, the memorial statue of Dr. Martin Luther King Jr. stands in quiet certitude, flanked by excerpts from Dr. King's inspiring speeches. Photo by Daniel Lobo, Creative Commons on Flickr.

As you round the point, watch for dark-green and white helicopters. Anacostia Naval Air Station, the Washington, D.C., home to the presidential flight group known as Marine Helicopter Squadron One (or HMX-1 Nighthawks), isn't far away. On the point across the channel from you is Fort Lesley J. McNair, with its ornate National War College building and neat brick Generals' Row. The Washington Channel on the east side of the park provides a safe harbor for private watercraft, rescue squads, and fishing vessels.

To your left, past a stop sign, are the park's golf course, miniature golf range, and swimming pool. Continue past the tennis complex then cross under the highway and railroad bridges on this leg of Ohio Drive. At the "T" intersection, walk straight across the road (this is still Ohio Drive), turn right on the sidewalk, and quickly turn left onto a narrow path leading down to the water's edge.

Metro riders, follow the sidewalk to your right to the traffic light at Maine Avenue SW. Cross the avenue and continue north on 15th Street (Raoul Wallenberg Place) SW, passing the Bureau of Engraving and Printing and the U.S. Holocaust Memorial Museum. Come to the corner of Independence Avenue and turn right at the red Forest Service building; retrace the two blocks to return to the Smithsonian station.

If you came by car, this will be your first close-up look at the Tidal Basin, so follow the walkway along its edge, past the Maine Avenue parking area and paddleboat kiosk. If you visit in early spring while the famed Yoshino cherry trees are in bloom, it might look as though huge, pale-pink snowballs are ringing the basin. (See "For the Love of Cherry Trees," on page 145.) Proceed along the water toward Independence Avenue. Turn left to cross the Kutz Bridge and continue your hike from the beginning of this trail's description.

MORE INFORMATION

The National Park Service maintains and administers East Potomac Park and the memorials along the Tidal Basin. For more information, visit nps. gov/nama or call 202-426-6841. Restrooms and water fountains are available at the memorials and at several locations in East Potomac Park. Park roads are sometimes closed due to flooding, and parking anywhere nearby can be difficult in spring, during cherry blossom time. For a classic D.C. experience, consider renting a Tidal Basin paddleboat (seasonal; fees apply) at the kiosk in the parking area along Maine Avenue SW. This hike is in the heart of Washington, D.C. where there are many museums and places of interest nearby. See map for further detail.

FOR THE LOVE OF CHERRY TREES

Eliza Scidmore, an American travel writer and photographer and the National Geographic Society's first female trustee, made her initial tour of Japan in 1885 with her brother George, a U.S. diplomat who lived in Japan at the time. She was enchanted by the beauty of the flowering cherry trees (*sakura*) she saw there—a poignant, centuries-old symbol of ephemeral life, love, and springtime in Japanese culture. Upon returning to Washington, D.C., she approached the superintendent of public buildings and grounds to propose that such trees be planted along the Potomac's riverbanks, which were then being reclaimed from swampland. The superintendent, and his successors for the next twenty-plus years, refused or ignored her requests.

Meanwhile, another world traveler, the Department of Agriculture botanist David Fairchild, also had taken a fancy to the fragile, delicately rosy, fleeting *sakura*. He made a test planting of 100 trees on his suburban Maryland estate and found them well suited to the local climate. For Arbor Day 1908, Fairchild presented cherry saplings to children from each Washington, D.C., school to be planted in their schoolyards, a common tradition in Japan. Fairchild also suggested transforming the speedway (along modern-day Independence Avenue SW) into a "field of cherries" and publicly lauded Eliza Scidmore as a great authority on Japan.

Scidmore then decided to plant *sakura* in the nation's capital, even if she had to raise the funds herself. In early 1909, she wrote to first lady Helen "Nellie" Taft. Mrs. Taft had also toured Japan, en route to Manila in 1899, when her husband had been appointed commissioner of the Philippines. Later, as the U.S. secretary of war in 1905, William Howard Taft had helped to negotiate the treaty that ended the Russo-Japanese War and had been warmly welcomed in Japan. The first lady was strongly interested in beautifying D.C. and embraced the cherry tree idea.

Suddenly *sakura* were all the rage. While visiting Washington, D.C., that April of 1909, the Japanese chemist and discoverer of adrenaline Jokichi Takamine heard of the plan and asked a friend, the Japanese diplomat Kokichi Midzuno, if the first lady would accept a donation of 2,000 cherry trees. Midzuno encouraged the gift and suggested making it in the name of the city of Tokyo. The first lady gladly accepted. A few days later, the superintendent of public buildings and grounds, Colonel Spencer Cosby, ordered the purchase of 90 Fugenzo cherries, which were planted south of today's Lincoln Memorial. (They have since disappeared.)

In January 1910, Tokyo's gift of 2,000 trees landed in Washington, D.C.—infested with invasive insects. President Taft ordered them burned, with the exception of a dozen or so that were planted experimentally in East Potomac Park. The destruction of the trees nearly set off an international incident. Letters of explanation and deep regret flew east and west between the secretary of State, Philander Knox; the Japanese ambassador, Viscount Chinda; the public grounds superintendent, Cosby; and the mayor of Tokyo, Yukio Ozaki.

Diplomacy saved the situation. Mayor Ozaki, wishing to show his gratitude to President Taft for the 1905 treaty, was gracious and undaunted. With Takamine's financial help, Tokyo generously gifted a second shipment of 3,020 trees—comprising twelve varieties, including 1,800 Yoshino cherry trees, with their famous single white-pink blossoms—that arrived in February 1912. On March 27, the first lady and Viscountess Chinda, the Japanese ambassador's wife, planted D.C.'s first two Yoshino cherries along the Tidal Basin's northern bank, near today's Martin Luther King Jr. Memorial.

Cherry blossoms quickly became a powerful tourist attraction—drawing humans and many other visitors. The small, bitter fruit serves as important food for birds, and in 1982, beavers were first spotted cruising the Tidal Basin for a potential home. Over time, they have managed to cut down more cherry trees than George Washington. When three beavers were humanely trapped in 1999 after getting their teeth into at least eight trees, their release location was kept top-secret due to heated controversy and a local desire for revenge against the vandals.

The National Park Service continues to propagate and plant cherry-tree grafts along the Tidal Basin, preserving the genetic line and incomparable loveliness. When postwar Japan asked for help in replacing trees damaged by World War II bombings, Washington, D.C., repaid Tokyo's gift with 55 cuttings from the Tidal Basin Yoshino trees in 1951 and another 2,000 in 1980. Thus the wheel of life continues to turn.

The expected life span of a Yoshino cherry tree is 45 years. Yet a century later, some 60 of the original 1912 trees, and possibly a handful of the diseased 1910 shipment, live on as a blooming testament to life and springtime—perhaps even to love.

This hike explores the natural beauty found in many lesser-known, peaceful, urban nooks and landscaped gardens along the National Mall.

DIRECTIONS

By train, take Metrorail's Blue, Silver, or Orange Line to the Capitol South station. Exit at 355 First Street SE, just south of the southwest corner of First and C streets SE. (Public parking in the city's tourist areas is very limited in availability and duration, so driving is discouraged for this hike.) *GPS coordinates:* 38° 53.143′ N, 77° 00.360′ W.

TRAIL DESCRIPTION

This urban walk takes you along a route ideal for appreciating the forethought of city planner Pierre L'Enfant (1754–1825), the classically trained French architect-engineer who enlisted with the Americans during the Revolutionary War. Following the war, in 1791 L'Enfant was appointed by President George Washington to devise a fitting layout for the new capital city of a brand-new nation. This route also features museums, memorials, and a plethora of natural retreats tucked amid the eager scrum of tourists from around the world.

Exit the Capitol South Metro station and walk left to the corner of First and C streets SE. Continue uphill one block along First Street SE, cross Independence Avenue, and follow the path leading diagonally left toward the U.S. Capitol's dome. These grounds, considered a jewel of landscape architecture, were designed by Frederick Law Olmsted, whose other credits include New York City's Central Park. Note how Olmsted's ironwork viewing shelter is placed perfectly for appreciating *Freedom Triumphant,* or simply *Freedom,* the 19.5-foot-tall bronze statue crowning the Capitol's cast-iron dome. Also look for the dozens of

LOCATION
Southeast, Southwest
Washington, D.C.

RATING
Easy to moderate

DISTANCE
3.7 miles

ELEVATION GAIN
70 feet downslope

ESTIMATED TIME
3 hours

MAPS
USGS Washington East, USGS Washington West; online: nps.gov/nama/planyourvisit/maps.htm

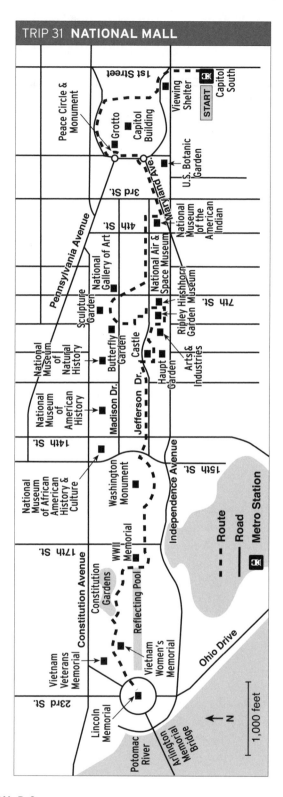

1st Street

Viewing Shelter

START

Capitol South

Peace Circle & Monument

Grotto

Capitol Building

U.S. Botanic Garden

3rd St.

Maryland Ave.

Pennsylvania Avenue

4th St.

National Museum of the American Indian

National Gallery of Art

National Air & Space Museum

Sculpture Garden

Ripley Hirshhorn Garden Museum

7th St.

Butterfly Garden

Castle

National Museum of Natural History

Jefferson Dr.

Haupt Garden

Arts & Industries

National Museum of American History

Madison Dr.

14th St.

National Museum of African American History & Culture

Washington Monument

15th St.

Independence Avenue

Route

Road

Metro Station

17th St.

WWII Memorial

Constitution Gardens

Constitution Avenue

Reflecting Pool

Vietnam Veterans Memorial

Vietnam Women's Memorial

Ohio Drive

23rd St.

N

1,000 feet

Lincoln Memorial

Potomac River

Arlington Memorial Bridge

memorial trees planted over the Capitol grounds. Many are the official trees of various states; others are dedicated to historical figures and events. Unfortunately, some of these trees have succumbed to storms or to construction of the Capitol's visitor center beneath your feet.

Cross the plaza lengthwise (watching out for official vehicles, which sometimes travel at higher speeds) and walk around the Capitol's north wing, pausing to enjoy the view westward down the Mall. You're standing upon what we know today as Capitol Hill, or what early Americans called Jenkins Hill and L'Enfant termed "a pedestal awaiting a monument." On this height, L'Enfant decided, would sit the "Congress House," honoring the American people, whose representatives would meet in the edifice. To the right is Pennsylvania Avenue, which leads to the "President's Palace"—now known as the White House. L'Enfant's street plan included wide avenues named for each of the states then existing, running diagonally across a grid of numbered and lettered streets. L'Enfant planned a long, open "grand avenue" running westward from the Capitol. Over time, this became the National Mall.

Proceed down Capitol Hill on the curving path toward a hexagonal red-brick structure, Olmsted's Summerhouse (often called the Grotto). Built over a natural spring, this is a cool, pleasant resting place where you can fill your water bottle (note: the fountains now flow with municipally treated water). Continue downhill into Peace Circle, named for Franklin Simmons's Peace Monument that depicts Grief sobbing on the shoulder of History in memory of sailors lost during the Civil War. The monument's Carrara marble has suffered serious degradation from acid rain and weathering; restoration efforts are underway to prolong the statue's life. Cross the circle toward the Capitol Reflecting Pool and turn back to see the West Front, where presidential swearing-in ceremonies have taken place since Ronald Reagan's first inauguration in 1981.

Facing the Mall again, walk south, to your left, toward the conservatory of the U.S. Botanic Garden, and enjoy its rooms of cacti, orchids, and desert and tropical plants. Outside you'll find inviting, open-air plots, including the quilt-inspired First Ladies Water Garden and a pesticide-free butterfly garden. Follow Maryland Avenue SW away from the Capitol, toward the yellow-beige National Museum of the American Indian. This building's flowing forms, designed in part by native people, represent natural elements, such as clouds and earth. Cross Third Street into the museum's entrance courtyard, looking along Maryland Avenue to see Nora Naranjo-Morse's organic sculpture *Always Becoming*, then walk around the building to enjoy the water feature, the fire pit, and the landscaping.

Now cross Fourth Street and continue along Jefferson Drive's southern sidewalk, observing a to-scale representation of the sun and the first planets of the solar system that stretches for blocks past the National Air and Space Museum. Cross Jefferson Drive and walk diagonally across the grassy Mall toward the corner of Seventh Street and Madison Drive NW. Just across Seventh Street is

The classic spire of the Washington Monument (as seen from the Lincoln Memorial, terminus of this hike along the National Mall) provides a classic vista of Washington, D.C., looking east past the Reflecting Pool toward Pierre L'Enfant's 2-mile-long grand avenue of green space. Photo by Brian Holland, Creative Commons on Flickr.

the southeast gate of the National Gallery of Art's whimsical Sculpture Garden. Enjoy splashing fountains in a large pool that becomes an outdoor ice-skating rink in winter. Many trees thrive here, including magnolias, cedars of Lebanon, and Kentucky coffees. Walk out to Madison Drive through the garden's southwest gate. Quickly turn right into the Butterfly Habitat Garden, where four different landscapes attract many of the 80 or so butterfly species seen in Washington, D.C. Return to Madison Drive and cross the grass back to the southern side of the Mall.

Head toward the doughnut-shaped concrete building, the Hirshhorn Museum and Sculpture Garden, and pause in its sunken sculpture garden on the north side of Jefferson Drive. Among 60 other works, you will find a piece by Auguste Rodin titled *Crouching Woman*. Cross Jefferson Drive and the Hirshhorn's fountain courtyard, turn right onto Independence Avenue SW, and turn quickly right into the Mary Livingston Ripley Garden. Ripley, an avid gardener and the wife of a former Smithsonian Institution secretary, planned a Victorian-style fragrant garden on this spot, which had been slated to become a parking lot. The garden path leads back to Jefferson Drive. Turn left, pass the Arts and Industries Building, and enjoy the Kathrine Dulin Folger Rose Garden's scented splendor.

Follow the path to the left (south side) of the red Maryland-sandstone Smithsonian Castle visitor center into the Enid A. Haupt Garden, with its old-fashioned, formal, clipped-shrubbery parterre beds. Note the entrances to two underground museums, the African Art Museum and the Sackler Gallery, as well as the Asian-inspired, compass-pointed, granite-and-water Moongate Garden. Walk around the Castle's west end and turn left to follow Jefferson Drive west across Fourteenth and Fifteenth Streets SW. Look across the Mall to your right to see the National Museum of American History and the newest Smithsonian Institution museum, the National Museum of African American History and Culture, with its three tapered levels enwrapped with bronze latticework—a tribute to ironwork crafted by enslaved people in the South.

Climb toward the base of the Washington Monument. When you arrive on top of the slope, try looking straight up at the monument. An odd trick of perspective makes it look like the obelisk is tipping over on top of you. Enjoy the 360-degree vista—north to the White House, east to the Capitol, south toward the Thomas Jefferson Memorial, west to the Lincoln Memorial and Reflecting Pool—then walk west downhill toward Seventeenth Street. Cross that street and proceed down the wide entrance avenue of the World War II Memorial. The memorial's green wall bears 4,048 golden stars, one for every 100 Americans lost in the war. Walk up the curving ramp to the left (past the Delaware column), through the Pacific arch, and around to the back of the green wall. You'll see a gate, inside which is one of two "Kilroy Was Here" inscriptions featured in the memorial. The long-nosed, mischievous Kilroy boosted morale during the war years, as soldiers cheerfully vied to see who could doodle him in the most unexpected and inaccessible places.

Proceed across the eastern end of the Lincoln Memorial's Reflecting Pool, and turn left onto the second path, which emerges at the edge of the Constitution Gardens pond, opened in 1976 for the national bicentennial. Its central island, dedicated to the signers of the Declaration of Independence and reached by a pedestrian bridge, is a haven for ducks and geese. Algae overgrowth has caused serious fish die-offs here; the National Park Service and the U.S. Fine Arts Commission are developing plans to deepen the pond and improve the habitat. When the path splits near a hexagonal snack bar, keep left, proceeding toward the Vietnam Veterans Memorial. This path leads you past the three nurses and the wounded soldier of the Vietnam Women's Memorial statue, by Glenna Goodacre. To your right, you have a full view of the polished black wall of the Vietnam Veterans Memorial, designed by Maya Lin. Continue west along this walkway toward the hike's terminus, the massive marble Lincoln Memorial.

Myths surrounding this memorial and fascinating coincidences in the president's life abound. Despite rumors to the contrary, there is not one step here for each year of Lincoln's life, although there is at his Kentucky birthplace. Nor has this marble Lincoln turned its back on the South, although Robert E. Lee lived for many years just across the Potomac at Arlington Plantation, now Arlington

National Cemetery. (See Trip 32: Arlington National Cemetery and Marine Corps War [Iwo Jima] Memorial.) Lincoln's statue actually faces east. Take time to ponder the president's own words from his Gettysburg Address and his second inaugural address—familiar yet poignantly powerful in their fuller context—that are engraved on the memorial's interior walls. Look down one of the step landings for the plaque marking the spot where Martin Luther King Jr. stood as he delivered his "I Have a Dream" speech in 1963.

You can hail a taxi on Constitution Avenue NW, a block to the north, or in the parking area just south of the Lincoln Memorial. Or hike a bit farther to a Metro station: Arlington Cemetery station (Blue Line) across Memorial Bridge in Virginia, or Foggy Bottom station (Blue/Silver/Orange Lines) about eight blocks north, at 23rd and Eye (letter I) streets NW.

MORE INFORMATION

For Metrorail information, call 202-637-7000 or visit wmata.com. Restrooms and water fountains are available in the U.S. Capitol Visitor Center (strict security screening is in effect), the U.S. Botanic Garden, the National Gallery Sculpture Garden, and the memorials. Note that leashed dogs are permitted outdoors on the National Mall, but not on Metrorail or in the museums. For current information and updates on tourism and special events in Washington, D.C., and on the National Mall, visit washington.org.

NEARBY

Take time to step inside the U.S. Botanic Garden in the shadow of the Capitol, at First Street and Maryland Avenue SW. Here you'll find vast rooms filled with tropical plants—including lemon and banana trees—plus orchids, cacti, bromeliads, and many more, each with its microclimate of proper temperature and humidity. Bring a book and relax by the soothing fountains, climb the catwalks in the rainforest room, or take in the special holiday displays of poinsettias, flowering bulbs, and other horticultural delights. Check out usbg.gov for details.

WHAT'S IN A NAME: MR. SMITHSON'S LEGACY

Inside the ornate red-stone Smithsonian Castle on the National Mall stands the crypt of James Smithson (ca. 1765–1829), the English gentleman scientist whose large fortune founded the Smithsonian Institution. Smithson never visited the United States during his life, and his moldering bones, resting here now, can't tell us what manner of man bestowed such an amazing gift.

Recent scholarship, however, delves into the enlightenment world of this previously shadowy historical figure. Born James (or Jacques) Louis Macie, he was the offspring of an illicit romance between the widowed aristocrat Elizabeth Macie and Hugh Smithson, the first Duke of Northumberland. Unacknowledged and unsupported by his father, James boldly took the family name Smithson in his 30s, after his parents' deaths.

As Macie, he had already gained renown for his work in the exciting new fields of chemistry and mineralogy. Following his student-prodigy career at the University of Oxford, a 22-year-old James was inducted into the exclusive, influential Royal Society and soon published the first of his many papers in its journal. On the strength of these accomplishments, plus his personal charm and exuberance, he embarked upon a grand tour of the European

continent, seeking scientific insights, kindred minds, and mineralogical specimens for his growing collection. He carried a portable laboratory, experimented with the properties of minerals (even tasting and sniffing them), and made strides toward systems of classification. He became friends with many of the era's brightest scientists. He witnessed events of the French Revolution and became a prisoner of war

Inside the Smithsonian Castle's north portico is the crypt of James Smithson (a.k.a. James Macie), the English gentleman-scientist and mysterious benefactor of the vast museum complex that bears his chosen name. Photo by Rain0975, Creative Commons on Flickr.

during Europe's lengthy Napoleonic Wars. He knew aeronauts, aristocrats, politicians, and inventors. But he had neither a wife nor children, and his one surviving blood relative, a nephew, died childless.

So, Smithson, a savvy investor, bequeathed in gold all of his wealth—about £105,000, or $508,000 at the time—"to the United States of America, to found at Washington, an establishment for the increase and diffusion of knowledge." It was to bear his chosen name. Astonished U.S. leaders wondered who he was, what he intended, and why. Some say he admired the young America's enlightenment-inspired ideals: a united country and open society, free from standing armies and the scourge of constant war. Others insist Smithson bore a grudge against the aristocratic privilege ingrained in England. "My name will live on in the memory of men when the titles of [my ancestors] are extinct or forgotten," he once vowed.

His bequest certainly made his name famous around the globe, creating what is today the world's largest museum and research complex. But his motive might always remain a mystery.

VIRGINIA

Even with its ever-intensifying suburban development, northern Virginia remains geologically and ecologically diverse, containing (from west to east) the Blue Ridge Mountains, the verdant hills and stream valleys of the Piedmont, and the tidal marshlands of the Atlantic coastal  plain. An obvious choice for nature lovers is to go west, away from the suburban sprawl to the farmlands and horse fields of western Loudoun and Fauquier counties. Here, hikers can enjoy the rugged spine of the Bull Run Mountains (at Bull Run Mountains Natural Area and Wildcat Mountain Natural Area) and the Blue Ridge Mountains (at Sky Meadows State Park, the third of our three AT-connected hikes, and at G. Richard Thompson Wildlife Management Area). Farther west and south is Old Rag Mountain in Shenandoah National Park, one of the best day hikes for overlooks and challenging, unique terrain in the Mid-Atlantic states. New to this edition are Signal Knob on the western face of the Blue Ridge, the most distant of all the trips listed here and the top hike for elevation gain, and Banshee Reeks Nature Preserve near Leesburg, a well-kept secret offering meadows, berry patches, and a scenic creek.

Closer to Washington, D.C., in busy Fairfax and Prince William counties, hikers can meander through the creased and folded landscape of the Virginia Piedmont, following stream valleys where old mills and mines reflect the way people once lived. Northern Virginia has its fair share of long out-and-back trails, frequented by bicyclists and hikers, including Washington & Old Dominion Trail and Cross County Trail, with its historic Colvin Run Mill; Mount Vernon Trail, paralleling the scenic Potomac River as it widens on its way south; and Bull Run–Occoquan Trail, which in some spots feels remote enough to rival the Appalachian Trail.

Meadowlark Botanical Gardens, by contrast, is a human-crafted haven of wildflowers, water features, and even a Korean bell garden. Hikers can also enjoy the inland offerings and largely forested areas of Huntley Meadows Park, Prince William Forest Park, and Manassas National Battlefield, where centuries-old hardwoods have survived the axes of settlers and the bulldozers of developers (but not always the incisors of determined beavers).

Farther upstream along the Potomac River, north of Washington, D.C., are the roiling waters of Great Falls National Park, Theodore Roosevelt's favorite spot to clear his head of the rigors of the presidency. In this same neighborhood are two lesser-known but challenging and worthwhile hikes: Scott's Run Nature Preserve and Riverbend Park, the latter of which we've incorporated in the Great Falls route. These hikes combine hilly climbs with walks along the Potomac River.

Along the Potomac south of D.C., facing east toward southern Maryland, are George Mason Plantation and Mason Neck State Park. Nesting in these tidal marshlands and delicate sandy cliffs are bald eagles, osprey, and great blue herons. Not far inland is Prince William Forest Park, once the training ground for eagle-eyed secret agents.

Closest to Washington, D.C.—and overlooking the ubiquitous Potomac, as well as the National Mall—is one of our new Virginia trips: a hike through Arlington National Cemetery and the Marine Corps War (Iwo Jima) Memorial. With its easy access to Metrorail, this trip could be just the place to begin your Virginia adventures.

32

ARLINGTON NATIONAL CEMETERY AND MARINE CORPS WAR (IWO JIMA) MEMORIAL

This Metro-friendly hike passes through some of the most hallowed and lovely hills in the nation, offering classic vistas of the capital city.

DIRECTIONS

Take Metrorail's Blue line to the Arlington Cemetery station. Use either exit and proceed along Memorial Avenue to the cemetery's welcome center through a gate on the left side of the roadway. If you choose to drive to Arlington Cemetery, the garage has limited parking for an hourly fee, and you can take the Metro back to the parking garage from Rosslyn station at the hike's terminus. Walk from the garage to the welcome center to begin your hike. *GPS coordinates: 38° 52.998′ N, 77° 3.946′ W.*

Arlington National Cemetery is an active cemetery hosting 25 to 30 burials a day, Monday to Saturday. Many individuals and families also come to visit the graves of loved ones interred here. Out of respect for those grieving, visitors are asked to yield right of way to funeral processions and to refrain from taking photos of funeral services or graveside visitors. Appropriate conduct is requested at all times while on the cemetery grounds. Security screening was introduced in fall 2016.

TRAIL DESCRIPTION

It might sound unusual to include a walk through a cemetery in a day-hikes guidebook, but Arlington National Cemetery is a special case. Its iconic American symbolism, its rich history, and its sheer beauty combine to make this a walk everyone should take at least once, at one's own pace to absorb all the place has to offer. Think of this trip as a guided historic hiking tour. The route encompasses the cemetery's most visited points of interest (the Kennedy

LOCATION
Arlington, VA

RATING
Easy to moderate

DISTANCE
4 miles

ELEVATION GAIN
600 feet

ESTIMATED TIME
3 to 4 hours, including sightseeing

MAPS
USGS Washington West, USGS Alexandria; brochure map at welcome center; online: arlingtoncemetery.mil

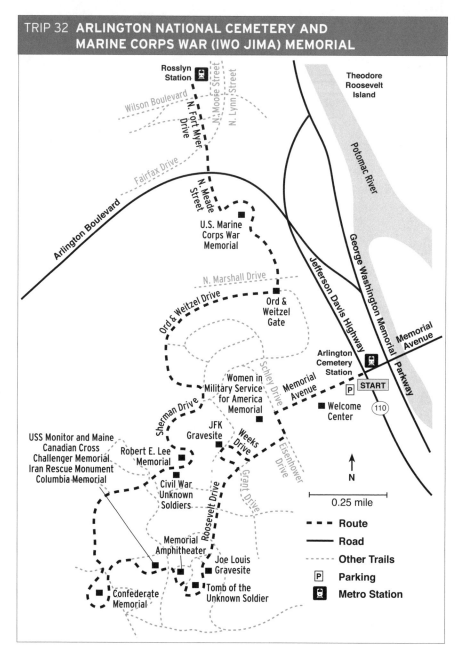

gravesites, the Tomb of the Unknowns, and Arlington House), along with some less-traveled pathways and lesser-known landmarks, before moving outside the gates to the massive Iwo Jima memorial.

This hike keeps mostly to paved walkways and is suitable for older children who are ready to take in the meaning of this place. The walk requires pedestrians to climb some steps and possibly to step off the pavement onto grass or gravel in a few stretches. Be prepared for a few inclines steep and lengthy enough to get most people huffing and puffing a bit.

Stop in at the cemetery's welcome center to fill water bottles, to pick up a map, and, if applicable, to inquire about the location of a relative's gravesite. A small exhibit hall offers rotating displays. Exit through the center's west doors (near the tram tour ticket window) and proceed straight ahead. When you come to a crosswalk, look to your right, toward the cemetery's gates, and note the golden seals of the branches of the U.S. military. Beyond those gates, glimpse the Women in Military Service for America Memorial, built into a hillside. The memorial hosts events, seminars, and exhibits exploring the experience of more than 2.5 million women in America's armed forces and support units, from the Revolutionary War through the present day. Of particular interest are the register inside the memorial building (where visitors can find service data, photos, and other media related to individual servicewomen) and the rooftop arcade of glass tablets inscribed with quotations from some of those women.

From the crosswalk, proceed directly up Roosevelt Drive and into the cemetery. Pause for a 360-degree view of the headstones that stretch in silent, precise rows in every direction, standing in for the fallen of all ranks and branches who themselves once stood in ready formation. Here and elsewhere during your visit, you can begin to grasp how many men and women have participated in our armed forces over the centuries, especially when you consider that this is just one of more than 100 national cemeteries and only the second largest. Note the marble headstones, provided by the U.S. government, all bearing the same set of information: faith symbols; name, rank, and service branch; notations of decorations, such as the Medal of Honor or the Silver Star; and on the reverse, the names of any spouses and dependent children interred with the servicemember. When you see sections containing only uniform grave markers, you're generally in either one of the newer or the older parts of the cemetery—in this case, where burials began just after World War II. Due to the heightened meaning of an Arlington burial, servicemembers interred here today must qualify for the honor under special rules. Active-service members who die in the line of duty, and any U.S. president, due to his or her commander-in-chief role, are automatically eligible for interment at Arlington, if desired. Two presidents—Kennedy and Taft—and three of five 5-star generals to date have had the honor of burial here.

Make your first right turn onto Weeks Drive and look toward Arlington House (the Custis-Lee mansion) atop the hill. You will visit the house later in the hike, but you won't see this view of it again. Note the flag in front of the mansion: If it's at half-staff, funerals are in progress in the cemetery. Proceed straight until you cross Sheridan Drive, toward the curving granite plaza at the gravesite of President John F. Kennedy and members of his family. Before mounting the steps or the circular ramp, look to your right, where the cemetery's section 5 contains the graves of several U.S. Supreme Court justices, including Thurgood

Sunrise bathes the U.S. Marine Corps War Memorial—often referred to as the Iwo Jima memorial—and its six flag-raisers, whose figures are roughly five times life size. Carved into the stone base are the names of Marine military engagements since the Corps's inception in 1775. Photo by Beth Homicz.

Marshall, the court's first African-American justice.

Proceed up to the Kennedy graves, where an eternal flame, ignited at the slain president's burial on November 25, 1963, illuminates his resting place. Next to him rests his widow, Jacqueline Kennedy Onassis. While she did remarry after the president's death, she was eligible for burial here because she was a widow again when she died in 1994. Remains of two of their children, a stillborn daughter and a son, Patrick, who died as an infant, were brought here following President Kennedy's death. Turn around toward Memorial Bridge to appreciate the vista along the National Mall. Several individuals who knew him have claimed that, while touring Arlington House earlier in 1963, President Kennedy remarked as he gazed over the Potomac that it was so beautiful there, "I could stay here forever." Quotations from the young president's speeches, engraved on the memorial wall, enhance the experience. If you are here in springtime, the tulip trees and flowering crabapples provide additional beauty.

Next, walk down the three steps toward the roadway but make a quick right along the cobblestone path, toward the white wooden cross marking the gravesite of President Kennedy's younger brother and U.S. attorney general, Robert F. Kennedy. During his own campaign for the presidency in 1968, Robert was shot as he exited through a back corridor of the Ambassador Hotel in Los Angeles. The white cross was installed at Robert's particular request. Also here is another simple marker to the youngest brother, Senator Edward "Ted" Kennedy (D-Mass), who died in 2009. Pause to enjoy the peaceful meditation pool that lies beneath several engraved quotations from Robert's speeches.

Take the steps out to the roadway and turn left, looking for the large headstone marking the grave of Michael Musmanno, a judge in the post-World War II Nuremberg trials following the fall of the Nazi regime. Make an immediate sharp right onto Grant Drive, walk past the tram stop, and look to your right for the headstone of Daniel "Chappie" James Jr., a Tuskegee Institute alumnus, decorated U.S. Air Force fighter pilot, and the first African-American to reach the rank of four-star general. Now look left at the equestrian statue marking the burial place of Sir John Dill, a British field marshal stationed in Washington, D.C., during World War II. When he died during his tour, he was granted burial at Arlington in keeping with the British tradition of laying soldiers to rest where they fell. Dill's is one of some two dozen graves of foreign officers in the cemetery.

Turn right, back onto Roosevelt Drive, and look to your left toward Chaplains' Hill. You might notice three identical tall stone markers standing side by side. These honor the military chaplains who died in the two world wars and in the Korean War. As you look around, you see many shapes, sizes, and colors of grave markers provided by survivors of the deceased. Proceed up the hill. When you come to a "Y" intersection, keep left then turn right onto a flagstone walkway. Now to your left, in section 7A, you'll notice a tall brown headstone with a bronze plaque for the world heavyweight-boxing champion Joe Louis. Louis's 1938 rout of former champ Max Schmeling of Germany humiliated the Nazis and helped make the "Brown Bomber" a favorite of U.S. GIs during World War II. Louis himself served in the war as a special assignment officer in a segregated unit and earned the Legion of Merit decoration. Turn left just past Louis's grave and continue uphill past a black headstone decorated with Air Force wings. This is the grave of astronaut Michael J. Smith, a naval aviator and the pilot of the ill-fated space shuttle *Challenger,* lost during its launch on January 28, 1986. Come to an elliptical lawn and proceed toward its far end, staying silent as you go. The Tomb of the Unknowns is at the top of the steps to your right, and a ceremony might be in progress. Continue uphill under several big, old maples then around to the right to approach the plaza in front of the tomb. Make sure no sentinels are approaching or exiting the enclosure, and when the way is clear, find a place on the marble steps from which to observe the changing of the guard.

The Tomb of the Unknowns was established following the First World War, when many American troops fell on foreign battlefields and were buried without identification. Grieving families thus had no closure for their losses. In 1921, the remains of one unknown American soldier were brought here to represent all those who never came home from that war. On the face of the tomb's white Colorado marble are the words: "Here rests in honored glory an American Soldier, known but to God." In the 1930s, an honor guard of soldiers from the 3rd U.S.

Infantry was posted to the tomb. Unknown soldiers from the Second World War and the Korean and Vietnam wars were later added, but the Vietnam unknown soldier's remains were later disinterred and identified with the aid of DNA testing technology as those of Lt. Michael Blassie of St. Louis. His former tomb will forever remain empty.

While on duty, the Tomb Guard sentinel performs a 21-step, 21-second walk before the tomb; turns to face the tomb; waits 21 seconds; turns again, shoulder rifle between tomb and onlookers; waits another 21 seconds; and repeats the walk in the opposite direction. With each step and pause, the soldier is intently focused, precise, and dignified in his or her movements, mentally counting the seconds while pacing out an endless 21-gun salute to fallen comrades. While the sentinel is prepared to defend the tomb, if necessary, his or her primary purpose is to guard a memory and a standard, rather than a physical structure.

The changing of the guard occurs hourly from October to March and every half hour from April to September. Be prepared to remain silent and standing for the solemn ceremony. Watch for the relief commander and the new sentinel to enter the enclosure and, if weather allows, to perform a white-glove inspection of the sentinel's rifle on the right-hand (south) end of the plaza. Following the guard change, wait for all but the newly posted sentinel to exit the enclosure before you attempt to leave the steps. Be advised that wreath-laying ceremonies often follow the guard change. It's worth remaining to observe one of these if you can; you'll get to hear an Army bugler blowing "Taps" after the commander asks you to place your right hand over your heart.

Now turn around and stroll through the Memorial Amphitheater, which hosts official ceremonies, such as the annual Memorial Day and Veterans' Day observances, when the president usually speaks and places a wreath at the tomb. Walk out to the roadway, Memorial Drive, and look across the road and off to your left at a short walkway bounded by draped chains. This is the grave of Audie Murphy, the most decorated American soldier of World War II. As you move now toward the tall white mast of the *USS Maine*, pause to visit the memorials to the crew of the space shuttles *Challenger* and *Columbia* on your right. The *USS Maine* Memorial remembers the 266 sailors who were lost when the ship, anchored in Havana, Cuba, in 1898, exploded and touched off the Spanish-American War with its rallying cry, "Remember the *Maine!*" Many jumped to the conclusion that Spanish forces, seeking to put down a Cuban bid for independence, had torpedoed or mined the American vessel, but more recent research suggests the explosion might have been caused by a coal-fired boiler malfunction aboard the ship.

Walk around the *Maine* mast to the circular driveway and out to Farragut Drive. Turn left and look across the road into section 13, noticing the white headstones with the letters "U.S.C.T." These represent U.S. Colored Troops: segregated Army units dating to the Civil War and the Spanish-American War. It wasn't until the Korean War in the early 1950s that America's military was fully integrated. At the intersection with McPherson Drive, turn left briefly to visit the Confederate Memorial and burial section. These 400 southern troops, mostly officers, were buried or reinterred here after Congress authorized a special section for the purpose in 1900. Watching over their peaked headstones is Moses Ezekiel's bronze statue of a woman embodying the South, intended to inspire "peace for the living and honor to the dead."

Return to McPherson Drive and turn left, walking through several older sections with big, old trees (and several headstones engulfed in their roots). Continue around the circle at section 14 and along to the intersection of Meigs Drive; turn right here. Watch for a large marker on your left bearing the name Doubleday; that's Abner Doubleday, credited with inventing the game of baseball. Come to the overgrown Old Amphitheater on your right, bear slightly left onto Sherman Drive, and turn right on the gravel path to visit Arlington House. Before you walk around to the front porch, look to your right into a grove of shrubbery to see the marker for a mass grave of 2,111 unidentified Union and Confederate soldiers recovered from Civil War battlefields. Stroll through the flower garden, noticing the ring of Union headstones around it, and out to the vista over the Potomac. Notice a table-shaped grave marker in front of the mansion. These are the reinterred remains of Pierre L'Enfant, designer of the city plan for Washington, D.C., who died as a pauper abroad but was later honored with a final resting place overlooking the city he created. (See Trip 31: National Mall.)

Pause for a walk-through of Arlington House, the memorial to Robert E. Lee, maintained by the National Park Service. Take in the family portraits and the period furniture, and stop for a moment on the wide wooden portico to enjoy the view. Exit to the back of the house for a visit to the Lee museum, kitchen garden, and slave quarters. Return to Sherman Drive, turning right and proceeding downhill past a heavily wooded area on your left. This is section 29, known as Arlington Woods and hotly defended by environmental groups as one of the best examples of old-growth, terraced gravel forest remaining in Virginia. Some of the old forest has been preserved as a buffer zone and an extended memorial to the Custis-Lee family. Turn left onto Ord & Weitzel Drive, pausing to view the Vietnam War Memorial Tree, and stroll along the curving road past the cemetery's Millennium Project on your left—an extensive effort to provide for future burial space and one that has consumed some of that old-growth forest.

Watch for the many small, block-shaped grave markers in this area and the standard-issue headstones marked "Civilian" or "Citizen." These graves belong to former slaves, many of them residents of the Freedmen's Village established on this site during the Civil War to resettle and educate formerly enslaved people. Now turn to your left to exit the cemetery through the Ord & Weitzel Gate, carefully cross the roadway, and proceed uphill toward the U.S. Marine Corps War Memorial. Look to your left to glimpse the square tower known as the Netherlands Carillon, containing 57 bells that were a gift from the people of the Netherlands to the United States following World War II.

You're approaching the largest bronze statue ever cast—and one of the most famous. Based on a Pulitzer Prize-winning photo by Joe Rosenthal of the Associated Press, the memorial depicts five Marines and a Navy medic raising an American flag atop Mount Suribachi on the Pacific island of Iwo Jima in February 1945. An initial amphibious landing on February 19, 1945, set off a brutal five-week-long push to secure the island as an Allied base despite the Japanese forces' entrenchments and hidden artillery. The photo—actually of a second flag-raising that day—was taken on February 23, five days into the battle. Three of the six men depicted were later killed in action on Iwo Jima.

As you come closer, walk around the circle to your right, watching to see if the flag seems to rise as you move—an optical illusion that has long delighted tourists. The piece's sculptor, Felix de Weldon, once scoffed at the urban legend suggesting there is an extra hand, possibly a hand of God, depicted among the figures. He denied he would have executed such a travesty of his masterwork. The men's figures are roughly five times life size, 32 feet tall, and their canteens would hold about eight gallons of water. Circle the statue to note all six figures and the names of major engagements of U.S. Marines since the inception of the Corps in 1775.

When you're ready to call it a half-day, walk past the parade ground, cross the parking area, and scramble up the wooded slope to North Meade Street. Turn right and walk about four blocks to the Rosslyn Metrorail station, which contains one of the world's longest continuous escalators at 207 feet.

MORE INFORMATION

Arlington National Cemetery opens daily at 8 A.M. and closes at 5 P.M. October to March and at 7 P.M. April to September. Admission is free. Call 877-907-8585. The changing of the guard takes place on the hour year-round and also on the half hour April to September. Restrooms and water fountains are available in the welcome center, the Women in Military Service for America Memorial, the Memorial Amphitheater, and Arlington House. Visit the Arlington National Cemetery website at arlingtoncemetery.mil to download the ANC Explorer smartphone app.

NEARBY

Just outside the cemetery gates along Va. 110 is the Pentagon, headquarters of the Department of Defense, with its 9/11 Memorial comprised of winglike benches in honor of each of the 184 souls lost here that bright September morning in 2001. Find more information at pentagonmemorial.org.

HOME FRONT LEFT BEHIND: ARLINGTON HOUSE AND THE LEES

Arlington National Cemetery, the final resting place today of more than 400,000 Americans, covers rolling hills that were once the plantation home of George Washington Parke Custis, the grandson of Martha Washington from her first marriage and the step-grandson of the first president. In 1802, Custis built a Greek Revival-style great house—known as Arlington House and, later, as the Custis-Lee mansion—atop the hill overlooking the new nation's capital, then still a village, and filled the chunky-columned residence with his collection of Washington family treasures.

In 1831, Custis's daughter, Mary Anna, married a young U.S. Army second lieutenant, Robert Edward Lee of nearby Alexandria, the son of George Washington's close friend, the cavalry commander Henry "Light Horse Harry" Lee III. The couple made Arlington their home for 30 years (although Lee was often away on army duty) until 1861, when civil war threatened to tear Virginia away from its neighbor across the Potomac.

Through his advisors, the new president, Abraham Lincoln, offered top field commands to a number of key military officers who might help keep their native southern states from seceding to form a separate country. One such officer was Colonel Robert E. Lee, by then a decorated soldier, a former superintendent (and distinguished alumnus) of West Point, and a well-known figure for subduing John Brown's assault on the federal arsenal at Harpers Ferry. (See "John Brown and the Assault on Harpers Ferry," on page 44.) While he thought secession unwise and hasty, Lee spent several agonizing days trying to decide his future. When he heard Virginia's legislature had voted to secede on the very day Lincoln's offer came, he chose to resign his U.S. Army commission rather than to "draw my sword upon Virginia, my native state." Lee accepted a post with the new Confederate army, knowing that by doing so he was perhaps leaving his home forever.

When Lee went off to fight in the spring of 1861, his family, including his increasingly ill wife, was forced to leave their home, too. Within weeks, Union troops had occupied the grounds and the house, using the site as a fort to protect the capital from southern invasion. Within two years, the swelling numbers of war dead prompted Union officials to seek additional burial places in or near the city. They didn't have to look far: Arlington Heights was just across the Potomac; it offered high ground free from the danger of flooded gravesites; it was already in Union hands; and it was the former home of a man seen by many Northerners as the greatest traitor since Benedict Arnold.

The Union managed to purchase the 1,100-acre plantation at public auction after ruling that owners of property inside Union lines had to appear in person to pay their property taxes. Lee himself couldn't risk enemy capture, and Mary Anna Custis Lee, the property's nominal owner, was by then an invalid, unable to travel. She sent a male relative to pay the $92.07 tax bill. The government refused the payment and seized the property. In 1864, the first military burials began on the Custis-Lee grounds. By the war's end, some 16,000 troops, mostly Union but also a few Confederates, had been interred here.

During the war, in addition to Union troops, another group took up quarters on these acres: the residents of Freedmen's Village, a government-run resettlement camp for the formerly enslaved people who lived and worked on the site, receiving training in various skills and education for their children. Originally intended as a temporary measure, the village remained more or less operative until 1900.

After the long and bloody war, and the surrender to Union General Ulysses S. Grant at Appomattox, Lee had no home to return to. He managed to make a new life in the small college town of Lexington, in the Virginia mountains 200 miles to the southwest of Arlington. His old friend and right hand, the Confederate General Thomas J. "Stonewall" Jackson, had spoken to Lee of the town's appeal. Before the war broke out, Jackson had lived in Lexington for more than a decade, teaching at Virginia Military Institute.

Lee accepted the post of president of Washington College in Lexington and moved there with his family in October 1865. He remained in that capacity until his death in 1870 from complications of a stroke. Stripped of his U.S. citizenship, the former general nonetheless strove to recruit northern students to the school—and insisted his southern neighbors make them welcome. Following Lee's death, the college's trustees voted to rename the school Washington and Lee University in his honor.

The general; his wife, Mary Anna; and six of their seven children are entombed in Lee Chapel on the university's campus. Lee's office remains much as it was on the day he died. The stable of his beloved horse, Traveller, still stands nearby, too.

Nearly twenty years after the war ended, Lee's eldest son prevailed in a lengthy litigation against the U.S. government over the loss of his family's old Arlington home, and in 1883, he accepted a compensation payment of $150,000 to the family. But neither he nor any of the Lee family ever slept under this roof again. In 1925, Congress designated the mansion for restoration, and in 1955, it became the official memorial in honor of General Lee.

33

PRINCE WILLIAM FOREST PARK

Prince William Forest Park is the largest forested region in the D.C. area. Its trails run along the north and south forks of Quantico Creek and span the hilly terrain in between.

DIRECTIONS

From the Capital Beltway, take Exit 170 on the inner loop of I-95/I-495 (or take Exit 57 of the outer loop of I-495) to go south on I-95 for about 20 miles. Then take Exit 150B onto VA 619/Joplin Road. Go 0.4 mile and take the second right into the park on Park Entrance Road. Proceed about 0.5 mile to the visitor center to check in (a 150-million-year-old piece of petrified wood is out front), then return west on the entrance road and take the first right into the Pine Grove parking lot. *GPS coordinates*: 38° 33.660′ N, 77° 20.989′ W.

TRAIL DESCRIPTION

Prince William Forest Park protects more than 15,000 acres in the middle of the busy I-95 corridor in Quantico, Virginia. The north and south forks of Quantico Creek flow through the park, and a large percentage of the 37 miles of hiking trails is along them.

This 7.9-mile hike traces the natural and human history of the park. The hike starts northwest along the south fork of Quantico Creek, travels east over forested hills that were once farmland, and returns southeast via the north fork of Quantico Creek. From the west end of the Pine Grove parking lot, cross an open field and start downhill on the western stretch of the yellow-blazed Laurel Trail Loop. The trees here are typical of the park's uplands: flowering dogwoods and hollies below, beech limbs spreading horizontally, and yellow poplars towering above. At 0.4 mile, just past the suspension bridge, turn left onto the white-blazed

LOCATION
Triangle and Quantico, VA

RATING
Moderate to strenuous

DISTANCE
7.9 miles

ELEVATION GAIN
600 feet

ESTIMATED TIME
3 hours

MAPS
USGS Quantico and USGS Joplin; free NPS map at visitor center; online: nps.gov/prwi/planyourvisit/maps.htm

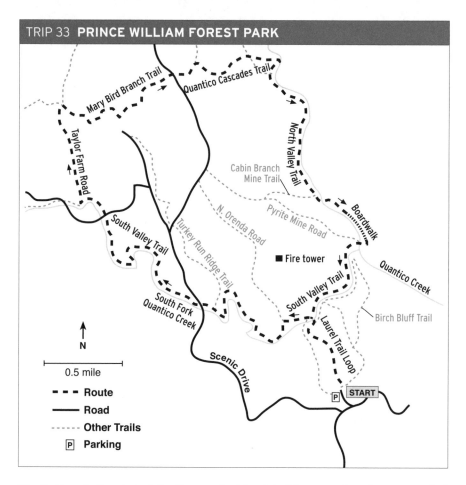

Mary Bird Branch Trail

Quantico Cascades Trail

Taylor Farm Road

North Valley Trail

Cabin Branch
Mine Trail

Pyrite Mine Road

Boardwalk

N. Orenda Road

South Valley Trail

Turkey Run Ridge Trail

■ Fire tower

South Valley Trail

Quantico Creek

South Fork
Quantico Creek

Birch Bluff Trail

Laurel Trail Loop

N

Scenic Drive

0.5 mile

P START

- - - **Route**

——— **Road**

- - - - - **Other Trails**

P **Parking**

North Orenda Road. At 0.6 mile, at a double white blaze on a beech tree, turn left onto the narrow South Valley Trail, which curves back toward the creek.

Follow the creek along its lush bank, catching views of several picturesque waterfalls streaming down from the cliffs on the opposite shore. At 1.1 miles, cross a small bridge over the Mary Bird Branch and immediately begin a steep rise up a ridge between the side and main streams, one of two big elevation gains on the south fork. Drop back down to a grove of sycamores, and at 1.4 miles, you reach the intersection with Turkey Run Ridge Trail.

Go straight to cross a bridge, a fire road, and then Scenic Drive, a 12-mile paved road circling the center of the park. Come to an area rich with knotty black birches, pass a spur trail that leads to parking lot B on Scenic Drive, and cross two small bridges over barely trickling side streams. This area is the fall line, where Quantico Creek plunges down erosion-resistant, gray-green boulders to the soft sedimentary rock of the coastal plain. Pass the spur to parking lot C and soon after, at 2.2 miles, cross another bridge over a side stream. Rise immediately on the second steep hill and return to the creek at a copse of holly,

Birch trees arc over the south fork of Quantico Creek in Prince William Forest Park. Hikers along the river are sure to see evidence of beaver activity: fallen trees, gnawed tree trunks, and small lodges. Photo by Stephen Mauro.

mountain laurel, and oak saplings. Continue as the creek becomes gradually more turbulent and boulder-strewn. Cross under Scenic Drive on a boardwalk. At 2.9 miles, reach the intersection with Taylor Farm Road.

Turn right onto the blue-blazed Taylor Farm Road and travel gradually uphill for 0.6 mile to High Meadows Trail. Turn right on this orange-blazed trail and meander downhill to Little Run. Turn left over the bridge and begin a sharp rise on a ridge where beeches cling tenuously to the edge. At 3.9 miles, reach Old Black Top Road. Turn right toward the ranger station; go 100 yards then turn left onto the red-blazed Mary Bird Branch Trail. This 0.5-mile trail, named for an early homesteader, goes downhill to a bridge. Cross a short boardwalk and climb the facing ridge, leveling out on top. Upon reaching Scenic Drive (the end of the Mary Bird Branch), cross at the crosswalk and head right (south), to a sign marking the start of Quantico Cascades Trail.

Follow the yellow-blazed Quantico Cascades Trail to Lake One Road, turn left at a double-blazed pine, and proceed 0.1 mile before turning right to reach the "Dinosaurs and Volcanoes" sign. Go steadily downhill, crossing North Valley Trail and continuing on Quantico Cascades Trail toward a hill in the distance. Reach the "Fall Line" sign and head downhill via a series of tight switchbacks, the steepest elevation in the park. At 5.1 miles into the hike, drop onto the rocks of the cascades and note the signing reading, "Power of Water." The slick, almost puttylike rock here is part of the Chopawamsic formation, the result of volcanic eruptions 500 million years ago. Go south along the creek (right) toward North Valley Trail, making sure not to head north on an unmaintained trail.

At 5.3 miles, turn left (south) at a "Y" intersection onto North Valley Trail. Pass a sign reading, "Coastal Plain," and continue following sharp bends in the creek, where massive upland boulders—more dramatic than the cascades to the north—create boiling mini rapids. Stop at a sign reading, "Pyrite Mine," and observe the concrete ruins of old mine buildings. Next, reach the bridge over North Fork Quantico Creek and turn left onto it to follow North Valley Trail to the north bank.

Follow the bank to a boardwalk bisecting a grove of tall pines. To the right is a denuded hill that was the site of the main pyrite mine, shut down in 1920. In 1995, the National Park Service built storm-water channels, planted 5,000 trees, filled the mineshafts, and buried the mine tailings (metal debris) in lime, all in an effort to regenerate plant and animal life. Continue on a boardwalk through more pines at the park's edge, following a depression from a narrow-gauge railroad that once serviced the mine. Turn right at a grove of rare redbuds and cross a bridge back to the south bank of North Fork Quantico Creek.

Twenty yards after the bridge, at 6.8 miles, turn left onto South Valley Trail. Travel for 0.9 mile back to the suspension bridge you saw earlier over South Fork Quantico Creek. Cross it, then return straight up the west edge of Laurel Loop Trail, reaching the parking lot at 7.9 miles.

MORE INFORMATION

Park entry is $7 per vehicle. In addition to the hiking trails, the park has 21 miles of bicycle-accessible trails, two large picnic pavilions, five historic cabins constructed by the Civilian Conservation Corps (see "Roosevelt's Tree Army: The Civilian Conservation Corps," on page 233) available for camping by advance reservation, and four campgrounds. For more information, visit nps.gov/prwi or call the park at 703-221-7181.

NEARBY

The National Museum of the Marine Corps, with its slanted spire evoking the flag raisings at Iwo Jima and visible from I-95, is a state-of-the-art facility whose galleries take visitors through the history and traditions of the Marine Corps. It's located adjacent to Marine Corp Base Quantico, home of the Corps's Officer Candidate School. See usmcmuseum.com.

The historic riverside town of Occoquan oozes a quaint yet eclectic vibe and offers waterside dining and shopping options. Rippon Lodge Historic Site in nearby Woodbridge is a peaceful attraction with its circa-1747 house on 43 acres, old family cemeteries, formal gardens, walking trails, and Potomac River vistas. Tours and special programs are offered seasonally. Visit discoverpwm.com to learn more about these and other area offerings

UNDER COVER: SPIES IN THE PARKS

In the days of the New Deal, President Franklin Delano Roosevelt's Civil Conservation Corps and Works Progress Administration built camps at Chopawamsic Creek (now Prince William Forest Park) and Catoctin Mountain (see Trip 14: Catoctin Mountain Park and Cunningham Falls State Park, on page 66). These facilities offered outdoor experiences for urban youth until the newly created Office of Strategic Services (OSS), the precursor to the Central Intelligence Agency (CIA), appropriated the sites in 1942 to train spies for World War II.

FDR wanted an American special-operations and secret-intelligence force to rival Great Britain's MI6, even though as recently as 1929, Secretary of State Henry Stimson had insisted, "Gentlemen do not read one another's mail." Longstanding U.S. policy eschewed peacetime espionage, so when FDR sought to establish OSS (initially called COI, for Coordinator of Information) in July 1941, prior to Pearl Harbor's bombing, he had to proceed with caution. He tapped an old law school classmate, the decorated World War I Colonel William "Wild Bill" Donovan, to lead the new organization. But Donovan and his aides had no experience building a spy agency. They looked to the Brits to learn a few tricks, then muddled through on their own.

The cabin camps (some of which are available today by reservation) served OSS's top-secret needs well: close to Washington, D.C., yet semi-isolated, with plenty of rugged terrain surrounding them. Recruits—mostly young, college-educated men—lived in the bugged, heavily guarded cabins and learned skills ranging from forgery to forest parachuting, covert radio operations to killing an enemy with a rolled-up newspaper. The Maryland and Virginia forest provided literal cover for fledgling undercover agents developing skills in stealth, concealment, and base-station setup. It was no cakewalk: Four men were killed, and many were injured during training. (The future CIA director William Casey sustained a broken jaw from a tripped booby trap.) In the dark of night, without warning, instructors rousted recruits from their bunks to face real-life, close-range pistol fire combat against "Nazi agents" who hid in a facility dubbed the House of Horrors.

Recruits practiced subtler covertness, too: befriending unsuspecting nearby townspeople, picking locks, spreading black propaganda (false information about an enemy), and sabotage tactics, such as planting sham explosives under local bridges. Known by code names only and restricted to gathering in groups of four or fewer, recruits were forbidden to discuss their assignments. Their purported final exam involved infiltrating an industrial target by gathering information on production and supply or by planning a sabotage. At OSS graduation parties, liquor flowed liberally, and candidates were unwittingly evaluated once again on how much they would reveal under the influence. Utter loyalty was the ultimate test and the final cover they would need to carry out their dangerous work.

34

SKY MEADOWS STATE PARK

Saved from development by the noted philanthropist Paul Mellon in 1975, Sky Meadows State Park offers an incredible blend of pastures and woodlands on the eastern slope of the Blue Ridge Mountains.

DIRECTIONS

From I-495 (Capital Beltway), take Exit 49 west onto I-66 then take US 17 north (Winchester Road) via Exit 23 toward Delaplane/Paris. Go 6.5 miles and turn left onto VA 710 into the park. The road ends at a parking lot near the Mount Bleak House and the visitor center. *GPS coordinates:* 38° 59.118′ N, 77° 57.523′ W.

TRAIL DESCRIPTION

Sky Meadows State Park comprises 1,864 mountain acres on elevations ranging from 600 to 1,800 feet. The park's trails ascend hilly, open meadows then travel through alternating woodlands and pastures at the top of the ridge, which affords stunning views of the surrounding countryside. Throughout the hike, note the great diversity in butterfly species, best enjoyed with close-focusing binoculars and a good field guide. Zebra swallowtails flutter across the trails with regularity, catching a hiker's eye with their majestic patterns of black-and-white stripes and splashes of red on the tails. The monarch butterfly is common in July and August; the ultra-rare giant swallowtail in August only.

Begin your hike at the northwest corner of the parking lot. Follow a connector trail that immediately veers left onto the gravel-surface Boston Mill Road. After a few hundred feet, climb the stone steps to the right and begin the 0.7-mile ascent on the red-blazed Piedmont Overlook Trail. Pass a wooden bridge over a brook and an old

LOCATION
Delaplane, VA

RATING
Moderate

DISTANCE
5.8 miles

ELEVATION GAIN
1,000 feet

ESTIMATED TIME
3 hours

MAPS
USGS Upperville; Potomac Appalachian Trail Club Map 8; map available at park; online: dcr.virginia.gov/state-parks/sky-meadows

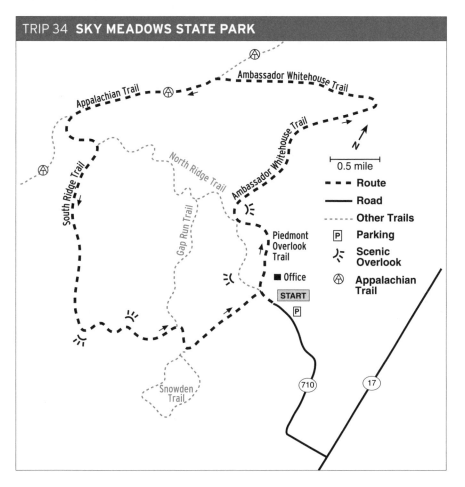

farm building. Continue on for a breath-taking view at Piedmont Overlook and survey the patchwork quilt of pastures and farm fields, interspersed with lakes and streams, stretching across the Crooked Run Valley below. George Washington mapped this area in the 1740s. In 1861, the valley served as the jumping-off point for Confederate soldiers en route to the Battle of Bull Run.

Continue on Piedmont Overlook Trail into a patch of woods, turn right onto the blue-blazed North Ridge Trail, and follow it 0.2 mile. Turn right onto the 1.1-mile Ambassador Whitehouse Trail. This trail arcs northward, crosses a clearing between wooded areas, and heads back into the woods. Keep your eyes and ears open for the ubiquitous red-headed woodpecker, a year-round resident whose drumbeat mating call reverberates through the park in spring and early summer. Blue jays, mockingbirds, and cardinals also abound year-round. A sharp curve left puts you back on open ground. After half a mile, turn left on the white-blazed Appalachian Trail (AT), which stretches south along the ridgeline. The AT extends 2,190 miles between Georgia and Maine; for a sample, simply follow its rocky path for a single mile, through old-growth

Sky Meadows State Park provides hikers with an appealing mix of mountain and pastoral terrain. As one of three Appalachian Trail-connected trips in this guidebook, it offers a good amount of elevation gain. Photo by Alex Ansley, Creative Commons on Flickr.

forest and along a fence line. Watch for a wooden stepladder that climbs the fence to your left. Reenter the woods, travel a few hundred feet, and turn left (east) onto North Ridge Trail. Continue 0.2 mile until you reach an intersection, with South Ridge Trail branching off to the right.

There's a bench here, and it is a great spot to rest and have some lunch before beginning the descent. Turn right onto the 1.6-mile South Ridge Trail and ease into a wide, soft-packed stretch that crosses a series of gentle streams. About halfway down the ridge, make a short side trip to see the ruins of Snowden Manor, a Federal-style house built in the 1860s and mostly consumed by fire in 1913, leaving only a fireplace and a chimney behind. Soon after, you come to another scenic view of the Crooked Run Valley. Then reach a small pond and, finally, an intersection with Boston Mill Road. Turn left (north) here and follow the gravel road half a mile to the parking lot. (Near the intersection of South Ridge Trail and Boston Mill Road is Snowden Trail, an optional 1-mile circuit hike through a mature oak forest.)

MORE INFORMATION

Sky Meadows State Park is open daily, 8 A.M. to dusk. Admission is $4 per vehicle on weekdays and $5 per vehicle on weekends. The park is home to a red-headed woodpecker sanctuary near the contact station at the southern end of the park, just off VA 710. The visitor center has nature and history exhibits, as well as a gift shop. For more information, visit dcr.virginia.gov/state-parks/sky-meadows or call 540-592-3556.

On weekends in spring, summer, and fall, naturalists lead excellent two- to three-hour programs on the diverse butterfly, bird, and wildflower populations, as well as the ecology of the park's streambeds. Astronomy Days take place from spring to fall, in conjunction with the Smithsonian's Albert Einstein Planetarium.

NEARBY

The neighboring hamlet of Delaplane holds its Strawberry Festival every Memorial Day weekend. The G. Richard Thompson Wildlife Management Area (Trip 38, page 189) is a short drive from Sky Meadows, and Signal Knob (Trip 4, page 17) is about 30 miles to the west, making for a nice weekend-getaway combo. This area of Virginia's Piedmont is also home to wineries, antique shops, and historic bed-and-breakfasts in its many small communities.

35

MASON NECK STATE PARK

Mason Neck State Park provides sanctuary for a stunning array of winged predators, including bald eagles, ospreys, herons, and hawks. Its trails traverse sandy beaches, a tidal marsh, and dense woodland.

DIRECTIONS

On the Capital Beltway, from Exit 170 on the inner loop of I-95/I-495 (or from Exit 57 on the outer loop of I-495), go south on I-95 for about 7 miles and take Exit 163 onto Lorton Road (VA 642). Turn left onto Lorton Road, travel 1 mile, turn right onto Armistead Road, and take the second right onto Richmond Highway (US 1). Go about 1 mile and turn left onto Gunston Road, which heads east onto Mason Neck. Travel 4.5 miles, past Pohick Bay Regional Park and Gunston Manor, and turn right onto High Point Road, which leads to both the state park and the wildlife refuge. Pass the park entrance and follow the road straight to the picnic area parking lot and visitor center. *GPS coordinates:* 38° 38.743′ N, 77° 10.330′ W.

TRAIL DESCRIPTION

Mason Neck State Park contains 1,825 acres of shoreline, marshland, and mixed hardwood forest on a peninsula that juts into the Potomac River 18 miles south of Washington, D.C. The nearby Mason Neck National Wildlife Refuge (to the south and east), Gunston Hall plantation and Pohick Bay Regional Park (to the northeast), and Meadowood Special Recreation Management Area (to the north) combine to protect 6,400 acres of the 8,000-acre peninsula. Each destination offers hiking trails (in addition to canoe and kayak launches, bike paths, picnic areas, and nature overlooks), but the state park has the best-maintained and most extensive trail system. It also has one of the highest concentrations of bald eagles in northern Virginia, with

LOCATION
Lorton, VA

RATING
Moderate

DISTANCE
5.4 miles

ELEVATION GAIN
250 feet

ESTIMATED TIME
2.5 to 3 hours

MAPS
USGS Fort Belvoir; map available at visitor center; online: dcr.virginia.gov/state-parks/mason-neck

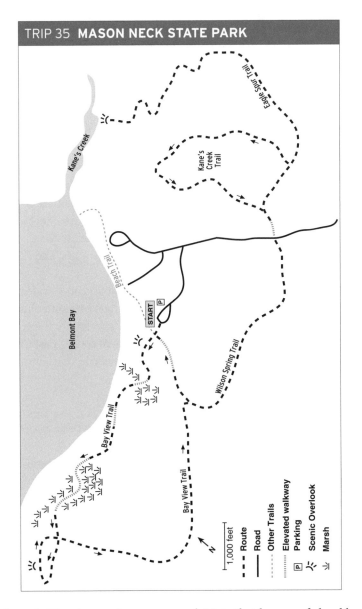

approximately 50 pairs nesting year-round. Note that because federal law mandates a 750-foot berth for bald eagle nests in national and state parks, trails are often relocated. Check with the visitor center for recent changes.

Begin the hike on the 1-mile, red-blazed Bay View Trail, which you can enter at the back left corner of the picnic area parking lot. This trail traces the shoreline of Belmont Bay, follows a creek upstream to a large tidal marsh, and passes into the forest. Begin by following the broad, dirt-and-mulch path a short distance along the cliff above the shore then ascend a series of wooden steps to a small bridge over a wet area. Continue on the sandy trail across a second wooden walkway, where stands of honeysuckle enliven the meeting of land and water. The walkway affords an excellent view of Belmont Bay. Note the gabion barriers slowing erosion on the shoreline. Mason Neck suffers from wave erosion caused by polluted waters, with many shore trees clinging to the tops of the sandy cliffs. Bay View Trail has to be periodically shifted inland due to cliff erosion. (Make sure to heed the postings for restoration areas.)

Arc back inland along a wooden fence and come to a boardwalk over a creek, where bay water flows into and out of the tidal marsh system, supporting a diverse wildlife population. Continuing on the boardwalk, enter a variegated tidal zone of spatterdock, wild rice, and cattail punctuated by wood duck habitats constructed as part of an Eagle Scout project. Take time to spot birds and other wildlife. During high tide, you might see large fish, including largemouthed bass, longnose gar, and carp, skirting underneath the planks of the boardwalk. At low tide, you sometimes can view frogs, snakes, and salamanders throughout the year.

At the end of the boardwalk, enter the woods and ascend wooden steps that transition to gnarled roots; forge straight ahead to an observation blind for more views of the freshwater marsh. Loop back around and follow the trail's winding path through a mature, upland, mixed hardwood forest, past an area that bears the marks of a 1986 fire. You still can see burn marks on the trees, and the

Mason Neck State Park's elevated boardwalks offer hikers the chance to observe waterfowl and other marshland species up close. Photo by Virginia State Parks, Creative Commons on Flickr.

reduced understory growth in this area has given rise to thriving blueberry and huckleberry bushes.

Return to the main Bay View Trail, then bear right onto the 0.5-mile, yellow-blazed Wilson Spring Trail. Walk along the leafy and root-covered trail as it alternately gains and loses elevation, crossing two wooden bridges over swampy runoff. Soon after the second bridge, cross High Point Multiuse Trail, a parking area, and the main entrance road. Continue on an elevated walkway and veer right onto the 1-mile, blue-blazed Kane's Creek Trail. Travel a quick 200 feet before turning right again, onto the 1.25-mile, white-blazed Eagle Spur Trail. This is a straight out-and-back hike and the most strenuous section. This trail hugs ridgelines and plunges down into small valleys, traversing intermittently flowing streams via wooden planks. Oak, beech, and sweetgum trees—the latter with their ubiquitous, spiky, ball-shaped seedpods—line the way, and red-backed salamanders swarm over dead logs and away from stomping feet, especially after a rainfall.

At the end of Eagle Spur Trail is an observation blind over Kane's Creek, a year-round nesting and roosting area for the magnificent bald eagle. Bald eagles are best spotted in the morning hours or at dusk, when park rangers lead guided tours to assist in observation. When you've had your fill of bird-watching, retrace the 1.25-mile hike down Eagle Spur Trail, turning right at the circular Kane's Creek Trail. This pleasant loop is fairly level and returns to Wilson Spring Trail. Retrace 0.5 mile down Wilson Spring Trail and turn right onto Bay View Trail, continuing over a boardwalk and back to the starting point.

MORE INFORMATION

Mason Neck's trails are open year-round, 8 A.M. to dusk. There is a per-vehicle fee to enter the park: in-state plates are $4 on weekdays, $5 on weekends; out-of-state plates are $6 on weekdays, $7 on weekends. All pets must be on a leash no longer than 6 feet at all times. The picnic area parking lot can fill on weekends or holidays; you can also start this hike at the Wilson Spring Trail parking lot, a short distance south on the entrance road. The park offers canoe and kayak rentals for access to Kane's Creek (April through October, weather depending), a perfect opportunity to spot bald eagles, ospreys, great blue heron, beaver, and even otters. Bicycles rentals are available for High Point Multiuse Trail. For more information, visit dcr.virginia.gov/state-parks/mason-neck or call 703-339-2385.

NEARBY

Pohick Bay Regional Park has excellent recreational facilities, including a water park, Frisbee golf, and a mini golf course. Also nearby is George Mason's plantation, Gunston Hall, which is open for tours and also offers a riverside bird walk (see Trip 41: George Mason Plantation River Walk, on page 203).

36

BANSHEE REEKS NATURE PRESERVE

If you're hoping to get off the beaten path and enjoy the beauty of northern Virginia, head to Banshee Reeks for a ramble through its mixture of fields and forests, where civilization feels a hundred miles away.

DIRECTIONS

From I-495 (Capital Beltway), take Exit 45A onto VA 267. Travel 22.5 miles then take Exit 3. Turn left onto Shreve Mill Road/VA 653. Turn right onto Evergreen Mill road and continue for 2.4 miles, at which point the entrance to the park is on the right, at 21085 The Woods Road. *GPS Coordinates:* 39° 1.720′ N, 77° 35.972′ W.

TRAIL DESCRIPTION

Banshee Reeks is a 725-acre preserve, an enclave of nature in sharp contrast to the subdivisions and housing developments springing up around it in Leesburg, Virginia. Despite the proximity to suburban neighborhoods, the landscape along these carefully maintained trails looks and feels remote, even a bit rough around the edges. With its restricted hours—open to the public only on Saturdays and Sundays from 8 A.M. to 4 P.M.—Banshee Reeks is likely to stay somewhat wild.

The Gaelic term *reeks* refers to the area's rolling hills, and a banshee is a female spirit. But the preserve's unusual name has less to do with a haunting than with an over-indulgence in a different sort of spirit. According to the park's website, the nineteenth-century owner of the farm that became Banshee Reeks spent an evening at the saloon in nearby Leesburg and, in his intoxicated state upon returning to the farm, mistook the howling of the wind for the shrieks of a banshee.

LOCATION
Leesburg, VA

RATING
Moderate

DISTANCE
5.2 miles

ELEVATION GAIN
215 feet

ESTIMATED TIME
2.5 hours

MAPS
USGS Leesburg; map by Friends of Banshee Reeks is available for free at kiosk in front of the visitor center; online: bansheereeksnp.org/Explore-Preserve/Trail-Maps

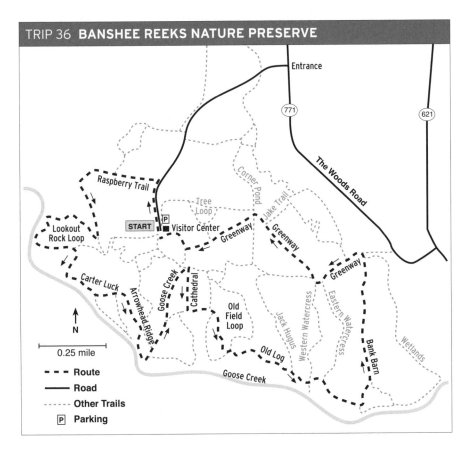

Although you won't see any ghosts in the preserve, its beauty is haunting. You are likely to glimpse a variety of wildlife as you hike through successional fields, meadows, and mixed hardwood forests. Located in the Piedmont ecosystem, the preserve is home to a broad spectrum of wildlife, including white-tailed deer, beavers, foxes, skunks, turkeys, and many other types of birds. A list of some 220 bird species that may be seen in the preserve is available at the kiosk in the parking area.

Some wildlife is a welcome sight, but other residents of the preserve are less welcome—ticks are prevalent here. As you drive in, you may see a sign reading "Designated tick area." Many of the trails pass through grassy fields where ticks may be abundant, particularly in spring and early summer. Wear long pants that are tight-fitting or tuck looser pants into high socks, and check for ticks when leaving Banshee Reeks. Alternatively, choose a winter weekend for your visit.

Parking is free near the visitor center, which is open only on the third weekend of each month, at which time there is also a volunteer day focused on trail improvements and other projects. A portable toilet by the parking lot provides restroom facilities when the visitor center is closed. From the parking lot,

Raspberry Trail runs parallel to the road as a mowed path through the grass. At the first left turn, look left for a broad view of the southwest and the Bull Run Mountains. The trail will climb gently as you begin this loop, with thorny bushes and scrubby growth lining the way. Summer brings an explosion of more than 190 species of wildflowers to the preserve. In August, also look for non-native Queen Anne's lace throughout the park.

At the intersection with Lookout Trail, continue on Raspberry Trail. The path remains straight and flat. Look left here to see the visitor center in the distance as the field slopes slightly down from the trail. At the next intersection, turn right onto Lookout Rock Trail. You'll leave the field behind, climbing gently on the rocky, rooted path. After you pass another intersection with Raspberry Trail, look for berry bushes lining the path as you descend to a "Y" intersection. A little ways to the right is a view of Goose Creek, a designated Virginia Scenic River that borders the south end of the preserve. The creek is calm in some places, but bear in mind that swimming is not allowed in the preserve. Keep an eye out for great blue herons, kingfishers, osprey, and bald eagles along the creek.

At the next intersection, turn right onto Carter Luck Trail. Watch out for thorns along the trail in this forested section. At the unmarked intersection, continue straight. Soon the trail widens, and at the marked intersection take a left to continue toward Arrowhead Ridge. The trail curves left, then right, heading into deeper forest. At the next intersection, turn left toward Goose Creek. Immediately cross a log bridge over a narrow tributary. From here, the trail winds and snakes through thick forest. In winter, you have a lovely view to the right where the tributary joins Goose Creek.

At the intersection of Carter Luck Trail and Goose Creek Trail, turn left onto Goose Creek Trail then turn left again to stay on this trail at the next unmarked intersection. At the intersection with Arrowhead Trail, turn right to stay on Goose Creek Trail, which climbs steeply. As you crest the slope on a broad, grassy path, look left for a view north, across the successional fields to the visitor center.

As you arrive at a farm and gate, take a sharp right onto Cathedral Trail and then another immediate right. Descend down a mowed corridor through a grassy field to a cluster of trees at the edge of a tall, thick forest. Turn left here to head toward the south end of Old Field Loop, first climbing gently then more steeply for a time. The path crosses a forested grove and winds over a small rise before descending to an intersection. Take a right onto Old Log Trail then an immediate left. This dirt trail, crisscrossed with roots, rises and falls before crossing a creek bed.

Soon after, turn right on the southern end of the Jack Hugus/Western Watercress loop. At the intersection with Western Watercress, stay right and cross a narrow creek. Arrive at the intersection with Eastern Watercress and Bank Barn trails. Bear right on Bank Barn Trail. This trail, which takes you

A hiker peers into an abandoned farmhouse just off the Greenway Trail, in Banshee Reeks Nature Preserve. The preserve, named for its rolling hills, was once a working farm. Photo by Annie Eddy.

north to the top of your loop, passes through strikingly beautiful tunnel-like vegetation, giving the impression of traversing a maze made of vines and trees.

At the next intersection, stay on Bank Barn Trail, turning left to head north. Climb moderately, emerging into a less forested area. When you reach the intersection with Wetlands and Greenway trails, take Greenway uphill to a cluster of old barns and buildings with nice field views on either side. Take a left to stay on Greenway, which takes you back to the visitor center; this trail is as wide as a single-lane road. Stay on Greenway for the remainder of your hike. Pass the north terminus of both East and West Watercress trails on your left, as well as intersections with Woodchuck Trail, Jake's Trail, Jack Hugus Trail, Corner Pond Trail, and Tree Loop. Stay straight, climbing gently and steadily. This part of the trail is very open, so you may wish to get out your sunscreen.

Pass through a field dotted with bluebird houses. Look left to see silos blanketed with native Virginia creeper vines. The trail crosses the access road that leads to the silos and ends at a "T" as the visitor center comes into view. Turn right onto the gravel road, which shortly curves around to return to the visitor center and parking area.

MORE INFORMATION

Dogs are allowed, but must be leashed. Bikes and horses are not allowed in the park. Although access to the park is generally limited to its weekend hours, visits by organized groups during the week are sometimes allowed by appointment. Contact info@bansheereeksnp.org to inquire.

NEARBY

Set in idyllic countryside, Banshee Reeks is surrounded by farms and vineyards. See virginia.org/winetrails for a vineyard near Banshee Reeks to sweeten your day trip.

37

BULL RUN MOUNTAINS NATURAL AREA

Bull Run, the closest mountain range to Washington, D.C., provides hikers with rugged— but not overwhelming—terrain, plus the ruins of a five-story gristmill dating to 1742.

DIRECTIONS

From I-495 (Capital Beltway), take Exit 49 west onto I-66. Go 27 miles and take Exit 40 (Haymarket). At the end of the exit ramp, turn left at the traffic light onto US 15 south (James Madison Highway). Go 0.5 mile to the next light and turn right onto VA 55 (John Marshall Highway) west. Go 2.7 miles (crossing railroad tracks at 2 miles) and turn right onto Turner Road. Follow it a short distance across I-66 then turn left onto Beverley Mill Drive. Go 0.8 mile to Mountain House at the end of the road. *GPS coordinates*: 38° 49.516′ N, 77° 42.183′ W.

TRAIL DESCRIPTION

Bull Run Mountains Natural Area consists of 2,500 acres near Haymarket, Virginia. Bull Run Mountains Conservancy (BRMC), a private nonprofit organization, protects the unique ecosystem through education, research, and stewardship, and manages public access to the southern 800 acres of the natural area. Hikers are required to sign a waiver-of-liability form, which protects the conservancy from potential lawsuits. BRMC's trails are on the north side of Thoroughfare Gap and are available anytime during daylight hours.

At the trail kiosk off the parking area, sign the liability waiver and pick up a map. The numbers on the map identify the trail intersections, and the legend at the bottom shows the trails by color code (except for Alternate Trail); hikers are cautioned to disregard any trail blazes painted on trees. Small colored disks identify trails at each intersection.

LOCATION
Broad Run, VA

RATING
Moderate

DISTANCE
3.5 miles

ELEVATION GAIN
810 feet

ESTIMATED TIME
2 to 2.5 hours

MAPS
USGS Thoroughfare Gap; free map at trailhead; online: brmconservancy.org

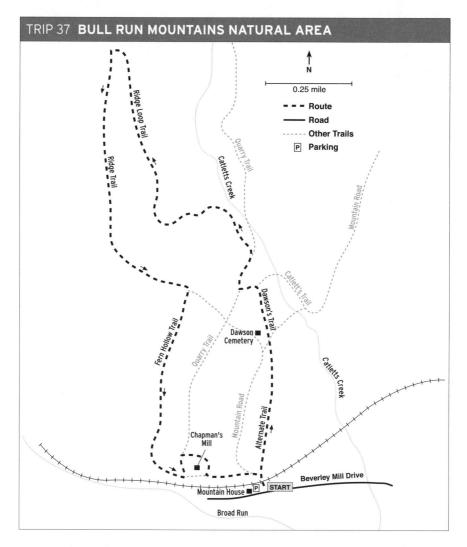

From the parking area, cross the railroad tracks and follow Alternate Trail to the right (north). The trail is narrow but well defined and moves gradually up the ridge at a moderate incline. At the large intersection marked with posts 6 and 7, follow the sign for Dawson's Trail and go straight through the inter-section down a wide path. Descend slightly into a small draw then over a small finger-shaped ridge. Note a small beech tree with a sign pointing the way to Dawson's cemetery. Turn right and walk 100 yards to visit it. More than 150 years old, the carvings on the gravestones seem remarkably well preserved, but BRMC personnel are certain they are authentic. Go back to Dawson's Trail, turn right, and proceed to intersection 11.

The trail map shows a left turn here onto Catlett's Trail, but the actual path is generally straight ahead. Follow Catlett's Trail 150 yards past a small stream to arrive at intersection 10. The brown sign on a large beech tree shows Quarry

Trail (or road) to the left; turn slightly right, off Catlett's Trail. At intersection 13, Quarry Trail crosses the stream to the right; turn left here onto Ridge Loop Trail. Twenty-five yards up the trail, cross the stream and climb steeply for about 100 yards. The grade lessens as you continue up the side of the ridge over exposed, jagged rocks. Bend to the left and follow the moderate incline. Exposed ledges—ancient quartzite transformed by heating and pressure into hard metamorphic rock—cover much of the side of the ridge. At the head (narrow point) of the draw, still on Ridge Loop Trail, turn right and continue up the side of the ridge.

The ridge is the southern extension of High Point Mountain. At intersection 14, turn left onto Ridge Trail, along the spine of the ridge. After a little more than half a mile, the trail turns left down the steep side of the ridge. At intersection 9, turn right onto Fern Hollow Trail and, within a few hundred yards, cross a short wooden walkway above a small stream. Descend gently down the hollow and cross a second wooden walkway above another small stream. The small concrete box cistern was built in the 1930s to hold water for the mill worker's house.

At the bottom of the hollow, near intersection 4 in a grove of young beech trees, is a dilapidated wooden house with a collapsed roof and walls. Until the nearby Chapman's Mill—built in 1742 and also known as Beverley Mill—was closed in 1951, a mill worker resided in this building. At intersection 4, turn

Hikers can catch glimpses of the historic Chapman's Mill, situated between Bull Run and the railroad tracks running along Bull Run Mountains Natural Area. Photo by Stephen Little, Creative Commons on Flickr.

left and cross a marshy streambed via a wooden walkway. The trail continues through more wet and muddy areas, but rocks, along with some logs, provide paths across. To the right are the railroad tracks you crossed at the beginning of the hike. Approach intersection 3 and notice the high stone walls of Chapman's Mill and the waters of Broad Run, which once powered that mill. At intersection 3, turn left onto Quarry Trail and walk a few hundred yards up a fairly steep hill to Quarry Trench, the site of the Battle of Thoroughfare Gap, a fierce Civil War battle that played an important role in the 1862 Second Manassas Campaign. Opposite the trench at intersection 5, a brown sign indicates Chapman Trail (not named on the trail map) to the right. The trail is not well defined, but following it about 800 yards down the hill leads to the Chapman Family Cemetery, surrounded by a stone wall. From the cemetery, retrace your steps about 100 yards and turn left down the hill along a narrow path to a large sycamore tree laced with creeper vines. At intersection 2, turn left onto Mill Trail (also not named on the trail map), where there is a large stone-lined pit on the right. Continue down the trail, cross a crooked wooden walkway, go past intersection 1 (staying to the right), then go over the tracks to the trail kiosk and parking area.

MORE INFORMATION

Pets are not allowed in the preserve. Visit brmconservancy.org to download a trail map, a release and waiver of liability, a calendar with public programs, and other information. Chapman's Mill is open on weekends and some holidays. Visit chapmansmill.org to learn about the mill's history and ongoing restoration efforts.

NEARBY

The village of The Plains, just a short distance to the west along VA 55 (John Marshall Highway), is an icon of northern Virginia's horse and hunt country. It hosts various equestrian events spring through fall at its Great Meadow venue, such as the Virginia Gold Cup steeplechase race the first Saturday in May. A seasonal corn maze run by locals is a harvest-time attraction. Check theplainsvirginia.com and greatmeadow.org for current information.

For one of the region's most enchanting scenic drives in any season of the year, continue north from The Plains on VA 626 (passing several wineries on the way) to another lovely country village, Middleburg, where you'll find taverns and antique shops to enjoy. See middleburgonline.com for details. Then take U.S. 50 east back toward Washington, pausing in the hamlet of Aldie to view another restored mill, the Aldie Mill; visit aldieheritage.com for information.

History buffs will be interested to learn that Aldie and Middleburg are among 57 historic towns included along a different sort of trail, the Journey through Hallowed Ground historic trail, which stretches 180 miles from Charlottesville, Virginia to Gettysburg, Pennsylvania. Find out more at hallowedground.org.

38

G. RICHARD THOMPSON WILDLIFE MANAGEMENT AREA

The trails at G. Richard Thompson Wildlife Management Area crest the Blue Ridge Mountains to reach heights of 2,200 feet above sea level. In springtime, the area is adorned with Virginia's best display of trillium flowers.

DIRECTIONS

From I-495 (Capital Beltway), take Exit 49 west onto I-66 then take Exit 23 toward Delaplane/Paris for US 17 (Winchester Road) north. Go 6.5 miles then turn left onto VA 688 (Leeds Manor Road) into the wildlife management area. After 2.5 miles, turn right into the Lake Thompson parking area, which contains two lots. Park in the northern lot near Lake Thompson. *GPS coordinates*: 38° 57.446′ N, 77° 59.327′ W.

TRAIL DESCRIPTION

The Virginia Department of Game and Inland Fisheries stewards 36 wildlife management areas (WMAs) across the state that encompass 200,000 acres of public land. To maximize hunting and fishing opportunities, WMAs introduce species, burn undergrowth, plant edible wildflowers, develop hedgerows, and stock ponds. Hunting is allowed, but hikers can enjoy one of northern Virginia's largest and best natural areas during open seasons by wearing bright safety clothing and staying on designated trails.

G. Richard Thompson WMA is broken into two tracts; the much larger southern tract has elevations between 700 and 2,200 feet above sea level, with the Appalachian Trail (AT) spanning the ridgeline for 7 miles on its western boundary. Generally speaking, as you go west, you go uphill. Eleven parking spots surround the area, and several trails running east to west connect the parking lots on either side.

LOCATION
Delaplane, VA

RATING
Strenuous

DISTANCE
8.8 miles

ELEVATION GAIN
1,750 feet

ESTIMATED TIME
4.5 to 5 hours

MAPS
USGS Linden, USGS Upperville; Potomac Appalachian Trail Club Map 8: Snickers Gap to Chester Gap; online: dgif .virginia.gov/wma/thompson/

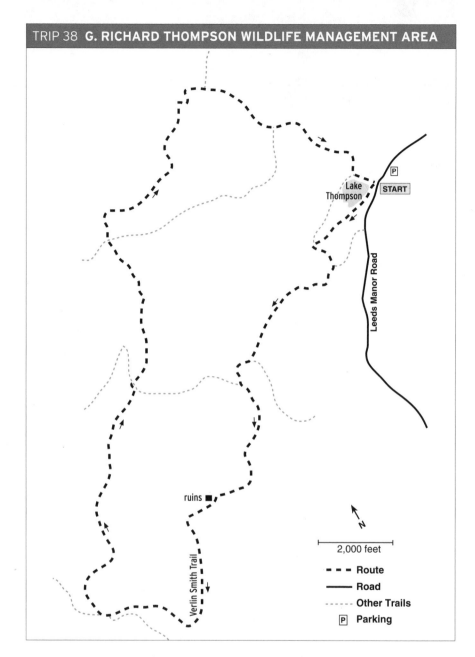

One of this hike's main attractions is the large-flowered trillium that blooms along the trail from late April to early June. Added to the trillium are dozens of other vibrant wildflowers, an impressionistic blend of showy orchids, yellow lady's slippers, sweet cicely, golden ragwort, lousewort, wild hydrangea, buttonbush, and fleabane. The final feather in Thompson's bountiful cap is its 10-acre Lake Thompson, which is stocked with trout as well as bluegill, sunfish, catfish, and bass.

A rugged dirt road in G. Richard Thompson Wildlife Management Area testifies to the preserve's unspoiled atmosphere. Mid-spring, look for abundant trillium blooming along the trails. Photo by Stephen Mauro.

From the parking lot, walk 100 yards down the gravel path to the lake and continue along the south shore. At the end of the lake, a deep ravine cradles the streambed, opening to the right. The ascent gradually becomes steeper until, at 0.6 mile from the starting point, another trail joins from the right, signaling a sharp shift to the left and the beginning of steep and rocky terrain.

Turn right at the "T" intersection onto the unmarked Verlin Smith Trail. Here the trail runs along a wire fence at the border of the WMA. Beyond the fence are open hillsides with farms, vineyards, and solar-panel-equipped houses. Travel uphill along the fence for 200 yards then veer right for a 0.5-mile climb, gaining 300 feet of elevation on a widening red-dirt trail to a convergence with another trail that comes in on the left and a clearing. Continue past granite boulders and curve gently to the left. At a dilapidated sheet-metal shack, turn left to stay on Verlin Smith Trail.

Go downhill. Kettle Run, a shaded stream, glides across the path. This is a good place to spot birds, box turtles, and snakes. Cross the stream and trek uphill again, passing through a clearing with dense, chest-high flowering plants. The trail levels out; at 0.2 mile from the clearing, it follows a rocky streambed for about 15 yards. Turn to the right to reach Wildcat Hollow Spring, which flows through granite boulders strewn across the path. Proceed on more sharp-edged rocks, traveling back uphill out of the ravine and along a gradual, narrow, and pleasant dirt trail. Swing abruptly right at a large clearing that on clear days affords a view of the humpback, twin-peaked Wildcat Knob in the distance. Soon the trail widens and becomes gravelly.

Under a grove of large-leafed yellow poplars, the white-blazed AT comes in from the left to combine with Verlin Smith Trail. This point marks the beginning of the journey along the rocky spine of the mountain. The smooth rock here makes this a pleasant perch, offering a moment of tranquility. Make sure to turn right 50 yards or so ahead onto the AT, as the wide Verlin Smith Trail continues straight to a parking lot. A little way ahead, the AT follows a rocky streambed along a gentle curve. Continuing on, the trail becomes rocky and steep, as hickories, white ash, chestnut oaks, and a few sassafras trees—the leaves of which make a tasty seasoning used by American Indians—crowd the path.

A blue-blazed trail (leading to more parking and a view of microwave/radio towers) breaks away to the left. Go straight, toward a pin cherry tree standing directly in the trail. Begin descending until you reach an intersection with a wide, gravelly spur trail. Turn left. (To the right, the trail returns to Verlin Smith Trail near the ruined shack.) Almost immediately, double white markers on a tree to the right mark the scenic byway of the AT. Proceed down a level path lined with tall hickories spreading horizontal limbs of thick foliage overhead—what AT thru-hikers call the Green Tunnel.

Just after an open clearing, another side trail intersects the path. Go straight. Pass a large, smooth boulder that looks like a Martian spacecraft. After an uphill stretch, a small, narrow trail breaks off to the left to yet another parking area. Again, stay on the AT as it veers right and begins a long, gradual descent. The ground alternates between sharp rocks and soft-packed dirt, with some dramatic granite boulders. At the "Y" intersection, go left to check out Dick's Dome shelter before proceeding on. In summer this section, unofficially known as Stone Wall Trail, is overgrown, requiring extra effort to move through the junglelike mass of clothes-grasping raspberry bushes and devil's walking stick. At points, the trail is completely consumed, making it difficult to locate its twists and turns.

Scramble over some old stone ruins. A connector trail spanning the WMA intersects from the right, opening a bigger, less-dense path ahead. On this downhill stretch, the trail alternates between dense vegetation and open areas. Descend to the lake and turn left along its eastern edge to return to the parking lot.

MORE INFORMATION

If you have time, scenic US 50 is the best way to reach Thompson WMA, passing through beautiful horse country. To learn more about the Thompson WMA, visit dgif.virginia.gov/wma/thompson. See Trip 34: Sky Meadows State Park and Trip 48: Signal Knob for hikes to combine in a weekend getaway. Many unexpected treasures await visitors along the side roads in these parts, such as the Apple House on VA 55 in nearby Linden, a good choice for a hearty Virginia breakfast or lunch—with or without cider donuts.

39

RIVERBEND PARK AND GREAT FALLS PARK

A hike from Riverbend to Great Falls offers dynamic, changing views of the Potomac River as it churns through class 5 rapids at Great Falls then flows into the narrow Mather Gorge.

DIRECTIONS

From downtown Washington, D.C., take US 50 (Constitution Avenue) west. Continuing as it becomes I-66, go over Theodore Roosevelt Memorial Bridge and keep right at the end of the bridge, merging onto George Washington Memorial Parkway north. Proceed 9 miles to I-495 (Capital Beltway), Exit 43. Cross I-495 and take the outer loop. Go 1 mile and take Exit 44 west, VA 193 (Georgetown Pike). Continue 4.6 miles on the Georgetown Pike, passing Great Falls Park on the right and turning right onto River Bend Road. Go 2.2 miles on River Bend Road, turn right onto Jeffery Road, and right again onto Potomac Hills Street, which ends at the visitor center. *GPS coordinates:* 39° 1.123′ N, 77° 14.787′ W.

TRAIL DESCRIPTION

Fairfax County's Riverbend and Great Falls parks, managed by the National Park Service, are only a few miles apart along the Virginia bank of the Potomac River. They are linked by the Potomac Heritage National Scenic Trail (PHNST). The main advantage of starting a hike at Riverbend Park is the free parking, as Great Falls National Park charges an entrance fee of $10 per vehicle, good for three days. For excellent hiking on the Maryland side of the Potomac at Great Falls, see Trip 20: Billy Goat Trail at Great Falls.

Starting along the relatively calm waters at Riverbend, this southward journey takes you by the Great Falls of the Potomac River and, equally dramatic, the Mather Gorge.

LOCATION
Great Falls, VA

RATING
Moderate

DISTANCE
6.8 miles

ELEVATION GAIN
1,100 feet

ESTIMATED TIME
4 to 4.5 hours

MAPS
USGS Seneca, USGS Vienna, USGS Falls Church; online: fairfaxcounty.gov/parks/riverbend-park/ and nps.gov/grfa

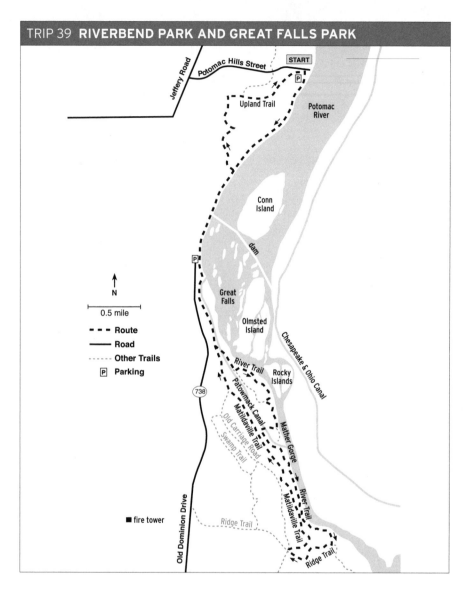

This trail also skirts the well-preserved remains of the eighteenth-century Patowmack Canal, a remarkable engineering feat begun by George Washington and now recognized as a National Historic Landmark.

From the parking lot, head toward the river and turn right on the PHNST to begin the 1.75-mile segment to the Great Falls visitor center. Walk past the boat launch and picnic areas to enter the riverside forest, where sycamore trees lean almost horizontally above the water, complementing the understory of tropical-looking pawpaw trees. At 0.5 mile, pass a side trail that leads to Weant Drive. Just after the intersection, ascend along a rocky ledge carved into the hillside. Note the exposed, 500-million-year-old metamorphic rock, formed when the African continent pushed into the North American continent and lifted

Formed of rock dating back some 500 million years, the Potomac's Great Falls beckons visitors with an otherworldly mystique and mesmerizing erosive power. Photo by Stephen Mauro.

the ocean floor. (See "Far Away in Time: The Geology of Great Falls," on page 197) At 0.6 mile, reach the intersection with Upland Trail, and at 0.9 mile, take a small bridge over a stream that marks the southern boundary of Riverbend Park. At the 1-mile mark is a small sign for Great Falls Park. An overlook offers a clear view of the aqueduct dam—the northern limit for boat traffic on the Potomac, due to the nearby falls—and of Conn Island in the center of the river.

After the dam, the trail follows a wide gravel service road. Abandon it at 1.3 miles with a slight left onto River Trail, a natural-surface trail that returns to the river (look for a river hazard sign at the split). At 1.5 miles, the remnants of the 200-year-old Great Falls Skirting Canal come into view on the left. The first structure is the wing dam, which funneled water into the canal built by the Patowmack Company between 1786 and 1802. When completed, the canal was 1,820 yards long and had five lift locks to carry boats past the falls to the gorge below. Eventually, however, canals were displaced by railroads, as year-round maintenance was too difficult and could not meet the demands of commercial transportation.

Follow the trail along the canal inland, crossing a bridge over Mine Run and reaching the visitor center at 1.75 miles. The center is worth a stop for its collection of artifacts from the amusement park that once existed at nearby Matildaville. South of the visitor center, go left across the canal bed and onto Patowmack Canal Trail, which offers access to three falls overlooks. Churning rapids tumble 40 feet in 200 yards through a maze of jagged, weather-beaten rocks. At average flow, the river cascades to a 25-foot-deep pool just below the falls, but after a snowmelt or heavy rains, it can swell and overflow the narrow Mather Gorge. A sign on Patowmack Canal Trail marks the water level during several heavy, twentieth-century floods, including the 1996 flood that put portions of Alexandria, Harpers Ferry, and the Chesapeake & Ohio Canal towpath underwater.

Proceed past a picnic area and turn left back to the blue-blazed PHNST as it forges uphill and begins to navigate around granite boulders. At 2.4 miles, descend to a wooden footbridge over a steep feeder stream, cross it, and climb back uphill to the cliffs above Mather Gorge, named for Stephen T. Mather, the first director of the National Park Service. At 2.6 miles, a sign signals a right turn back over the canal cut. Upon leaving the canal, turn immediately left to continue on the PHNST, following what becomes a tree-lined bluff above Mather Gorge. Soon the thin gorge widens into the larger Potomac Gorge, marking a point where the river crosses the fall line between the Appalachian Piedmont and the Atlantic Coastal Plain. At 2.9 miles, the blue-blazed trail reaches a road that leads down to Sandy Landing. Cross it diagonally to the right and follow the trail into a small ravine and up the opposite side. Continue, passing through a notch in a spine of boulders. With the river to the left, follow the path along the slope and up to Cow Hoof Rock. From here, follow the blue blazes uphill past a faint intersecting trail from the right. Continue to the "T" intersection and turn right onto Ridge Trail. At 3.3 miles is a five-way intersection: Turn slightly right here onto Old Carriage Road. Take an immediate right onto Matildaville Trail, which passes through the indistinct ruins of a town founded by the Revolutionary War commander "Light Horse" Henry Lee, who named it for his first wife. Just north of the ghost town, return to the Old Carriage Road and go past the visitor center.

Continue on the trail. At 5.8 miles, turn left where a sign marks the beginning of Upland Trail. Ascend the rocky path away from the floodplain to an upland forest of oaks, hickories, and beeches. Cruise along the streambed to your right then turn right onto a smoother stretch of Upland Trail. Next cross an east-west path that leads to Weant Drive. Continue downhill, still on Upland Trail, and at 6.1 miles, come to a "T" intersection that faces a streambed with a ridge rising behind it. Turn left (northwest) to stay on the marked Upland Trail. At a "Y" intersection, continue to the right and cross the streambed, climbing through a rich carpet of ferns to the top the ridge. Upon arriving at another "T" intersection, go right then turn right again at the "Y" intersection to travel back to the Riverbend visitor center.

MORE INFORMATION

Riverbend Park is open from 7 A.M. to dusk and offers canoe and kayak rentals from May to October, as well as a number of exercise classes and expert-led bird-watching excursions at the nature center. Leashed dogs are permitted. Visit fairfaxcounty.gov/parks/riverbend or call 703-759-9018. For information about Great Falls National Park, visit nps.gov/grfa or call 703-757-3103.

FAR AWAY IN TIME: THE GEOLOGY OF GREAT FALLS

If the rocky channel carrying the roiling Potomac River through Great Falls seems like a vision from a cruder world, far away in time, that's only natural. More than 500 million years ago, the long-vanished Iapetus Ocean covered this spot. Its floor was a layer of graywacke, or mud and sand coalescing into sandstone. The ocean's underlying crust eventually shifted and sank, scraping against the hard edge of Taconia, one island of a volcanic archipelago whose tectonic plate was on the slow move toward present-day North America. The ensuing collision helped build the Appalachian Mountains 450 million years ago. Meanwhile, the approaching crust acted like a bulldozer, pushing chunks of graywacke into an underwater heap. Tectonic pressure and volcanic heat churned and melted this sedimentary rock into metamorphic rocks: metagraywacke, gneiss, and schists.

Migmatite, 460 million years old, is heavily folded layers of medium-gray metagraywacke, with wispy swirls of other rock types (granite, schist, quartz) injected by volcanic activity deep beneath Earth's surface then cooled as pressure pushed the mass away from its heat source. Also look for 530-million-year-old amphibolite, a metamorphic hornblende rock with an igneous protolith (source rock) and a dark-gray, hammered surface. Sedimentary graywacke still appears in bed formations; the coarser the grain of a layer within a bed, the longer ago the particles settled—as long as 600 million years back into Earth's past.

The rocks of the Mather Gorge Formation, just downstream from Great Falls, contain veins of whitish quartz, pink feldspar, deep-red garnet, mica, and other minerals. Lamprophyre dikes—near-vertical layers of 360-million-year-old igneous rock forced upward by heat into cracks in surrounding rock—stretch across Mather Gorge from Maryland to Virginia, noticeably misaligned. One possible explanation is that a fault line beneath the river sliced through the gorge, making the lamprophyre shudder from side to side. Lamprophyre's presence is often linked with gold deposits; indeed, gold was mined for decades along the Maryland bank of the falls.

Much of this geologic richness lay buried until the last ice age, 20,000 to 30,000 years ago. Before that time, the Potomac flowed across a higher, broad valley. Dropping sea levels and massive snowfalls caused the river to flow stronger and cut deeper, exposing the bedrock. Over millennia, erosion formed successive river terraces that are still visible today.

40

HUNTLEY MEADOWS PARK

Huntley Meadows is a 1,400-acre natural oasis in the heart of suburbia, less than a mile from the hustle and bustle of US 1. A prime birding location, it contains a large freshwater marsh that supports more than 200 species.

DIRECTIONS

From I-95/I-495 (Capital Beltway), take Exit 177 south onto US 1 (Richmond Highway). Travel 3 miles through a series of traffic lights then turn right onto Lockheed Boulevard. Go 0.7 mile to the "T" intersection with Harrison Lane. Turn left into the park's main entrance. The visitor center parking lot is ahead. *GPS coordinates*: 38° 45.611' N, 77° 05.736' W.

TRAIL DESCRIPTION

The trails at Huntley Meadows Park do not cover great distances but feature scenic boardwalks traversing the 500-acre freshwater marsh. Managed by the Fairfax County Park Authority, the park is located in Hybla Valley, between Old Town Alexandria and Mount Vernon. This lowland area, formed by an ancient shift of the Potomac River, hasn't always been a nature lover's paradise. Human endeavors—farm fields and dairy pastures, a prospective airpark for zeppelins, a federal public roads test zone, a National Guard antiaircraft site, and a Naval Research Laboratory radio communications test site—previously held sway over the land. In 1975, President Gerald Ford authorized the transfer of the land to Fairfax County for $1. Over the years, suburban development has increased surface runoff and, coupled with the introduction of enterprising beavers, greatly expanded the park's wetlands.

Begin the hike at the Lockheed Boulevard parking lot and walk a short distance to the visitor center.

LOCATION
Alexandria (Hybla Valley), VA

RATING
Easy

DISTANCE
1.5 miles

ELEVATION GAIN
Minimal

ESTIMATED TIME
1 hour

MAPS
USGS Alexandria, USGS Mount Vernon; map available at visitor center

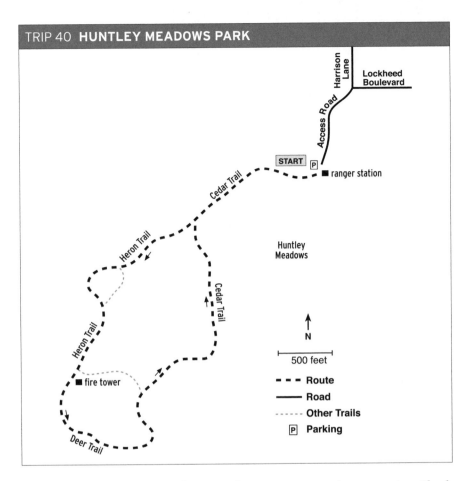

Bird-watchers and photographers use the center as a rendezvous point. Check the nature logbook, peek at the bird feeder outside the window near the main desk, and visit the gallery for rotating photography exhibits on Huntley Meadow flora and fauna.

Exit the visitor center and start down Cedar Trail, a gentle avenue through the woods to the wetlands. Cross a nineteenth-century ditch-and-berm used to drain the lowland for farming and travel through young sweet gum and maple interlaced with shaggy-barked grape vines. This young edge habitat, preferred by marsh rabbits, house sparrows, and indigo buntings, soon gives way to mature, broad oaks. After passing five small location markers, turn right onto Heron Trail and reach the wooden boardwalk at the wetland's edge.

On the right side, a few feet down the boardwalk, stands one of the park's few sycamore trees, a stalwart sentinel over Barnyard Run, a small lazy stream, as it enters the marsh. Take time to enjoy the unique watery ecosystem from the boardwalk. Dense stands of cattail, buttonbush, swamp rose, and lizard's tail thrive here, acting as natural filters for runoff from the surrounding suburbs and helping protect the Potomac River and Chesapeake Bay. Watch for

A great blue heron stalks prey along the edge of a marsh in Huntley Meadows Park. The park attracts water species of many kinds—including industrious beavers. Photo by Bobistraveling, Creative Commons on Flickr.

animals that feed on these plants: beavers, otters, muskrats, frogs, turtles, herons, ducks, geese, and songbirds.

Reenter the woods for a few hundred feet before returning to the open air. Follow the boardwalk to a two-story observation blind. Forest in every direction ensures the tranquility of this spot, where the park holds early-morning yoga classes in the spring. After leaving the blind, the serpentine boardwalk parallels the forest edge at the point where Barnyard Run exits the marshland and makes its way toward Dogue Creek (named for an American Indian tribe known as Dogue, Doag, and Tauxenent) at the western edge of the park. To the right, intricate beaver lodges nestle against the marsh edges. Beavers reentered Huntley Meadows in the 1970s and built this 450-foot-long series of dams that dramatically increased the volume of water in the wetlands.

Both the boardwalk and Heron Trail end at the edge of the forest, where the 0.4-mile Deer Trail begins. At the start of this loop, two informal trails break off in succession on the right. These untended 1.2-mile out-and-backs reach a fence on the western edge of the park, extending the hike but also guaranteeing muddy boots.

Continue past a swale on the right where blue flag, a native iris, and rhododendron bloom as early as April, luring white-tailed deer to the area. Farther along, dead pines and live gray-barked beeches surround a meadow with blue-bird nesting sites. At the next intersection, turn right onto Cedar Trail and make the return trip to the visitor center (or loop around again to the boardwalk). Dead oaks in this area, felled in the early 1990s by a rare disease, provide nesting sites for barred owls and several types of woodpeckers, including the large and awesome pileated woodpecker. Upon returning to the visitor center, take a break, mark any nature sightings in the logbook, and be sure to ask the resident naturalists about any unknown species you encountered.

MORE INFORMATION

Huntley Meadows is located at 3701 Lockheed Boulevard, Alexandria, VA 22306; use this address to find the park on a GPS device. There is no fee for parking. Dogs on leashes are allowed. The park features a 1.2-mile dual-use hike and bike trail, accessed from South Kings Highway. The park has excellent educational programs for the entire family, ranging from site-specific bird-watching to teen night hikes. Hours vary by season. Note that the visitor center is closed on Tuesdays. For more information, visit fairfaxcounty.gov/parks/huntley-meadows-park or call 703-768-2525.

NEARBY

Restaurants, historic attractions, hotels, and parks are all plentiful in Alexandria and along US 1. Just a few miles south are George Washington's Mount Vernon and Grist Mill, worth a day trip in their own right. A stone's throw from the park entrance, uphill along Harrison Lane, is Historic Huntley. Built in 1825 by George Mason's grandson, it is now listed on the National Register of Historic Places and is open to the public.

WORKING LIKE BEAVERS

Meet *Castor canadensis*: North America's largest rodents and nature's corps of engineers. Industrious enough to create an 850-meter-long dam—visible from outer space—in Canada's Wood Buffalo National Park and intelligent enough to build their dams arced into oncoming water flow, beavers are considered a keystone species. Where they build dams, they also build local populations and enhance the diversity of frogs, fishes, insects, and birds.

The beaver's anatomy is uniquely specialized: a flat tail for balance, steering, and communication (tail-slapping warns other beavers of danger); webbed posterior feet for paddling; and continuously growing incisor teeth. One beaver can gnaw down 200 trees in a year, and its teeth will still be in fine working condition.

Castoreum, an oily substance long used in perfume making, is secreted by glands near the beaver's tail. Spread over the coat during grooming, castoreum waterproofs the fur, making the pelts excellent outerwear for the animals—and irresistible to trappers, who also considered the scaly tail a delicacy. Endangered by the 1930s then reintroduced beginning in the 1960s, beavers have come back with gusto.

These water-loving rodents alter their surroundings by making dams and transport canals. A beaver family will also build a multiroom lodge with underwater access tunnels as its dwelling and operations base. The animals use various materials in construction: deciduous trees, stones, grasses, mud, waterlogged wood, even trash and animal carcasses. Beaver pairs take turns chomping and resting; just a few hours' work will bring down a tree, leaving behind a telltale pointed stump.

Beaver dams and the resulting ponds help in denitrification, or the filtration of water containing toxins from farmland and highway runoff. The ponds provide beavers with wide, navigable waters offering safe harbor and escape from predators. Trouble can arise for humans, however, when beaver dams cause flooding in agricultural lands, leading to crop losses; when beavers take down rare or valuable trees, as happened in Washington, D.C.'s Tidal Basin in 1999; and when resulting wetlands erode bridge foundations, levees, and railway trestles. Trapping and removing the animals is only a temporary solution. Other beavers are likely to move into the area, and any survivors tend to produce larger litters as compensation for the loss in numbers.

41

GEORGE MASON PLANTATION: RIVER TRAIL

Nestled within this historic Virginia plantation is a brief, peaceful ramble to the Potomac River that brings you face-to-face with deer, herons, and bald eagles.

DIRECTIONS

From I-495 (Capital Beltway), take I-95 south to Exit 163 and turn left onto VA-642 toward Lorton. Continue 0.4 mile then turn right onto Lorton Market Street. After 0.6 mile, continue onto Gunston Cove Road then onto VA-242 E/VA-600/Gunston Road. The entrance to George Mason Plantation, 10709 Gunston Road, is on the left after 3.4 miles. *GPS coordinates*: 38° 39.841' N, 77° 9.586' W.

TRAIL DESCRIPTION

George Mason is best known for writing the Virginia Declaration of Rights in 1776, during the midst of the American colonists' struggle for independence from Britain. James Madison later adapted the wording of the articles in Mason's declaration into the U.S. Bill of Rights. Mason's ideals of liberty and justice seem to have stood in contrast to his status as the owner of an active slave plantation; an apparent distaste for the institution never compelled him to offer his slaves freedom. Today, the plantation is maintained as a historic site, recognizing the paradox between Mason's higher ideals and the harsh realities of a slave plantation.

The property's River Trail is a short but rewarding trip to the shores of the Potomac River. Park in the large lot in front of the visitor center. If you would like to tour Gunston Hall, the restored Georgian-style mansion on the property, admission is $10 per adult. The plantation also offers a $5 grounds pass, which entitles you access to the museum, grounds, and trails—everything except the

LOCATION
Lorton, VA

RATING
Easy

DISTANCE
2.5 miles

ELEVATION GAIN
86 feet

ESTIMATED TIME
1.5 hours

MAPS
USGS Fort Belvoir; free map available at the Visitor Center; online: gunstonhall.org/index .php/visit/grounds-map

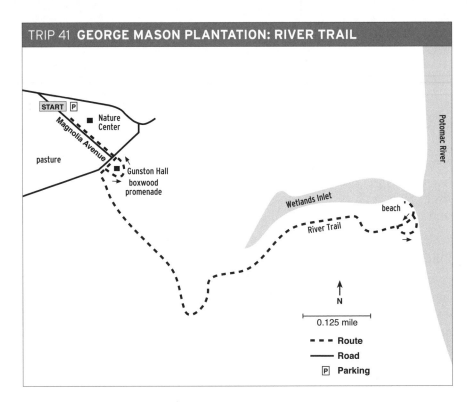

main house. If you think you'll want to see Gunston Hall at a later date, save your grounds pass and present it upon your return to receive a discount on the full-price entrance fee.

Head to the right of the visitor center and proceed down the magnolia-lined carriage road to Gunston Hall. In George Mason's days, cherry trees, not magnolias, lined this central road. Mimicked by a wide hallway inside the house, this carriage road was the property's backbone. Head to the right of the residence; at the site of the Old Barn, turn left, following signs to River Trail. Take a right down the rutted, overgrown path to a clearing with a bluebird house in the middle. Several birdhouses line a large section of the grounds; they are an effort by a group of volunteers, including members of the Virginia Bluebird Society, to support a once common bird whose natural habitat has been diminished by agriculture.

Continue into a mowed clearing fringed with forest and cross it toward the sign for River Trail. Look left for a nice view of the slope up to the main house and the fenced fields that surround it. The narrow, heavily forested River Trail is not especially well traveled; a stick may avail the warding off of cobwebs. The trail becomes less distinct and narrower as it curves to the right through patches of holly plants and ferns then crosses a narrow creek, marked by wooden posts on either side.

Pass the intersection with the trail that leads to the deer park. Like his contemporaries, George Mason kept an area stocked with ornamental native deer, and many still populate this area. Continue to the right on River Trail, heading slightly downhill, then cross a wooden railed bridge over a dry creek bed. The trail curves sharply to the left soon after, and water comes into view on your left. This wetlands inlet, branching off the Potomac, is home to lush plant life and many birds. Listen for frogs; you may also see herons, bald eagles, hawks, and ospreys. The undisturbed nature of the trail and the presence of fish in the water make it an excellent place to spot birds of prey. The trail follows the edge of a low ridge, elevated above the inlet, with views of the plantation on the left as you climb the rooted, mossy slope.

The trail descends to the right before circling and climbing again; you may begin to hear the hum of motorboats on the Potomac. The trail twists to the left, back toward the inlet. After another lovely view of the wetlands on the left, emerge at the end of the trail with a panoramic view of the river. Clamber down a short, steep slope to a beach with soft sand. The view is excellent from this vantage point. When the water is low enough, a few steps along the water's edge to the left brings you to the mouth of the wetlands inlet, offering the chance to see myriad birds.

The boxwood hedges that line the promenade behind Gunston Hall date to the time of the eighteenth-century plantation owner George Mason.

When you are ready to return, head back up the steep slope, keeping left of the trail you arrived on. Climb a short slope toward an old picnic area with an elevated view of the river. From there, with the picnic tables on your left, go straight to rejoin River Trail at the bottom of a short slope; turn left to go back the way you came.

When you arrive back at the entrance to River Trail, head straight up the hill and turn right at the bird box at the top of the rise. With Gunston Hall before you, turn right to walk through its garden. This short, boxwood-lined promenade, thought to date to the days of George Mason himself, offers a view over the deer park and the Potomac.

MORE INFORMATION

The grounds are open from 9:30 A.M. to 6 P.M. daily, except Thanksgiving, Christmas, and New Year's Day. The mansion and museum close at 5 P.M. daily.

NEARBY

If you would like to see more of the plantation property, Bluebird Trail is a 2.25-mile loop around the grounds. Although the trail is not marked on the map, it's easy enough to stay on course. Just follow the birdhouses. If you would like to add some variety to a longer day trip, Mason Neck State Park and Pohick Bay Regional Park are both close by.

42

WILDCAT MOUNTAIN NATURAL AREA

Wildcat Mountain Natural Area offers strenuous but scenic woodland hiking in the Blue Ridge foothills. John Trail climbs to a 1,000-foot-high ridgeline where farmers once lived and worked.

DIRECTIONS

From I-495 (Capital Beltway), take Exit 49 west onto I-66. Go 31 miles and take Exit 28 (Marshall). Turn left at the end of the exit ramp onto US 17 (Winchester Road) south and go a quarter-mile. Turn right onto VA 691 (Carters Run Road), go 5 miles, and turn left onto England Mountain Road (a private paved driveway). Follow the driveway past a house on the left with a pond and park just after it, at a small parking lot on the right near a kiosk. *GPS coordinates*: 38° 47.543′ N, 77° 51.590′ W.

TRAIL DESCRIPTION

In the 1960s, The Nature Conservancy began managing 655 acres in the Broken Hills range of northern Fauquier County—its first nature preserve in Virginia. Known as the Wildcat Mountain Natural Area, it is home to a wide variety of plant and animal life. Stands of old oak and hickory trees mix with younger pines, beeches, hickories, and oaks; foxes, deer, squirrels, raccoons, and even bobcats and an occasional black bear make their homes here.

The trail from the parking lot traverses between England and Rappahannock mountains; it was cleared as a farm road more than 250 years ago, when settlement began in the region. Old stone walls marking homesteads, and farm and orchard boundaries still can be seen, although many of the small farms were abandoned after the Civil War. Logging and apple growing continued into the 1940s, and a nineteenth-century farmhouse and springhouse remain, both in surprisingly good condition.

LOCATION
Warrenton, VA

RATING
Moderate to strenuous

DISTANCE
3.4 miles

ELEVATION GAIN
840 feet

ESTIMATED TIME
2 hours

MAPS
USGS Marshall; free map at parking area information kiosk; online: nature.org/ourinitiatives/regions/northamerica/unitedstates/virginia/placesweprotect/wildcat-mountain-natural-area.xml

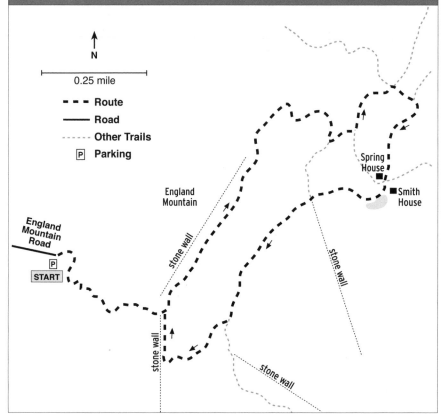

The trail map available onsite shows a preferred route marked in yellow; green-and-yellow, diamond-shaped signs on the trees point out the direction of this trail.

Head up the gravel road about 500 yards to the "T" intersection, turn right, and walk 500 yards more to the trailhead. This is where the going gets difficult. Turn left and climb 100 yards almost straight up a steep, rocky, narrow trail. The trail sometimes goes straight up and sometimes cuts diagonally across the ridge. Turn sharply to the left where logs on the right mark the first switchback. The second switchback begins at a right turn around a large tree. Continue and take the third switchback back to the left. Trail marker signs guide you up the steep ascent, which is strewn with fallen logs and large rocks. In some sections, the trail consists of exposed rock ledges. This first third of a mile includes twelve switchbacks and 420 feet of elevation gain.

At the top of the ridge is a long, straight, high stone-wall fence in good condition running to the right and left. Step through the disassembled section of the wall and take the trail to the left that leads down a gentle, wide, and well-marked path through the quiet, deep woods. The trail parallels a stone wall on the left;

One of Wildcat Mountain Natural Area's old stone fences reminds hikers of the mountain's past as a farm and orchard, before other kinds of trees retook the land. Photo by Stephen Mauro.

in some sections, a barbed-wire fence marks the boundary of the nature area. England Mountain stands on private property, past the stone wall to the left, 200 yards through the woods. After walking half a mile down the broad, flat area, follow the gentle descent along a finger of the ridge.

The trail then goes down a short, steep section and turns right onto an old farm road. Cross two streambeds, turn left, and proceed up a moderate incline. Next, turn right, continue up the hill, and turn left at the intersection. In about 50 yards, look for a green-and-yellow trail marker that confirms this as the main trail. Continue down into a ravine and back up to the next intersection. Here the preferred route is to the right, but another option is to take the farm road to the left and cross two more streambeds that are dry most of the year. At the John Trail sign, turn right, walk 100 yards up the broad path, and turn right at the T intersection.

Walk up a slight hill about 500 yards, passing several large yellow poplars, to reach the Smith House, probably abandoned for 50 years but in remarkably good condition. On the west side of the very old stone-and-mortar foundation, the plaster covering the stone used to form what looks to have been a map of the United States. However, weathering has caused the "Northeast" to crumble away. Behind the Smith House stands a chimney that appears to mark the former location of an older farmhouse. As you return to the trail, turn right down the small draw and walk 60 yards to see the Spring House, used to keep meat, fruit, and dairy products from spoiling with the use either of pond ice brought up the mountain or of flowing water supplied by a spring that has since dried up.

Returning to the intersection in front of the Smith House, turn right and follow the trail across the top of the earthen dam. To the left is the often dry bed of a small reservoir that once served the Smith House. Take the trail downhill and follow it, walking through the opening in another stone wall. The trail, which is an old farm road, slowly moves up the hill and turns right up a narrow path. Hike past oak trees, beech trees, and flat rock ledges until you come to another stone wall. Turn right at the stone wall and follow the path beside the wall for 200 yards. At the break, turn sharply left and head down the steep, winding path with a dozen switchbacks that you climbed on your way up. At the gravel road, turn right and then left to return to the parking area.

MORE INFORMATION

Wildcat Mountain Natural Area is open year-round, dawn to dusk. Dogs are not allowed in the natural area. Visit The Nature Conservancy website for more information on the history of the preserve and the steps the conservancy is taking to acquire surrounding portions of land and allow for natural succession: nature.org/ourinitiatives/regions/northamerica/unitedstates/virginia/placesweprotect/wildcat-mountain-natural-area.xml.

NEARBY

Warrenton, the county seat of Fauquier County, offers an appealing Old Town section featuring art galleries, shops, and a Civil War museum in the Old Jail. Also in town is the grave of Confederate cavalry raider, lawyer, and "Gray Ghost" John Singleton Mosby, a familiar name around these parts. The visitor center provides detailed information, including a map of the Fauquier Wine Trail—there are over two dozen wineries in this county alone and nearly 70 vineyards within an hour's drive. See warrentonva.gov/visitors/index.php and visitfauquier.com for the latest information.

Also refer to the Nearby section of Trip 37 (Bull Run Mountains Natural Area) for ideas to craft a relaxing weekend stay in this scenic and idyllic region. From Warrenton, head north on U.S. 17 to Marshall, then travel east on VA 55 (John Marshall Highway) toward The Plains.

43

WASHINGTON & OLD DOMINION TRAIL AND CROSS COUNTY TRAIL

This out-and-back covers a good distance of mostly level ground on two county-spanning trails, ideal for setting a steady, easygoing pace. At its midpoint is a well-preserved eighteenth-century mill.

DIRECTIONS

From I-495 (Capital Beltway), take Exit 49 west onto I-66. Take Exit 62, VA 243 (Nutley Street), north toward Vienna. Go 1.0 mile and turn right onto Maple Avenue (VA 123). Then go 1.0 mile more and turn right onto Park Street. Travel two blocks and turn right into the Vienna Community Center parking lot. *GPS coordinates*: 38° 54.037′ N, 77° 15.607′ W.

TRAIL DESCRIPTION

Washington & Old Dominion (W&OD) Trail is a paved hike-bike path that follows the former roadbed of the W&OD Railroad for 45 miles through northern Virginia. The full trail's southeastern end is at Arlington in the Shirlington business district, and the northwestern end is the small town of Purcellville, 9 miles from the Blue Ridge Mountains. Fairfax County's full Cross County Trail (CCT) travels through 40 miles of mostly stream-valley parkland from the Occoquan River to the Potomac at Difficult Run. This hike starts in Vienna and leaves W&OD Trail at Difficult Run to follow CCT, which was begun in 1999. The hike ends at the historic Colvin Run Mill. Keep in mind that portions of the CCT flood after heavy rains, so waterproof hiking boots are ideal.

From the community center parking lot, turn right onto the asphalt W&OD Trail, hiking below large electric transmission towers. At 0.2 mile, cross Maple Avenue (Chain Bridge Road), which is the main north–south

LOCATION
Vienna, VA

RATING
Easy

DISTANCE
12 miles

ELEVATION GAIN
230 feet

ESTIMATED TIME
4.5 to 5.0 hours

MAPS
USGS Vienna; official Northern Virginia Regional Park Authority W&OD trail guide; online: wodfriends.org, fairfaxcounty.gov/parks/cct

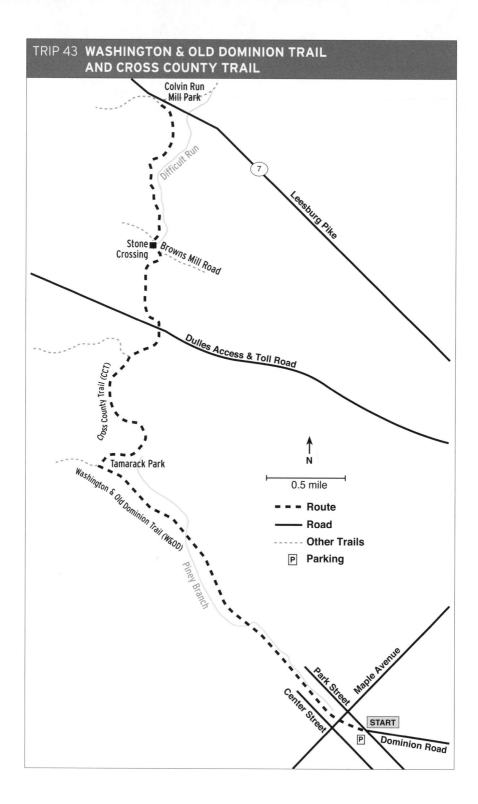

TRIP 43 **WASHINGTON & OLD DOMINION TRAIL AND CROSS COUNTY TRAIL**

Colvin Run Mill Park

Difficult Run

7

Leesburg Pike

Stone Crossing

Browns Mill Road

Dulles Access & Toll Road

Cross County Trail (CCT)

Tamarack Park

N

0.5 mile

- - - Route
——— Road
- - - - Other Trails
P Parking

Washington & Old Dominion Trail (W&OD)

Piney Branch

Park Street

Maple Avenue

Center Street

START

P Dominion Road

artery through Vienna. One block beyond Maple Avenue is Church Street, site of the historic Freeman House, a town museum and gift shop selling regionally produced books and handcrafts (open on afternoons from Wednesday to Sunday). At 0.6 mile is another well-preserved building, the eye-catching, circa-1859 Vienna train station, which features a brightly painted mural. The last train departed from this station in 1967. Today, the building houses items from its heyday and a scale-model version of the W&OD line through Vienna in the era of steam locomotives; the building is open to the public just a dozen times per year. (Go to www.nvmr.org for more information.)

At mile marker 12 (12 miles from the trail's start in Alexandria), an equestrian trail begins, paralleling the asphalt trail and, in sections, offering a nice alternative path with some elevation change. Pass the entrance to Northside Park at the 1.0-mile mark of this hike. Here the trees are nestled close to the trail on the right, but an open hill studded with power lines falls away to the left and offers little shelter on sunny days. Informative signs about the flora and fauna of Virginia's northern Piedmont make it worthwhile to stop on this portion of the trail. You may view dragonflies, for instance, and learn that their wings beat 50 times per second.

Two miles into the hike, the green space increases on either side of the trail, indicating Clarks Crossing and Tamarack parks. At 3 miles, cross a bridge over Difficult Run and go about 100 yards before swinging right onto CCT. This 40-mile-long trail connects Fairfax County north to south, and this section is

Colvin Run Mill, circa 1813, serves as this hike's turnaround point. The working mill makes a pleasant spot for a picnic, with tours and a gift shop available. Photo by Mike Bryan, Creative Commons on Flickr.

known as Difficult Run Stream Valley Trail because it adheres to its namesake stream until its confluence with the Potomac River in Great Falls. The trail is red blazed and well marked with metal poles sporting the CCT logo. The trail is intermittently maintained, but expect some overgrowth and don't expect snow to be cleared in the winter. Snow isn't the major obstacle, however; in spring and after heavy rains, Difficult Run often overflows and leaves low-lying sections of the trail under several inches of water. Wear solid, waterproof boots for the slogs through these sections.

For the first mile after leaving W&OD Trail, the trail snakes along the side of a hill with nice views of Difficult Run below to the right and suburban homes above to the left. After crossing a tributary of Difficult Run, turn right onto a gravel path and then cross fast-moving Difficult Run over a series of round, concrete steps. Walk onto a small bridge over swampy lowland before forging across another trail intersection to reach the Dulles Toll Road overpass. North of the toll road, turn left at the T intersection in a suburban neighborhood and follow a fairly level asphalt trail. At about three-quarters of a mile north from the toll road, recross Difficult Run for the final time, over a series of boulders. Immediately after, pass Browns Mill Road. The trail gradually edges westward away from Difficult Run and soon reaches a pleasant grove of pines and cedars that makes for the quietest and most secluded section of the hike. At the 6-mile mark, come to Colvin Run Road and its intersection with the busy Leesburg Pike. This stream once powered Colvin Mill, a restored early-eighteenth-century mill just across the pike and up Colvin Run Road. Decide here if you'd like to make a stop. After visiting the mill and its surroundings, turn around at this point to make your return.

MORE INFORMATION

The park is open year-round, from dawn to dusk. Admission is free. Dogs are permitted on leashes. For more information, visit novaparks.com/parks/washington-and-old-dominion-railroad-regional-park. Also visit the Friends of W&OD Trail at wodfriends.org or call 703-729-0596. See the Fairfax County Park Authority website (fairfaxcounty.gov/parks/cct/) for information and maps relating to CCT.

NEARBY

Colvin Run Mill Park includes the circa-1811 gristmill, a miller's house, a charming country-style general store, and a barn. Open Wednesday to Monday from 11 A.M. to 4 P.M. The fee is $7 for adults ($5 for children) for a worthwhile, hands-on tour of the milling process. At certain times of the year, actual grain milling, open to the public, occurs at the site. The general store sells the freshly ground wheat, cornmeal, and grits, as well as refreshments. Call 703-759-2771 or visit the Colvin Run Mill Park website (fairfaxcounty.gov/parks/colvinrunmill/) for information.

44

BULL RUN–OCCOQUAN TRAIL

Traveling through a swath of rural land in the Bull Run and Occoquan River watersheds, Bull Run–Occoquan Trail can seem as remote in places as the Appalachian Trail.

DIRECTIONS

This hike requires a car shuttle between two points—Bull Run Regional Park and Hemlock Overlook Regional Park. Head for Hemlock Overlook first. From I-495 (Capital Beltway), take Exit 49 west onto I-66. From I-66, take Exit 53 (Centerville), VA 28 south. Stay on VA 28 (Centerville Road) for 2.5 miles, turn left onto Compton Road, and then, at a T intersection, turn right onto Clifton Road. Go 1.8 miles, through the town of Clifton, turn right onto Yates Ford Road, and travel 1.4 miles to the parking lot at the Hemlock Overlook park entrance. *GPS coordinates*: 38° 46.007′ N, 77° 24.302′ W.

To reach Bull Run, return north on VA 28 and turn left onto US 29 south (Lee Highway). Go 2.3 miles and then turn left onto Bull Run Post Office Road. Stay straight where the road jogs slightly left (avoiding a sharp left); go over I-66 and past the entrance station. Continue 1.6 miles and then park at the waterpark on the left (the trail begins just ahead to the right). *GPS coordinates*: 38° 48.149′ N, 77° 28.572′ W.

TRAIL INFORMATION

This 17.5-mile overall path follows Bull Run in the north and the Occoquan River farther south, through the longest stretch of undeveloped land within an hour of Washington, D.C. The Northern Virginia Regional Park Authority (NVRPA) manages 4,000 woodland acres in these watersheds, including, from north to south, Bull Run, Hemlock Overlook, Bull Run Marina, Fountain-

LOCATION
Manassas, VA

RATING
Moderate

DISTANCE
7.8 miles

ELEVATION GAIN
470 feet

ESTIMATED TIME
4 hours

MAPS
USGS Manassas; map in NVRPA brochure available at entrance booth; online: novaparks.com/parks/bull-run-occoquan-trail

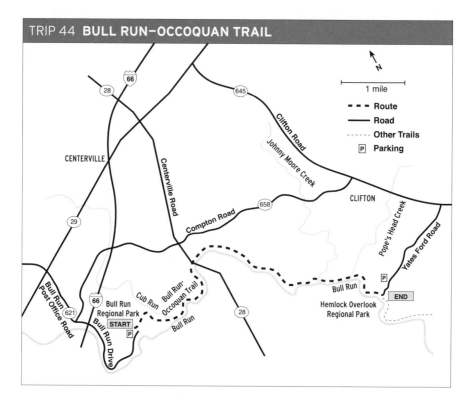

head, and Sandy Run regional parks. Bull Run–Occoquan Trail, maintained by the Potomac Appalachian Trail Club, goes through all the parks except Sandy Run. The trail's terrain alternates between flat river bottomland and rocky hills and ravines, with dramatic elevation changes especially evident in the northern section described in this hike, between Bull Run and Hemlock Overlook regional parks.

From the swimming pool parking lot, proceed 100 feet down the road to an information sign and small wood bridge beneath a willow oak. This is the start of the blue-blazed Bull Run–Occoquan Trail. Begin on the wide dirt trail, taking wooden ramps over swampy areas, and turn right at the T intersection with Cub Run. In April and early May, the forest floor around this portion of the trail erupts in thousands of Virginia bluebells, shade-loving wildflowers that American Indians used as a dye. The purple flower of the pawpaw tree—rather dark and mournful, like a fading red rose—and white flower of the dogwood tree add springtime color here and elsewhere on the trail. Cross a clearing for electricity pylons, after 0.8 mile turn left at a second T intersection, and cross Cub Rub on a suspension bridge near its confluence with Bull Run. Notice the steep, rocky opposite bank of Bull Run—the uneven terrain here differs from the gentle course of the river near its origin west of Dulles Airport. From its headwaters, Bull Run drops 1,280 feet through the Piedmont plateau to the coastal plain of the Potomac River.

Start along Bull Run's eastern shore, alive with scraggly river birch, tall sycamore, and stout Shumard oak. At 1.4 miles, go under Ordway Road and across a warped bridge. Several hundred yards on, at a point where the husk of a sycamore stretches halfway across Bull Run, follow the blue blazes left and uphill. Climb to a cedar grove and then descend back to Bull Run as it flows under Centreville Road (VA 28). This junction was the site of the Civil War battle of Blackburn's Ford, where inexperienced New York troops under Israel B. Richardson stumbled into a brigade of Confederates concealed in the woods. Richardson was later mortally wounded at the Battle of Antietam (see Trip 15: Antietam National Battlefield).

Continue to a "T" intersection and turn left uphill (marked by double blazes). Moving from the water, proceed up and down steep terrain, following a twisting trail. Pass a Civil War artillery emplacement under large tulip trees and then, at 3.7 miles, cross concrete steps over fast-flowing Little Rocky Run, where clear water snakes its way around dirt shoals. Turn left at double blazes and cross a fire road several hundred yards on under old-growth giants. Proceed up and down a series of broad hills carved by trickling, rocky streams. A bed of brown fallen leaves and a shimmering green canopy of chestnut oaks, pawpaw, and mountain laurel color the steep landscape.

Reach Bull Run again a little past the 5-mile mark—more bluebell patches here in the spring—and follow the riverside hornbeam, birches, sycamores, and oaks for 0.3 mile before veering left away from the horse trail that follows the river. Climb astride gurgling miniature waterfalls, cross the rocky stream on wood planks, and mount wooden steps up a steep-sided draw. Loop over a small hilltop and head back downhill. Reach a low floodplain where old rusty engine parts share the forest floor with low-growing, foul-smelling skunk cabbage. At 5.7 miles, cross Johnny Moore Creek on stone pillars.

Bull Run–Occoquan Trail provides stretches of peaceful hiking that can feel nearly as remote as the Appalachian Trail. Photo by TrailVoice, Creative Commons on Flickr.

Come back to Bull Run at an embankment where a side stream flows in and, at the 6-mile mark, reach the rusting but still operating railroad bridge of the Norfolk Southern Railroad (Amtrak and Virginia Railway Express trains cross here on their way to Washington, D.C.). Inspect the crumbling stone foundations of the Civil War-era Orange & Alexandria Railroad trestle, a strategic point only a few stops from the vital hub of Manassas Junction. (See Trip 49: Manassas National Battlefield Park.) Go underneath the trestle past small but sporting rapids and then traverse a grassy open expanse with the tracks on the left and Bull Run on the right. Reach and cross Pope's Head Creek near its confluence with Bull Run, taking care on its steep banks and slick stone pillars.

Continue on crumbly substrate at the bottom of a sharp, hemlock-lined cliff to the left. The dark-green, conical hemlocks—not poisonous, the leaves are used in tea—are complemented by diamond-barked flowering dogwoods. At 7.1 miles, come to what looks like a hollowed-out concrete bunker—the remains of the first hydroelectric plant in Virginia, built in 1925. This plant supplied power to Clifton, the first town in Fairfax County to receive electricity.

Go uphill alongside the plant (downriver) and then head left uphill at a blue blaze on a sharp rock. Curve along a narrow stretch lined with mountain laurel and go left at the sign Hemlock Overlook/Yates Ford Road, leaving the blue blazes to follow yellow blazes directly atop a rocky streambed. Go 0.5 mile uphill to the parking lot at Hemlock Overlook Regional Park.

MORE INFORMATION

Bull Run–Occoquan Trail is accessible to horseback riders as well as hikers. Biking is prohibited on this segment of the trail (but is allowed on a 6.4-mile leg farther south, from Bull Run Marina to Fountainhead Regional Park). Dogs are permitted, but must be leashed. Bull Run and Hemlock Overlook regional parks are open year-round; admission to Bull Run is free to Fairfax, Loudoun, and Arlington county residents, $7 for nonresidents. (Both Bull Run and Hemlock Overlook regional parks have shooting centers, and rifle reports can be heard in the vicinity.) Bull Run Regional Park offers a waterpark, among other attractions, and Hemlock Regional Park boasts an outdoor education center with zip lines and a ropes course (advance booking usually necessary). Visit websites for Bull Run Regional Park (novaparks.com/parks/bull-run-regional-park; phone: 703-631-0550) and Hemlock Overlook Regional Park (novaparks.com/parks/hemlock-overlook-regional-park; phone: 800-877-0954). Also see the Bull Run–Occoquan Trail website (novaparks.com/parks/bull-run-occoquan-trail; phone: 703-250-9124) for an interactive map of the entire trail.

NEARBY

Occoquan Water Trail comprises 40 miles of Bull Run and the Occoquan River. Kayak and canoe access points along Bull Run–Occoquan Trail include: Bull Run Regional Park, the VA 28 intersection, the Bull Run Marina, Fountainhead Regional Park, and Lake Ridge. (Fees may apply.) Occoquan Water Trail continues around Mason Neck to Pohick Bay Regional Park. Visit the Occoquan Regional Park website (novaparks.com/parks/occoquan-regional-park/things-to-do) for more details.

45

SCOTT'S RUN NATURE PRESERVE

Scott's Run Nature Preserve offers strenuous hiking along bluffs and ridges overlooking the Potomac River near Washington, D.C.

DIRECTIONS

From I-495 (Capital Beltway), take Exit 44 west, VA 193 (Georgetown Pike). Proceed past the first small parking lot for Scott's Run Nature Preserve (on the right, 0.3 mile from I-495) and turn right into the second main lot (1.0 mile from 1-495). The turnoff is hidden from view just after the Swinks Mill Road sign on the left and just before a large sign on the right for Betty Cooke Bridge. *GPS coordinates*: 38° 57.528′ N, 77° 12.301′ W.

TRAIL DESCRIPTION

The swath of wilderness now called Scott's Run Nature Preserve, once known as the Burling tract, was the scene of controversy in the 1970s when housing developers came knocking. Determined local environmentalists and high school students saved it from suburban sprawl. This 385-acre preserve has scenic views of Scott's Run, the Potomac River, a small waterfall, the remains of an old homestead, and a grove of old-growth eastern hemlocks. The latter's ancestors migrated here during the last ice age, and the trees stand as a reminder that this region long ago was in a subarctic, or boreal, climate zone—equivalent to that of interior Alaska today. Geology lovers will find the preserve's wild, craggy rock formations appealing and fascinating. The preserve's southern section lies on a major fault line dating back 520 to 570 million years (see the essay "Far Away in Time: The Geology of Great Falls" on page 197). Trailing arbutus, Virginia bluebells, and trillium bloom on the steep hillsides. Scott's Run itself starts near the parking lots of the Tyson's Corner shopping center, flows north

LOCATION
McLean, VA

RATING
Strenuous

DISTANCE
3.1 miles

ELEVATION GAIN
710 feet

ESTIMATED TIME
2 to 2.5 hours

MAPS
USGS Falls Church; online: fairfaxcounty.gov/parks/ scottsrun/trails

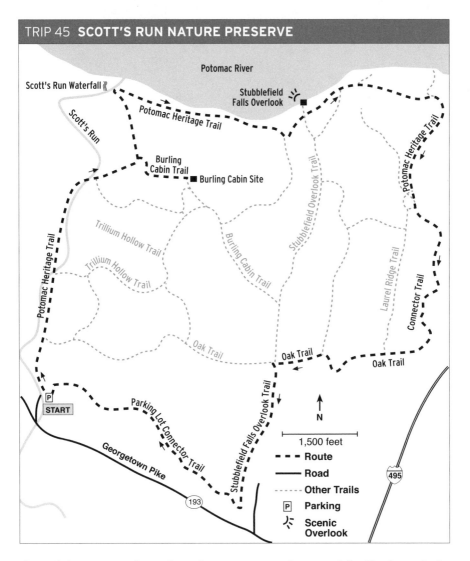

Potomac River

Scott's Run Waterfall

Stubblefield
Falls Overlook

Scott's Run

Potomac Heritage Trail

Potomac Heritage Trail

Burling
Cabin Trail

■ Burling Cabin Site

Potomac Heritage Trail

Stubblefield Overlook Trail

Trillium Hollow Trail

Burling Cabin Trail

Trillium Hollow Trail

Laurel Ridge Trail

Connector Trail

Potomac Heritage Trail

Oak Trail

Oak Trail

Oak Trail

P
START

Parking Lot Connector Trail

Stubblefield Falls Overlook Trail

N

1,500 feet

- - - **Route**
— **Road**
····· **Other Trails**
P **Parking**
⅄ **Scenic Overlook**

Georgetown Pike

193

495

through business parks and condominium complexes, and finally through the nature preserve and over the waterfall as it empties into the Potomac.

Scott's Run Nature Preserve is interlaced with trails—about 25 intersections and 40 segments ranging from easy to very difficult. The trails are blazed to match the colors shown on the online trail map, but they are not signed. Maps are also posted near the parking lots and at several locations in the preserve. Note that on weekends, the easier trails can be crowded with families and groups.

This hike largely follows the looping Potomac Heritage Trail, with a side visit to the Burling Cabin site, and returns via Oak Trail and the Parking Lot Connector Trail. From the main parking lot, start on the wide, rocky, light blue-blazed Potomac Heritage Trail, which runs parallel to Scott's Run through a small, steep-sloped valley. The wooded slopes are crowded with sycamore,

Scott's Run cascades down a rocky ledge to flow into the Potomac River from the streamhead near Tyson's Corner shopping center. Because the stream picks up pollution from storm runoff and other sources, swimming and wading is prohibited. Photo by DW Ross, Creative Commons on Flickr.

yellow poplar, chestnut oak, American beech, and various pines. In 400 yards, the trail crosses Scott's Run via short concrete posts that act as stepping-stones. Continue with the streambed on the right for 600 yards until the trail splits. Take the right fork across Scott's Run again by means of concrete posts and then climb a moderately steep hill.

A sign at the next trail junction describes the community protests that blocked development in the area. Take the wooden steps on the right along the green-blazed Burling Cabin Trail for a 300-yard out-and-back hike to a hilltop, where the chimney is all that remains of the old Burling house. Edward Burling was one of the founders of the iconic Washington, D.C., law firm Covington and Burling. The house here hosted politicians seeking to escape the pressures of the capital during the early 1900s. Return to the steps and turn right downhill, following the Potomac Heritage Trail to the Potomac River bank. At water's edge, look to the left to see the 30-foot-high waterfall where Scott's Run flows over the rock ledges into the Potomac River.

Turn around and follow a narrower segment of Potomac Heritage Trail that runs along the riverbank, taking in the scenic views of the Potomac, where strong river currents flow through the Stubblefield Falls. Take the small connector trail on your left to visit the Stubblefield Falls overlook, then return by following yellow-blazed Stubblefield Falls Overlook Trail just 60 yards back to Potomac Heritage Trail. Turn left on Potomac Heritage Trail to continue your hike through a grove of large pawpaw trees and past steep rock ledges on the right. Continue along the riverbank, across an intermittent stream, and follow the light blue blazes as the trail bends to the right.

This section of the Potomac Heritage Trail runs sharply uphill at first, through some challenging rocky terrain likely to put you on hands and knees. Crawl along a stream running through the rocks. Hike up the side of the hill to the first ridge, where you'll see red blazes for Laurel Ridge Trail on your right. Follow the Potomac Heritage Trail's light-blue blazes slightly left (southeast) about 100 yards to the next ridge, then continue uphill to one of the higher elevation points, 276 feet above sea level, as the topography eases up approaching this vantage point.

At this point, you'll leave the Potomac Heritage Trail. From the ridgetop, take the connector trail leading southwest toward the next high point. Follow this pleasantly curving trail 200 yards, then turn right on the royal-blue-blazed Oak Trail.

Now the terrain runs level to just slightly rolling for some 250 yards, until you come to a downslope where the trail bends left, then crosses a small stream and makes a hairpin turn to the right as it climbs up the opposite bank. Pass a connector trail on the right. Next, come to a four-way intersection with yellow-blazed Stubblefield Falls Overlook Trail and follow it to the left (south). This trail ascends toward the preserve's highest point, 328 feet of elevation, and along it you can spot a number of stately homes just outside the preserve boundary. Arrive at the first, smaller parking lot on Georgetown Pike and then turn right onto purple-blazed Parking Lot Connector Trail, which leads back into the woods and parallels the road down a shallow ravine. Cross the streambed and walk up the other side of the ravine through beech, poplar, and oak trees. Where the trail drops down into a second ravine, take the left fork to avoid crossing the stream at the bottom of the gully. Continue with the streambed to the right and a small ridge sloping up to the left, blocking the sound of traffic on the pike. End at the long set of wide, wooden steps leading down a steep hill to the big parking lot.

MORE INFORMATION

Both parking lots are often full on weekends, so arrive early. Despite its splendor, Scott's Run is polluted, and swimming or wading is prohibited. In times of heavy or sustained rain, dangerous flash flooding can and does occur; use caution and common sense. Visit the Scott's Run Nature Preserve website (fairfaxcounty.gov/parks/scottsrun/) or call 703-759-9018 (the Riverbend Park office, which oversees the preserve) for more information.

NEARBY

For a longer hike, try combining a circuit at Scott's Run with an out-and-back on the Potomac Scenic Heritage Trail, either west toward Riverbend Park and Great Falls Park (Trip 39), or east toward Turkey Run Park, Potomac Overlook Regional Park, and Theodore Roosevelt Island (Trip 25). Meadowlark Botanical Gardens (Trip 50) and the Washington & Old Dominion and Cross County trails (Trip 43) are also nearby.

46

MOUNT VERNON TRAIL: FORT HUNT PARK TO MOUNT VERNON

The southern end of Mount Vernon Trail connects Fort Hunt Park to George Washington's Mount Vernon estate and offers continuous views of the Potomac River.

DIRECTIONS

From I-95/I-495 (Capital Beltway), take Exit 177B onto northbound US 1. At the first light, turn right onto Franklin Street, drive three city blocks, and turn right onto South Washington Street, which becomes the George Washington Memorial Parkway southbound. Proceed on the parkway for almost 6.0 miles, then take the right exit into Fort Hunt Park. Turn right at the "T" intersection onto the road that circles the park and then take the first left into the parking lot. If the lot is full, proceed to the next lot along the circle. *GPS coordinates*: 38° 43.015′ N, 77° 3.006′ W.

TRAIL DESCRIPTION

The 3.4-mile stretch of Mount Vernon Trail from Fort Hunt Park to Mount Vernon follows the scenic George Washington Memorial (GW) Parkway along a gentle bend in the Potomac River, over land that once constituted Washington's 8,000-acre Mount Vernon plantation. The GW Parkway, built with limited access in a time before wide-lane interstates, opened in 1932 to connect the capital with Mount Vernon. The full 18.5-mile-long hike-bike trail described here was built in 1973, giving nonmotorized travelers a chance to enjoy the parkway. The National Park Service (NPS) manages both the trail and the parkway.

This hike starts with a loop around Fort Hunt Park before going out-and-back to Mount Vernon. Start at the first parking lot on the circle. Turn left onto the paved circle and pass a tiny brick outbuilding, staying to the left where the road becomes one-way to allow vehicular traffic

LOCATION
Mount Vernon, VA

RATING
Moderate

DISTANCE
8.2 miles

ELEVATION GAIN
400 feet

ESTIMATED TIME
3.5 to 4 hours

MAPS
USGS Mount Vernon; online: nps.gov/gwmp/planyourvisit/maps.htm

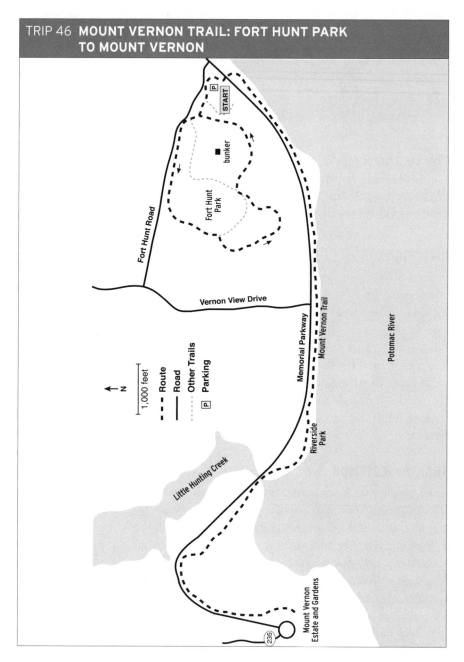

Fort Hunt Road

P
START

bunker

Fort Hunt Park

Vernon View Drive

Memorial Parkway

Mount Vernon Trail

Potomac River

Riverside Park

Little Hunting Creek

N

1,000 feet

- ■ - Route
——— Road
········· Other Trails
P Parking

235

Mount Vernon Estate and Gardens

to pass on the right. After passing horse stables for the U.S. Park Police on the right, come to a parking lot and turn right onto a side road. After a few hundred yards, turn right at a conspicuous yellow-blazed oak tree onto a dirt trail that enters the woods. Follow this well-marked and maintained trail for a short corkscrew stroll. Stay straight ahead at a point near a picnic table where the trail forks in three directions (no blazes here). After a few more turns and a bridge

Hikers pause for a rest along the Mount Vernon Trail. Photo by Binibining Beth, Creative Commons on Flickr.

crossing, the yellow-blazed trail ends. Turn right and enjoy an easy uphill for a quarter-mile before taking another right back onto the paved circle. Break the circle with a right onto the entrance/exit road that leads to the GW Parkway.

Watch for a concrete bunker on the right, an imposing reminder that the park was once Fort Hunt. It was built in 1893 to protect Washington, D.C., from sea invasions. In the 1930s the fort-quartered Civilian Conservation Corps (CCC) workers planted trees along the GW Parkway. During World War II, the fort reverted to the U.S. Army, serving as a detention and interrogation center for Axis prisoners of war.

Walk just past the intersection with Fort Hunt Road and then turn right onto Mount Vernon Trail toward the benches and information kiosk—a good place to pick up NPS maps of Mount Vernon Trail and GW Parkway and prepare for the 6.8-mile round-trip. Continue underneath a Depression-era stone bridge and over a long wooden boardwalk with views of Fort Washington, across the Potomac on the Maryland bank, through the trees to the left. This circa-1809 fort was destroyed by its fleeing garrison during the War of 1812 and later rebuilt to resume guard of this narrow channel of the Potomac. Fort Hunt was constructed to complement it from the wide river's opposite bank.

Mount Vernon Trail has an exciting, almost metropolitan feel—bicyclists and joggers, picnickers and anglers comingle, making people-watching a fun element of this hike. The trees offer intermittent shade; the CCC (Civilian Conservation Corps) planted many of these trees in the 1930s, including oak, maple, beech, elm, cherry, and sycamores. Birds of prey such as ospreys and red-tailed hawks perch in the trees or patrol the water, and occasionally a resident pair of bald eagles dubbed George and Martha (the names stay the same even when a new pair forces out the old) can be seen. Continuing on the trail, sometimes traversing boardwalks over marshy areas redolent with the scents of earth, leaves, and brackish water, you pass mile markers, stately homes, the Cedar Knoll restaurant, Riverside Park, and a large stone bridge over Little Hunting Creek (a Potomac tributary that begins at Huntley Meadows Park; see Trip 40).

Much of this area was part of Washington's River Farm. Over time, Washington amassed some 8,000 acres and more than 300 enslaved people. He lived at Mount Vernon from the 1750s until his death in 1799—when he wasn't away fighting the American Revolution, representing Virginia in the Continental Congress, or serving as the first president. The grounds became a laboratory for his beloved economic and agricultural experiments, such as whiskey-distilling and importing plant varieties from other countries. The first president worked his entire adult life to make the Potomac River the preeminent trade corridor in the nation, connecting Washington, D.C., with frontier settlements to the west.

Now turn uphill and away from the river, passing a series of boardwalks lined with majestic beech trees. The uphill becomes steep and then reaches benches, a water pump, and an information kiosk next to one of Mount Vernon's large parking lots. Continue to Mount Vernon's large circular driveway and directly to the entrance gates. Then retrace the route to return to Fort Hunt Park.

MORE INFORMATION

Fort Hunt Park, a unit of the GW Parkway, is open year-round from 7 A.M. to sunset, and ranger-led programs are available; call 703-235-1530. The park hosts summertime concerts on certain Sundays and has several picnic areas for families or small groups. Visit the Fort Hunt Park website (nps.gov/gwmp/ planyourvisit/forthunt.htm) or call 202-439-7325 for a schedule.

NEARBY

Mount Vernon's inner grounds, mansion, pioneer farm, Donald W. Reynolds Museum and Education Center, and tomb are open to the public 365 days a year (admission fees apply). A visit to Mount Vernon in itself can take a full day, so do plan your time accordingly. The estate's food court and gift shops are open to the public at no charge, and restrooms are available in the gift shop building. In 2007, Mount Vernon opened fully functional reconstructions of Washington's eighteenth-century gristmill and distillery, which are open to the public and located 2.7 miles west of the estate's main entrance on Mount Vernon Memorial Highway (VA 235). Visit mountvernon.org or call 703-799-8688.

47

OLD RAG

Old Rag Mountain, a set of strenuous rock scrambles on an eastern spur of the Blue Ridge Mountains in Shenandoah National Park, is one of the Mid-Atlantic's most popular hikes.

DIRECTIONS

From I-495 (Capital Beltway), take Exit 49 west onto I-66. Go 11.5 miles, and exit onto westbound US 211. After 29 miles, turn left onto US 522 in Sperryville; drive 0.8 mile and turn right onto VA 231. Go 7.5 miles and turn right onto Sharp Rock Road. Proceed 1.2 miles and turn right onto Nethers Road. After 2.0 miles, reach the lower lot and fee station. (*Note*: The upper lot has been permanently closed.) *GPS coordinates*: 38° 34.255′ N, 78° 17.145′ W.

TRAIL DESCRIPTION

Old Rag Mountain is a solid hour and a half from Washington, D.C.—one of the farthest afield of all the trips in this guidebook. However, the unique challenge of hiking to its summit is worth traveling the distance. Old Rag is an outlying mountain on the eastern edge of the Blue Ridge. It is an extremely old formation, the result of tectonic forces in play more than a billion years ago during the Grenville orogeny. For the past 200 million years, the crystallized granite has been exposed to weathering at the surface, and for the past 50 years or so, recreational hikers have made Old Rag the most popular destination in Shenandoah National Park.

To avoid the largest crowds, do this hike in the middle of the week or in wintertime (but don't risk it when wet or icy conditions prevail). During weekends in summer and in autumn "leaf season," expect large crowds and queues forming at the difficult tunnels and ledges. Also, to mitigate the effects of overuse at Old Rag, avoid

LOCATION
Etlan, VA

RATING
Strenuous

DISTANCE
8.8 miles

ELEVATION GAIN
2,510 feet

ESTIMATED TIME
6 to 7 hours

MAPS
USGS Old Rag Mountain; Old Rag Road and Trail map available at fee station in lower parking lot; online: nps.gov/shen/planyourvisit/maps.htm

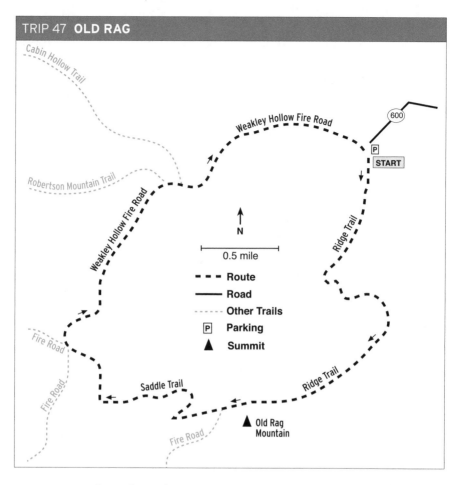

camping anywhere along the route (camping is specifically prohibited above 2,800 feet of elevation). Note that the narrow passes make for tight squeezes even for an average-sized adult. Be advised also that the rock scrambles do demand good upper- and lower-body strength.

From the lower parking lot, hike 0.8 mile up Nethers Road, keeping the Hughes River on the right until arriving at the trailhead for the blue-blazed Ridge Trail. From here, it's a 2.7-mile climb to the summit, with the first 0.7 mile on a gently ascending trail through a dense hemlock forest. At this point, the trail narrows into a rock-studded path lined with large boulders—hints of the demanding terrain to come. Finally, proceed along swooping, mountain-laurel–lined switchbacks, past several overlooks at the tree line.

The 2,800-foot elevation mark is indicated by a No Camping sign, and the path becomes composed entirely of granite at this point. Here the real fun begins! At first, simply step from boulder to boulder, but then, after rounding a broad slab providing an eastward vista, begin a mile-long scramble west through a challenging granite obstacle course. For this section, it is necessary to variously crawl on all fours beneath rock overhangs, drop into crevices, clamber up narrow chutes, leap over cracks, shimmy along edges, and hoist yourself up onto ledges. Make sure to locate the next blue blaze before making a move, and on crowded days, be conscious and considerate of other hikers.

At 3.2 miles, emerge from the first stretch of rock labyrinth onto the minor summit, a large flat area with views in all directions. Next, continue on a less-intense rock scramble for 0.3 mile to reach the 3,268-foot summit of Old Rag. Climb one of the series of steep rock piles on the right to reach the mountain's highest point (3,291 feet), being especially careful on windy days. Take time to eat lunch—and rehydrate—while reveling in the views.

The remaining 5.3 miles are downhill. From the summit, continue the circuit on the blue-blazed Saddle Trail. After 0.4 mile, pass Byrds Nest Shelter #1, a barnlike stone hut built in 1934 by Civilian Conservation Corps workers from rock off the mountain. Look for table mountain pines, which are unique to the high elevations of the Appalachian chain. Following another 1.1 miles of bracing switchbacks through heavy forest, reach Old Rag Shelter.

From here, the trail widens and follows a forestry road for 0.4 mile to the intersection of the Berry Hollow fire road (left), Old Rag fire road (straight), and Weakley Hollow fire road (right).

This intersection was the site of the now long-vanished village of Old Rag. The small settlement was once industrious, boasting two stores, two churches, at least one school, a post office, and a number of private homes. The roads through the hollows date to the 1750s. But the longtime residents and their town were wiped off the map in

Hikers eagerly queue up to navigate the rock "tunnels" along Old Rag's strenuous trail. On busier days, human traffic bottlenecks here, as some crevices are just wide enough for one person at a time. Photo by Ryan Somma, Creative Commons on Flickr.

1935 to make way for the national park. (See "Roosevelt's Tree Army: The Civilian Conservation Corps" on page 233.) Pay attention at this intersection; it is known to confuse hikers. Turn right onto the Old Rag Road, proceed just 75 feet, and then turn right again onto the yellow-blazed Weakley Hollow fire road. The walk grows gentler now. Watch for wildfowl, such as grouse and wild turkeys, along this stretch; woodpeckers are also frequent companions. After 1.4 miles, pass Robertson Mountain Trail and, within 200 yards, Corbin Hollow Trail. Continue for 1.1 miles on the broad path through old-growth forest, making several crossings over Brokenback Run, before returning to the upper parking lot.

MORE INFORMATION

The entrance fee of $20 per vehicle is good for one week of access to Shenandoah National Park. Dogs are not permitted on Old Rag. For more information about the Old Rag area, visit nps.gov/shen. For detailed information on preparing to hike Old Rag, including a safety video, visit nps.gov/shen/planyourvisit/old-rag-hike-prep.htm. The U.S. Geological Service has an interesting, detailed hike brochure and geologic history of the mountain, available online at pubs.usgs.gov/of/2000/of00-263/of00-263.pdf.

NEARBY

From the junction with Robertson Mountain Trail, it is 1.0 mile to the 3,296-foot summit of Robertson Mountain. White Oak Canyon and Cedar Run trails also are nearby; they follow steep, cascading rapids on the east side of the Appalachian ridge.

ROOSEVELT'S TREE ARMY: THE CIVILIAN CONSERVATION CORPS

In March 1933, new President Franklin D. Roosevelt knew unrest was brewing nationwide among unemployed youth and World War I veterans, who were caught in an economic depression growing ever more severe. The previous year, his predecessor, Herbert Hoover, had faced a desperate band of 17,000 former soldiers marching into Washington, D.C., insisting upon immediate payment of a service bonus promised to them but not redeemable until 1945. The regular Army soon forcibly evicted this "Bonus Army." Several people were killed, including at least one child, and many were wounded.

A landed gentleman himself, FDR also felt grave concern about the soil erosion then decimating midwestern farmlands (due largely to logging and plowing), leaving their inhabitants in a swirling dust bowl without livelihood or sustenance. Appreciative of outdoor life, FDR also wished to make nature's benefits accessible to more Americans. He now perceived a supply of hungry young men who could help him address these issues, and quickly proposed the Emergency Conservation Work Act, providing for "a civilian conservation corps, to be used in simple work…of definite practical value." A month later, the first work camps began springing up within a day's drive of Washington, D.C.—ideal for showcasing Roosevelt's brainchild to important foreign and domestic visitors. Camps were soon established in all 48 states and several territories.

Members of the new Civilian Conservation Corps (CCC) were paid $30 a month ($25 of which was sent directly home); they lived under military-style conditions. Single men aged 18 to 25 from needy families could and did enlist eagerly for six-month tours, for up to a total of two years. Veterans of World War I, single or married, soon were also allowed to join. By summer 1933, 250,000 men had been mobilized. While integration had been stipulated, the CCC's 200,000 black workers were primarily housed in separate (but, progressively for the time, equal) camps, at equal pay. A distinct division, mostly working in western states, was also established for 85,000 American Indians.

Organized labor objected to low CCC wages and government-paid skills training that allowed these young men to compete unfairly with union members, so FDR cleverly appointed a union leader to head the program. Some complained that CCC workers would bring trouble to host communities; camps were placed strategically to win support. Others, fearing the totalitarian wave engulfing Europe, saw in FDR's plan shades of Hitler's *Arbeit macht frei* ("Work sets one free") propaganda, or of Mussolini's private army.

But most CCC workers and their families were simply grateful. About 70 percent of enrollees arrived malnourished and poorly clothed. Interviewed later, they universally recalled the muscles, skills, and pride they developed; the tangible results of their work; and the abundant, tasty food provided to them. One laborer interviewed for a PBS television documentary reminisced that it was "the only time in my life I'd ever had two pairs of shoes! And three squares [meals] a day…I really had it made!"

In today's Shenandoah National Park, home of Old Rag Trail (Trip 47), the CCC established ten camps. Their members initially worked to build fire towers, log comfort stations, trails, and picnic areas. They also cleared understory forest growth, transplanted nursery and wild stock into eroded spots, and removed blight-damaged chestnut trees. CCC workers later labored "straightenin' the curves, flattenin' the hills" to help build Skyline Drive and constructed roadside scenic overlooks that had not been included in the parkway's initial plans. They also erected many of the park's buildings, from chestnut they felled nearby and from handmade wood-grain concrete shingles. They engraved the park's trademark chestnut-wood signs and forged iron hinges, latches, tools, and sign brackets still in use today.

Strenuous objections came from farmers and other rural residents whose lands the state and federal governments seized to create these new recreation areas. The issue went to the Supreme Court; landowners lost. A few residents were granted life interests in their properties, but most were not so fortunate; many whole towns and settlements died out.

Nationwide, CCC workers planted more than 3 billion trees, fought forest fires, carved erosion-control channels, built retaining walls, dug irrigation waterways, erected fire towers, quarried stone, stocked fishponds, and aided in disaster relief and cleanup. They helped build the presidential retreat Shangri-La (now Camp David) and portions of the Appalachian Trail. They created some 800 parks.

The CCC workers came, 3 million strong, to grow stronger in both body and spirit. Then came another world war; many CCC workers joined the armed forces as their civilian corps was demobilized. CCC camps were then used to house conscientious objectors, interned Japanese-Americans, and German POWs. But, as FDR intended, the CCC's good works remain for outdoor-lovers today.

48

SIGNAL KNOB

This challenging but rewarding loop follows rugged trails, with viewpoints overlooking the Shenandoah Valley and Strasburg, Virginia.

DIRECTIONS

From I-495 (Capital Beltway), take I-66 west heading into Virginia. Take Exit 6 for US 340/US 522 toward Front Royal/Winchester. Turn left onto US 340/US 522 south and continue for 1.2 miles. Turn right onto VA 55 West/West Strasburg Road and continue for 5.1 miles. Take a left onto VA 678/Fort Valley Road. Continue for 3.4 miles. The parking lot is on the right off VA 678, marked with a sign for "Massanutten Trail/Signal Knob." *GPS Coordinates:* 38° 56.102′ N, 78° 19.174′ W.

TRAIL DESCRIPTION

Signal Knob was a strategic viewpoint during the Civil War used by Confederate troops to observe battles in three counties in the Shenandoah Valley below and to plan attacks, including an unsuccessful surprise attack attempted by General Jubal Early in 1864. This rugged loop takes you up the Massanutten National Recreation Trail past the Buzzard Rocks Overlook and Signal Knob viewpoint, which is the northernmost summit of Massanutten Mountain; it then joins with the Tuscarora Trail to climb across the Meneken Mountain ridgeline and return to the parking lot. The loop comes in just shy of 11 miles; the terrain is, at times, an all-rock treadway requiring you to leap from rock to rock, so it is best to leave at least seven hours to complete the hike. Be aware that the mileage on signs in the Elizabeth Furnace Natural Area is rounded; refer to the park map and this guide for more accurate mileage counts.

LOCATION
Fort Valley, VA

RATING
Strenuous

DISTANCE
10.7 miles

ELEVATION GAIN
2,680 feet

ESTIMATED TIME
7 to 7.5 hours

MAPS
USGS Fort Valley West; National Geographic Trails Illustrated Maps #792

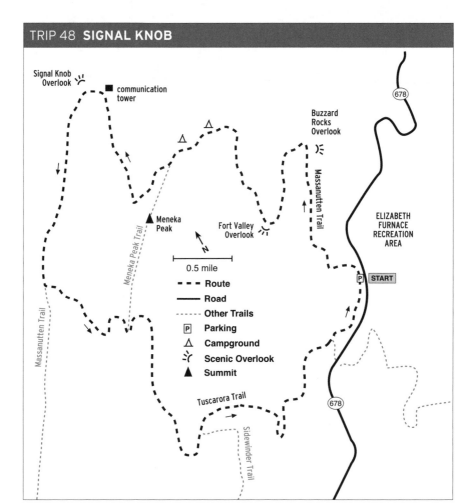

Signal Knob Overlook

communication tower

Buzzard Rocks Overlook

678

Massanutten Trail

ELIZABETH FURNACE RECREATION AREA

Meneka Peak

Meneka Peak Trail

Fort Valley Overlook

N

0.5 mile

- - - Route
—— Road
······ Other Trails
P Parking
△ Campground
⋛ Scenic Overlook
▲ Summit

Massanutten Trail

P START

Tuscarora Trail

Sidewinder Trail

678

The orange-blazed Massanutten Trail begins to the right of the parking lot, climbing moderately through a deciduous forest. Pass a camping area on your right as you follow the narrow, rocky trail; continue to climb as a streambed drops away on the right. At the first intersection, stay right to follow the orange blazes; shortly, you pass an old stone house on the left.

Turn right to cross an often-dry streambed bordered by a rock wall and continue climbing up a sandy slope with rocky areas mingled with mossy forest on either side. You are now on the east side of Massanutten Mountain, with a steep slope dropping to your right. Look to your right in this section for your first glimpses of valley views to the east. Continue climbing, curving around the mountainside.

The trail gradually grows rockier as it emerges into a more open section, with several pleasant views of the valley on your right. After climbing steadily for the first 1.5 miles, take a break at the unmarked but impressive Buzzard Rocks overlook, where you can gaze over the valley at the distant cliffs. Also at this spot is a campsite with a large fire pit. The trail hairpins sharply to the left at Buzzard Rocks; continue to follow the orange blazes.

Climb on a gently rising, pitch-pine-flanked, upper switchback. The treadway becomes increasingly rocky, requiring some scrambling; your progress is likely to be considerably slower in this section as you approach Signal Knob. As the trail takes a tight turn in a leafy grove, it passes through another col of rocks with a view of the valley, still climbing gently; the grade eventually becomes less steep, but the trail remains rocky. Curve around to the right on the ridge, passing another view of the valley, and then climb to the marked Fort Valley Overlook at 2.2 miles; there is a slightly overgrown but far-reaching view of the Shenandoah Valley and the town of Fort Valley. At the overlook, the trail curves sharply to the right to head north.

The trail rises gently on rocks through another open area; pick your way over the rough terrain with the valley now to the left. As the large boulders give way to smaller rocks, the trail continues to climb, though more gently, entering a thick forest of mountain laurels. In spring, these shrubs are festooned with pink blossoms. Here, the trail narrows and becomes more gentle, occasionally widening as the view of the valley disappears. Pass a campsite with a fire pit on the right before the trail once again becomes slightly steeper and rockier.

Another campsite, this one with a view, appears on the right, after which the trail flattens out for a time. Underbrush diminishes as the trail passes a third, more shaded campsite. Soon after, orange and white blazes appear together, and you come to the sign for the intersection with the white-blazed Meneka Peak Trail. This trail goes left to the summit of Meneka Peak, cutting off the Signal Knob viewpoint. Continue straight on the orange-blazed Massanutten Mountain Trail for the 1.1 miles remaining until Signal Knob. Look to the right through the trees for a view of a faraway tower on a peak at the point where a rock slide intersects the trail. Pass through varied sections of forest and lush beds of ferns. The trail descends slightly to curve around the ridge; a carpet of blueberry bushes flanks the trail as it rises and falls.

The trail flattens for a section; here, it is open on both sides, although the view is obscured by young trees. Pass another campsite on the left. Soon after, the WVPT public television tower comes into view. The sign indicates that you have come 5 miles; this is rounded up, and at this point you have gone approximately 4.5 miles. Behind the tower is a view of the valley, partially obscured by power lines; a better view awaits at Signal Knob. Pass the tower and bear right at the fork to continue on the orange-blazed trail. Very soon, arrive at the marked Signal Knob Overlook with its stunning view of Strasburg and the Shenandoah Valley.

Head to the left to continue on the orange-blazed trail, which soon joins the wide, descending gravel fire road. After the rugged ascent to Signal Knob, you can walk easily and quickly on this descent; look right and left to see thistles and, in August, Queen Anne's lace. After you have walked 1.3 miles from Signal

A hiker approaches the Signal Knob overlook at the northernmost summit of Massanutten Mountain. During the Civil War, Confederate troops used this strategic viewpoint to observe battles in the Shenandoah Valley below.

Knob, the blazes turn from orange to blue-and-orange; soon after, arrive at the intersection with the blue-blazed Tuscarora Trail. Turn left onto this trail, which leads 0.8 mile to the wooded ridgeline of Meneka Peak.

Cross a shallow creek and then climb on the narrow, gravel-strewn path. Tuscarora Trail climbs through lichen-covered, boulder-strewn areas, becoming steadily steeper and rockier for the loop's last major ascent. Loop left and right on well-placed switchbacks, curving around the ridge and climbing steadily as the view begins to open up behind you. The view on this ascent is the only one you'll get on Meneka Peak, so snap a photo as you pause for water.

The ridgeline of Meneka Peak is marked only with a sign pointing to Elizabeth Furnace Picnic Grounds. The woods thin out a bit, but it is viewless; you have now gone 6.6 miles. Here, Tuscarora Trail intersects with the white-blazed Meneka Peak Trail. Continue on Tuscarora Trail, descending and occasionally climbing on the rugged path, which narrows as it dips back into the forest but remains quite rocky. The rocks gradually diminish and the path becomes sandy as it passes through a burned-out section with new growth. Cross a wet patch on slippery rocks and then climb slightly again, passing a dip in the land. As the trail flattens out, a view opens up through the trees ahead and the valley comes into sight on the left. The trail, descending again on switchbacks, winds past occasional dizzying glimpses of the valley, framed by pitch pines laden with pine cones.

When you have gone 1.9 miles from the ridgeline of Meneka Peak, arrive at the intersection with the pink-blazed Sidewinder Trail, which departs to the right; stay straight to continue on Tuscarora Trail. You now have 2.2 downhill miles remaining. Come to another intersection with a white-blazed trail on the right; again, continue straight to stay on Tuscarora Trail.

Cross a shallow brook on a large, flat rock; the trail curves to the right and soon passes another campsite on the left. Continue to descend more gently on switchbacks, circling around a deep valley on the right with a view of a rock-strewn streambed. The trail parallels VA 678 for the last mile, so expect to hear some distant traffic noise. Pass a deep pit on the left as the trail widens; shortly after, intersect a shallow gorge on the left.

When you arrive at the next intersection, take a left to rejoin the orange blazes for the remaining 0.5 mile back to Signal Knob parking. The trail has been rerouted in several areas to deter ATVs, but is well blazed. Descend, at first gradually, but then more steeply, on switchbacks. Pass a turnoff on the right for group camping; continue straight past this and cross a rocky streambed. To the right, come into view of VA 678 and continue to hike parallel to the road. At the sign for Tuscarora and Elizabeth Furnace, hang right to emerge on the opposite side of the parking lot from where you entered.

MORE INFORMATION

Bears are present throughout George Washington National Forest. Seeing them can offer the thrill of wilderness within a short drive of the city, but respect these impressive animals by keeping your distance. Park staff recommend wearing bells and making noise to ensure you do not surprise a bear. Never come between a mother bear and her cubs.

NEARBY

The Elizabeth Furnace Natural Area includes several old pig iron and smelting areas featuring shorter hikes, and the Elizabeth Furnace Picnic Area is expansive and enjoyable. For those seeking a different type of adventure, Shenandoah, Luray, and Skyline caverns are nearby.

49

MANASSAS NATIONAL BATTLEFIELD PARK

The rolling hills of Manassas National Battlefield Park offer the perfect mix of nineteenth-century historical interpretation and opportunities for forested solitude.

DIRECTIONS

From I-495 (Capital Beltway), take Exit 49 west onto I-66 to Exit 47 (Manassas). Go north on VA 234 (Sudley Road). The park entrance is 1.0 mile ahead on the right. *GPS coordinates*: 38° 48.761' N, 77° 31.300' W.

TRAIL DESCRIPTION

The open hills and forested patches of Manassas National Battlefield Park offer the intrepid hiker food for thought and memory as well as a physical workout. The lay of the terrain in this hike played a major role in the Battle of First Manassas on July 21, 1861—the first major battle of the Civil War. Bull Run, the small creek meandering through the area, forced advancing Union troops to waste valuable time searching for a ford where they could cross it with their artillery and supply wagons, and the hills to the south offered the Confederates high ground from which to inflict punishment and eventually drive the bluecoats back. First Manassas Trail, a 5.4-mile trek over this terrain, visits Bull Run and several of the most hotly contested points of the battle. Even those not interested in military history will feel a tangible link to the past while standing on ground where 38,000 Federals and 32,000 Confederates fought with a savage intensity for which neither side was really prepared.

First Manassas Trail starts to the right of the visitor center between a stand of oaks on one side and the statue of Confederate General Thomas J. "Stonewall" Jackson—who earned his famous nickname in this battle—on the

LOCATION
Manassas, VA

RATING
Moderate

DISTANCE
5.4 miles

ELEVATION GAIN
900 feet

ESTIMATED TIME
3 to 3.5 hours

MAPS
USGS Gainesville; online: nps.gov/mana/planyourvisit/maps.htm

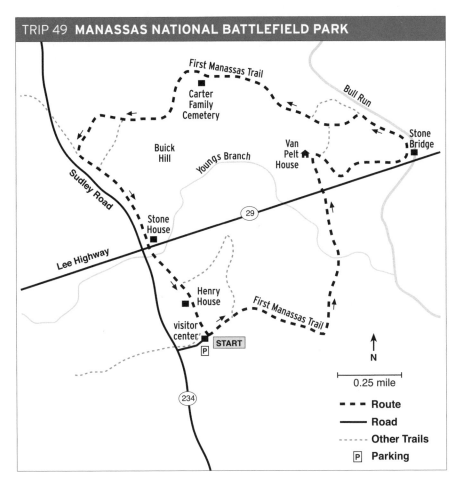

other. Follow the broad, grassy path straight ahead toward a line of cannons. The higher, unmowed grass on either side re-creates the sea of weeds through which the soldiers waded during the fighting. Enter the woods where Jackson earned his nickname "Stonewall" for shoring up the Confederate line: "There stands Jackson like a stone wall," cried his colleague, General Barnard Bee. Bear right on the mulch path denoted by a blue-blazed marker. The cool, shaded covering here is courtesy of a diverse range of pines, cedars, hickories, American elms, persimmons, and a few black walnut trees. Soon the mulch changes into gravel, with ash trees set directly in the path. Cross two wooden bridges over dry-in-the-summer streambeds. An old bench sits right before the bridges.

Turn 90 degrees left at the clearing, making sure to take the first left onto the small dirt path rather than the second left onto a wider gravel road. A little way ahead is a concentrated pine grove. Cedars, oaks, and a few sassafras shrubs mark the way on the right, and a small clearing opens on the left. The trail returns to gravel here. Trees pop up here and there in the clearing on the left, marking the early succession of field to forest. At the end of the clearing, where

The Stone House on Manassas National Battlefield served as a refuge for soldiers wounded in the first conflict here, in July of 1861. Today the house is flanked by a pair of silver maple trees. Photo by Stephen Mauro.

a large black walnut unfurls its canopy of crowded compound leaves, turn left over a dry streambed toward another open clearing and then immediately right (a marker denotes the turn). Travel over the Youngs Branch (a tributary of Bull Run) on a wooden bridge shaded by elms and hickories. Turn left onto a gravel path near another marker and arrive soon in the middle of a large, open field. Rows of cedars and pines come and go on the right, and two benches sit under the shade of a single cedar—a perfect spot for lunch. Cross US 29 (Lee Highway—a major thoroughfare) and go up a short rise. Make sure to go straight where a dirt path diverges sharply to the right. Pass a squat tree that gives off a silver sheen—an illusion maintained by the silvery underside of its leaves—and turn right up a rise to the Van Pelt House site, a small clearing surrounded by big-leafed redbud trees. This site served as the battle headquarters of Confederate General Nathan Evans, whose South Carolinians cleared timber from the ridge on the western slope all the way to Bull Run to enable fields of fire. Follow a sign for the Stone Bridge pointing right and descend a sharp slope to a raised walkway over damp lowland. This leads to the Stone Bridge, the original structure defended by the Confederates.

Turn left on the gravel road in front of the bridge and follow Bull Run. Go left at the Farm Ford and ascend the gravel slope. Turn left again at the top of the hill and then turn right back onto the larger trail that comes directly from the Van Pelt House. This habitat where trees and grass meet is replete with chickadees, bluebirds, mockingbirds, sparrows, robins, and red-tailed hawks. Travel slowly downhill past a law enforcement office on the left and plunge into the woods on a mulch path that travels by giant yellow poplars, a few sycamores, and, even rarer, a chestnut oak. The trail passes the Carter House, a few ruins standing in a depression. After 4.0 miles on the hike and 0.75 mile on the broad mulch path in the woods, on the left pass the George Stovall Marker for a Georgian who died on the spot and whose last words, according to the marker, were "I am going to heaven." This is the wooded saddle of Matthew's Hill. Markers to the 8th Georgia, 4th Alabama, 71st New York, and 2nd New Hampshire commemorate the tough fighting. Emerge from the woods and proceed straight onto a mowed portion of grass. Head toward a few of cedars on the rise ahead and continue down Matthew's Hill to the Stone House, an original antebellum home, which was in the thick of the carnage and served as a Union hospital through numerous engagements. Cross US 29 at the traffic light and then cross a wooden bridge over Youngs Branch again, heading uphill over ground where Union forces retreated. Arrive at Henry House, a postwar stand-in for the original—where octogenarian Judith Henry was killed by a bullet aimed at snipers firing from her home—and continue past it, back to the visitor center.

MORE INFORMATION

There is no admission fee to visit Manassas National Battlefield Park, but donations are gratefully accepted. The Henry Hill visitor center, open daily from 8:30 A.M. to 5 P.M. (closed Thanksgiving Day and Christmas Day), offers a six-minute fiber-optic battle map experience and a more in-depth 45-minute orientation film. The National Park Service gives daily tours of both the First Manassas and Second Manassas battlefields, and a number of living history reenactments and events take place during the year. Visit the website (nps.gov/mana) for a tour schedule and to download podcasts about the two battles. Call the park at 703-361-1339 and press 0 for assistance.

During winter, the hiking trails, rolling hills, and bridle paths draw cross-country skiing and snowshoeing enthusiasts.

NEARBY

The historic downtown district of Manassas, a few miles south on VA 234 (Sudley Road), boasts an appealing array of eateries, brewpubs, and shops, along with the Manassas Museum and the Payne Memorial Railroad Heritage Gallery—the latter located in the city's renovated train station and showcasing 150 years of railroad history in the Manassas area. For local African-American history, stop by the Manassas Industrial School & Jennie Dean Memorial, a five-acre archaeological park located on the original site of a school founded through the efforts of Jennie Dean, a former slave.

Also nearby is the inviting fieldstone Ben Lomond Historic Site, a farmhouse turned Civil War hospital, where visitors can view handwritten notes from soldiers. Gardening enthusiasts will enjoy the site's 5,200-square-foot Old Rose Garden, one of the nation's largest public gardens devoted to antique rose cultivars. Check out visitmanassas.org and discoverpwm.com for more information on these and other attractions.

"FIRSTS" OF THE FIRST BATTLE OF MANASSAS

The picturesque rolling hills around Manassas Junction, or Bull Run, were the site of many military "firsts." Most notably, the first major land engagement of the War Between the States took place here on July 21, 1861. Many people—whether Confederate or Union—expected the battle to be an occasion for celebration. Each army was certain that it could easily beat the enemy in one battle, although the sides were, in President Lincoln's words, "green alike." Drilling, discipline, and practice were sorely needed, but the feverish public on each side demanded a swift victory.

Major changes to battlefield strategy and tactics were also needed, and possible, because railroads had recently become an important aspect of the American landscape and economy. Military leaders were just beginning to appreciate the iron lines' value and utility in wartime. Wishing to control the railroads as a step toward capturing the enemy capital at Richmond, Union General Irvin McDowell moved his army of 35,000 volunteers—the largest army ever fielded in America at that time—southwest from Washington, D.C., toward the Manassas rail junction, where 21,000 Confederate troops under Brigadier General Pierre G.T. Beauregard (McDowell's West Point classmate) were encamped.

Some of those Union soldiers, marching slowly toward their first face-off with the Rebels, dawdled in the sultry heat to pick blackberries. But at their first taste of war, they and their counterparts in gray quickly realized the seriousness of their situation. The ensuing battle demanded the first train movement of troops into combat in U.S. history, as the Confederates hurried General Thomas J. (soon to be known as "Stonewall") Jackson's brigade in from the Shenandoah Valley to reinforce Beauregard. Well-to-do civilians, including members of Congress, drove out to the battle grounds in carriages laden with picnic baskets and champagne, then—as defeat loomed—clogged the roads while fleeing alongside frantic Union soldiers toward the safety of their capital (in perhaps the earliest recorded American traffic jam). Routed, the Union army handed the southerners their first major land victory, although both sides made serious errors and sustained unexpectedly heavy losses.

Another transportation mode first entered American military usage at the First Battle of Manassas, when McDowell requested aerial reconnaissance by Professor Thaddeus Lowe's balloon *Enterprise*, which was then on a demonstration tour in Washington, D.C. Lowe was one of several aeronauts seeking a Union government contract to create an Army Balloon Corps. From a tethered balloon, airborne telegraphy was even possible. On July 24, after the battle, a second balloon recon mission by Lowe relieved northern terrors by reporting that the victorious Confederates weren't massing for attack, and President Lincoln appointed Lowe the Union Army's chief aeronaut.

Back on the ground, wig-wag semaphore signaling—the use of large, square, colored flags waved in code patterns—was being employed in combat for the first time. And the battle's chaos, smoke, and blunders influenced another sort of flag: Confederates realized that their original "stars and bars"—a blue field and ring of white stars in the upper left, with three horizontal red-white-red stripes—resembled much too closely the U.S. banner. The Rebel battle flag design was soon changed to the red field with a saltire of crossed diagonal stars and bars still recognized today.

First mentioned in accounts of the 1861 battle here at Manassas was the Confederates' infamous, unnerving Rebel yell. No one is sure today how the yell really sounded. Union soldiers in the field, writing in letters and journals, described it as like a rabbit's scream or an Indian war whoop or a Highlander's attack cry. One insisted that when it sounded, "a peculiar corkscrew sensation . . . went up your spine," and another taunted, "If you claim you heard it and weren't scared, that means you never heard it!"

Local grocery merchant Wilmer McLean also learned about wartime beginnings, and endings, in a very personal way. McLean and his wife lived on the Manassas battlefield at the time of the first battle there. They later moved south to Appomattox—to a house eventually chosen to host Lee's formal surrender to Grant in 1865. After the surrender, McLean reportedly quipped, "The war began in my front yard and ended in my front parlor." Actually, both McLean houses hosted generals. During First Bull Run, the McLeans' home was commandeered as a headquarters for Beauregard, who later recalled, "A comical effect of this artillery fight was the destruction of the dinner of myself and staff by a Federal shell that fell into the fireplace of my headquarters at the McLean House." But by the time second Manassas occurred, in late August 1862, both armies had learned the true cost of war—and for many, it was no longer so easy to joke about.

50

MEADOWLARK BOTANICAL GARDENS

Meadowlark Botanical Gardens offers inviting trails that meander among trees, shrubs, and wildflowers indigenous to Virginia's wetlands and Piedmont region. Also look for a Korean bell garden and eighteenth-century log cabin.

DIRECTIONS

From I-495 (Capital Beltway), take Exit 47 (Tysons Corner) west onto VA 7 (Leesburg Pike). Drive 3.0 miles (passing Tysons Corner Mall) and turn left onto Beulah Road. Then drive 1.0 mile to the garden entrance on the right. *GPS coordinates*: 38° 56.250′ N, 77° 16.955′ W.

TRAIL DESCRIPTION

Meadowlark Botanical Gardens, 3.0 miles west of Tysons Corner in the heart of northern Virginia, is a small suburban park (95 acres) that combines the beauty of botanical gardens with several miles of wooded trails. Managed by the Northern Virginia Regional Park Authority (NVRPA), Meadowlark has a unique native plant collection. A camera in your day pack is a must.

This hike is 3.8 miles long and includes a short inner loop as well as a longer outer loop. Exit the visitor center through the side door near the small gift shop, walking around the garden area to the atrium building. Follow the path to the seasonal plantings and the herb garden, using the tour map and the numbered signs along the path.

From the herb garden at the top of the knoll, look to the southwest for a picturesque view of the Great Lawn area—three small lakes, gazebos, and more gardens and nature areas. Head left toward Lake Gardiner and take the path to the right around the lake. On the other side of the lake, turn left and take the bridge to the tiny island in the lake. Follow the path to the other side of Lake

LOCATION
Tysons Corner, VA

RATING
Easy

DISTANCE
3.8 miles

ELEVATION GAIN
360 feet

ESTIMATED TIME
2 hours

MAPS
USGS Vienna; free map in visitor center; online: novaparks.com/parks/meadowlark-botanical-gardens (scroll past the fee schedules for the map link)

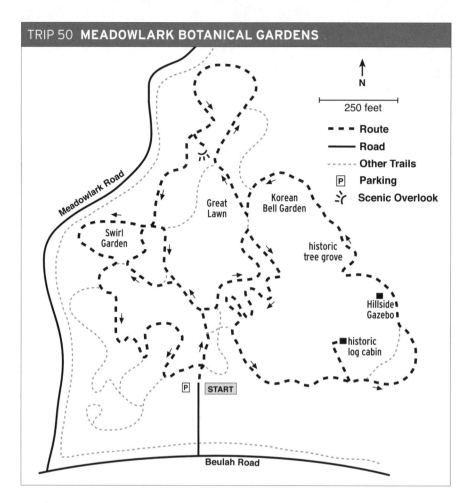

N

250 feet

- - - Route

—— Road

····· Other Trails

P   Parking

Scenic Overlook

Meadowlark Road

Great
Lawn

Korean
Bell Garden

Swirl
Garden

historic
tree grove

Hillside
Gazebo

historic
log cabin

P   START

Beulah Road

Gardiner and turn left up the hill, back to the herb garden. Then head down the slope along the path toward Lakes Caroline and Lina. The path curves to the right and then to the left, passing two intersections. Stay to the left each time. Near the corner of Lake Caroline (with the gazebo in the middle), turn sharply right to the Conifer Collection and walk a couple of hundred yards past the collection on your left, turning right and then left to the Springhouse and Hosta Gardens. On the left side of the path down in the creek bed are the ruins of the eighteenth-century springhouse that supported the farmhouse up the hill. Leaving the springhouse, the path zigzags through the wooded area until it reaches the Perennial Color Border area.

Follow the path to the left, keeping the atrium to your right. Continue to follow the path as it curves to the left and then to the right until it crosses a service road. In this area of rare chestnut trees, find signs about the husband-and-wife team, economist Gardiner Means and social historian Caroline Ware, who bought this farmland in 1935. About 30 years ago, Ware donated the land to the NVRPA, which added a 21-acre parcel to the Means-Ware farm. The resulting public gardens and park wonderfully showcase the beauty of the Virginia Piedmont region.

After visiting the cabin, return to the asphalt path. Turn left and follow the path about 30 yards to the start of Fred Packard Grove Nature Trail. (Packard was an executive director of the NVRPA.) On the right is the dirt trail leading into the woods. Climb slightly and then turn left down the hill and across a bridge over a dry streambed. Follow the path, continue up the hill across another bridge, and go back out to the asphalt. Turn right on the path and pass the Hillside Gazebo on your left. Next, pass an area on the left of trees native to Virginia, several of which are identified by signs.

The path curves to the left around a large meadow. A side spur trail on your left leads into the Korean Bell Garden, which boasts a solid, ornately carved, hand-built pavilion containing the massive 3-ton *Bell of Peace and Harmony*, cast in Korea by masters of the art and donated by the local Korean community. This bell garden is the only one of its kind on the East Coast. Continuing back along the main path, follow it around the bell garden and bear left at the "Y" intersection to proceed toward the Butterfly Garden and Hosta Garden. Where the four paths come together at the southern end of the Hosta Garden, turn right 180 degrees and follow the path along the bank of Lake Caroline. Near the gazebo bridge, turn right toward Lake Lina and the Virginia Native Wetlands

Visitors of all ages will find appeal in the gazebos and nooks of Meadowlark Botanical Gardens' 95 acres, with displays ranging from historical to whimsical. Photo by DC Gardens, Creative Commons on Flickr.

area. Walk along the boardwalk beside the lake and take in the numerous bald cypress trees. Native water plants flourish during the summer, and pitcher plants, cardinal flowers, iris, rush, aromatic bayberries, cattails, and numerous sedges line the shores. The wetlands are also habitat for turtles, brown water snakes, frogs, native fish, and several types of herons and perching birds.

As the trail leaves the Virginia wetlands, look for a sign for a nature trail that enters a young forest. Take it and head gradually uphill along a high fence at the boundary of the park. Cross a bridge over a dry creek bed and follow the signs for the nature trail straight across the gravel path and along the edge of the park. Take the right fork down the hill to the asphalt path that leads from Lake Gardiner. Turn right on the path and follow it. On the right is the Experimental Meadow, a monarch butterfly migratory way station. From here, take either the mowed path that winds through the meadow or stay on the asphalt path along the lake to the Children's Interactive Garden. Past this, turn right at the next intersection. At the tree line, take the dirt trail to the left into the Potomac Valley Native Plant Collection and pick up a pamphlet with a diagram showing where examples of 16 native trees and shrubs can be found along the trail.

Turn left in front of the second bridge and follow the trail up a gradual incline, back out to the asphalt path. Turn left here to return to the visitor center, following the path around the gazebo and going left again at the next intersection past the carved wooden totem pole and the sign for the azaleas and rhododendrons.

MORE INFORMATION

The park opens at 10 A.M. and closes between 5 P.M. and 8 P.M., depending on the month. The entrance fee is $5 for adults and $2.50 for children and seniors. Annual passes are available for $25 for an individual and $35 for a family. Note that dogs are not permitted in the gardens, but are welcome on Perimeter Trail.

The gardens offer ample facilities. In addition to the visitor center with a gift shop and educational programs, an atrium with an indoor tropical garden can be rented for weddings and other functions, as can the Korean Bell Garden pavilion. The gardens include picnic areas, restrooms, a half-dozen gazebos, and a large parking lot. The park also offers gardening and horticulture workshops and summer concerts. Call 703-255-3631 for information.

NEARBY

Wolf Trap National Park for the Performing Arts, a favorite live performance venue for musical acts, is just a stone's throw away in Vienna. This is a perfect year-round destination for a picnic while enjoying your favorite musicians' stylings, from classical to hip-hop to opera, folk, and jazz. Check out wolftrap.org for schedules and tickets.

APPENDIX
FURTHER READING

HUMAN HISTORY

Carton, Evan. *Patriotic Treason: John Brown and the Soul of America*. New York: Simon & Schuster, 2006.

> A sympathetic look at Brown that is objective enough to allow for individual reader conclusions, this biography provides perspective on the man, his family, and his ethics.

Chambers, John Whiteclay II. *OSS Training in the National Parks and Service Abroad During World War II*. Washington, D.C.: National Park Service, 2008.

> Covers the creation of the Office of Strategic Service, how the parks were converted into spy training facilities, and the details of training activities in camps as well as in local towns and businesses. Available online at nps.gov/history/history/online_books/oss/index.htm.

Ewing, Heather. *The Lost World of James Smithson: Science, Revolution, and the Birth of the Smithsonian*. New York: Bloomsbury USA, 2007.

> A fascinating, deeply researched journey into Smithson's late-Enlightenment world and the optimistic spirit of its scientific vanguard; the greatest contribution to date to our knowledge of the Smithsonian's benefactor.

Henson, Matthew. *A Negro Explorer at the North Pole*. Montpelier, Vt.: Invisible Cities Press, 2001 (reprint).

> Henson's autobiography, originally published three years after the successful expedition to the Pole, tells the full story that Peary wouldn't—or couldn't—such as the discrimination Henson faced for most of his long life.

Johnson, Dolores. *Onward: A Photobiography of Matthew Henson*. Washington, D.C.: National Geographic Children's Books, 2005.

> Tells a strong story and provides rare photos of Henson and Peary's expeditions and of the Inuit guides who helped them reach the Pole. Geared toward young people, but worth a read by anyone.

Mayer, Henry. *All on Fire: William Lloyd Garrison and the Abolition of Slavery*. New York: W.W. Norton & Company, 2008.

> A powerful read that shines much-needed light on the abolition movement, especially noteworthy for its in-depth treatment of John Brown and his plots.

McIntosh, Elizabeth P. *Sisterhood of Spies: The Women of the OSS.* New York: Dell Publishing/Random House, 1998.

> Although the female members of the Office of Strategic Service don't seem to have trained in Prince William Forest or Catoctin Mountain parks, this is a compelling, entertaining set of tales by a female OSS and CIA veteran.

McPherson, James M. *Battle Cry of Freedom: The Civil War Era.* New York: Oxford University Press USA, 2003.

> An excellent in-depth, one-volume overview of the events leading up to, and the political and military conflicts of, the War Between the States.

Rountree, Helen C., ed. *Powhatan Foreign Relations, 1500–1722.* Charlottesville, Va.: University of Virginia Press, 1993.

> One of the very few published books touching upon the Piscataway people and their lands, traditions, migrations, and relations with neighboring tribes.

Smith, Richard Harris. *OSS: The Secret History of America's First Central Intelligence Agency.* Guilford, Conn.: Lyons Press, 2005.

> Considered by many to be the authoritative work on the OSS's creation and operations, it tells of interagency rivalries as well as behind-the-lines derring-do.

Stone, Robert, director. *American Experience: The Civilian Conservation Corps* (DVD). PBS Home Video, 2009.

> Documents the reasons behind the CCC's creation, and the impacts on its members nationwide. Many interviews with CCC veterans.

Tayac, Gabrielle, and Schupman, Edwin. *We Have a Story to Tell: The Native Peoples of the Chesapeake Region.* Washington, D.C.: National Museum of the American Indian Education Office, 2006.

> An educator's guide geared toward high school students, with good depth and insight into the historical and current-day challenges faced by regional tribes.

NATURAL HISTORY

Allaby, Michael. *Temperate Forests* (Biomes of the Earth Series.) New York: Chelsea House, 2006.

> A general textbook on flora and fauna for Grades 7 and up, with good basic information on beavers, riparian zones, and more.

Choukas-Bradley, Melanie. *City of Trees: The Complete Field Guide to the Trees of Washington, D.C.* 3rd ed. Charlottesville, Va.: University of Virginia Press, 2008.

Astonishingly in-depth and invitingly written, this guide spotlights the plants—and the larger-than-life personalities—that have made Washington the beautiful city it is today.

National Geographic Society. *Wild Animals of North America*. Washington, D.C., National Geographic Society Book Division, 1998.

A beautiful pictorial look at beavers and other wildlife, with entertaining informational tidbits.

Reed, John C. Jr., Sigafoos, Robert S., and Fisher, George W. *The River and the Rocks: The Geologic Story of Great Falls and the Potomac River Gorge*. Washington, D.C.: United States Geological Survey, 1970.

The classic study of Great Falls geology, fascinating and not too technical. Available online at nps.gov/history/history/online_books/grfa/contents.htm.

INDEX

ABOUT THE AUTHORS

Beth Homicz received a Bachelor of Science in Language from Georgetown University in 1990 and qualified for her Washington, D.C., professional tour guide license in 1994. For seventeen seasons, she led some 15,000 visitors, from many nations and all walks of life, on lively, memorable custom adventures among the cultural and historical sights of the nation's capital and the East Coast.

Beth has written for *The Washington Post*, penned a regular column for *Destinations* magazine, and published articles on topics ranging from political strategy to relationship-based marketing. She has created and delivered staff-development programs in effective writing for several federal agencies, including the U.S. Department of Defense, the Bureau of the Census (U.S. Department of Commerce), the National Credit Union Administration, and the Environmental Protection Agency.

Currently, Beth lives beside a creek in rural Virginia, works as an award-winning reporter for a community newspaper, and has a novel in progress about the Underground Railroad.

Annie Eddy is a writer and hiking enthusiast living in Baltimore. She started camping before she could walk and went on her first backpacking trip at the ripe old age of 4. Since then, she has hiked thousands of miles. After graduating from Williams College, she relocated from New England to Baltimore and has thrown herself into discovering the area's natural features and helping her city friends explore the great outdoors, issuing them flashlights and bug spray along the way. Her professional pursuits include blogging for Impact Design Hub, a media platform for designers working for social change, and co-coordinating the annual Writing from Nature workshop. She is currently the Office Manager for the Inner Harbor Project, a youth-led, research-based organization working to improve relationships among teens, police, and store owners in Baltimore's Inner Harbor.

AMC'S POTOMAC CHAPTER

Started in 1984, this is the southernmost chapter of the Appalachian Mountain Club. Its 2,400 members—mostly from Washington, D.C., Maryland, and northern Virginia—engage in various activities, including day-hiking, backpacking, paddling, biking, and social get-togethers. The chapter also organizes conservation initiatives and offers education and leadership opportunities.

To view a list of AMC activities in Washington, D.C., Maryland, northern Virginia, and other parts of the Northeast, visit trips.outdoors.org. To learn more about the Potomac Chapter, visit amc-dc.org.

AMC BOOKS UPDATES

AMC Books strives to keep our guidebooks as up-to-date as possible to help you plan safe and enjoyable adventures. If after publishing a book we learn that trails are relocated or route or contact information has changed, we will post the updated information online. Before you hit the trail, check for updates at outdoors .org/publications/books/updates.

While hiking or paddling, if you notice discrepancies with the trail description or map, or if you find any other errors in the book, please let us know by submitting them to amcbookupdates@outdoors.org or in writing to Books Editor, c/o AMC, 5 Joy Street, Boston, MA 02108. We will verify all submissions and post key updates each month.

AMC Books is dedicated to being a recognized leader in outdoor publishing. Thank you for your participation.

APPALACHIAN MOUNTAIN CLUB

At AMC, connecting you to the freedom and exhilaration of the outdoors is our calling. We help people of all ages and abilities to explore and develop a deep appreciation of the natural world.

AMC helps you get outdoors on your own, with family and friends, and through activities close to home and beyond. With chapters from Maine to Washington, D.C., including groups in Boston, New York City, and Philadelphia, you can enjoy activities like hiking, paddling, cycling, and skiing, and learn new outdoor skills. We offer advice, guidebooks, maps, and unique lodges and huts to inspire your next outing. You will also have the opportunity to support conservation advocacy and research, youth programming, and caring for 1,800 miles of trails.

We invite you to join us in the outdoors.

YOUR CONNECTION TO THE OUTDOORS

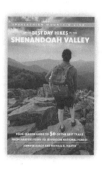